1-14-70

GOOD TALK 2

GOOD TALK 2
An anthology from BBC Radio

edited by

DERWENT MAY

TAPLINGER PUBLISHING COMPANY
NEW YORK

First Published in the United States in 1970 by
TAPLINGER PUBLISHING CO., INC.
29 East Tenth Street
New York, New York 10003

© Victor Gollancz Ltd., 1969

SBN 8008–3577–8

Library of Congress Catalog Card Number 69–11983

Printed in Great Britain

CONTENTS

IV—IMAGININGS

FOREWORD

THE FIRST VOLUME of *Good Talk*, published last year, received a warm welcome from both the public and the reviewers, and, as was hoped, it has become possible to continue with the venture as an annual. This second selection consists entirely of new talks, all of them broadcast since the spring of 1968. Again I have sifted a very large number of scripts, and hope that the talks I have chosen represent the best of the 'output'—as BBC idiom describes it—both on the Third Programme and Radio 4. Certainly, as before, they cover an extraordinary range of topics, and I have only grouped them loosely into sections. This year 'Personalities', 'Problems', 'Travels' and 'Imaginings' seemed good heads. The *Times Literary Supplement*'s review of last year's *Good Talk* said that if it became an annual it would be 'particularly helpful to the trend-watchers'. I haven't deliberately kept those alert if nervous readers in mind; but looking back across my choice as I write this foreword, I think I can say that it does reflect many preoccupations and styles of the late Sixties. There is a good deal of scepticism shown here about the immediate past, of anxiety about the future: an intense scrutinising of the facts, and a refusal to take on trust either traditional values or revolutionary values, is to be seen in many of these talks. At the same time there is plenty of entertainment.

My first acknowledgment must be, as before, to the BBC producers who found and no doubt in some cases groomed these speakers; my next, to the speakers themselves for their cooperation. The BBC colleagues who helped me last year did the same this year, and I record my gratitude again. I must add my thanks to my secretary, Mrs Rosalind Davies.

Acknowledgments are also due to the editor of *The Listener*, in which some of these talks were printed; and to Messrs Faber and Faber, who will be publishing the autobiography of René Cutforth of which his talk, in some form, will constitute a part.

DERWENT MAY

7

I
PERSONALITIES

John Wells and Richard Ingrams

A MAN APART—A SOUND PORTRAIT OF AN ENIGMA OF THE TWENTIES

Last year's Good Talk began with a sound portrait of Evelyn Waugh. A more mysterious figure from the same epoch is described here. Richard Ingrams is the editor of Private Eye, of which John Wells was also formerly a co-editor; together they wrote the play, Mrs Wilson's Diary.

NARRATOR: 'If he had not lived, it would have been necessary to invent him.' These words were not written about Basil Vacuum, they were written about Our Lord. Nevertheless, it would be possible, though perhaps improbable, to say the same about Basil. To a whole generation, Vacuum represented a style of life that was as impalpable as it was inscrutable. And the irony of it is that were he alive today, and able to listen to this programme, he would undoubtedly enjoy the last laugh. Who knows but that in some Elysian smoking-room, tuned in on who knows what ethereal wave-length, sipping a frosted glass of nectar on the rocks, and looking out, with his un-forgettable brown eyes, over the fields of Arcady, Basil may even now be revealing his long yellow teeth in an immortal smile, and murmuring once more the phrase that calls him back to all of us: 'Hullo, ducky, how's tricks?' Basil Vacuum was born, like many of his contemporaries, on 12 November 1906. After an unusual childhood, spent in the bosom of his nanny, Florence Cavendish-Bendix, he was eventually sent, much against his will, to Trouser Lodge, a little-known preparatory school in the hinterland of Ashby de la Zouch. Conrad Plume takes up the tale.

CONRAD PLUME: I think I shall always remember him, not for what he did at school, but for the rather bizarre reasons that led up to his premature departure. (Offside. Free kick. You'll take it, will you, Parker?) I think it was quite clear to us from the very beginning that Vacuum, or 'Tartie' as he was known to masters and boys alike, was going to make his mark on the Head Master, Canon Wildboor. (Wilkinson, put Jenkins down, will you, and I'll have that marline spike, I think. Thank you. And Jenkins, you run along to matron. All right, crawl along then. Don't waste my time, little boy.) Of course I don't think it's fair to say that Vacuum was wholly evil. I would be the last to condone arson in any of its many forms, but the old school buildings in Vacuum's day were a deplorable example of Lavatory Gothic, and it is true that the Padre was to say the least of it a little over-enthusiastic in trying to get through to some of the younger boys. (Will the B Team kindly put those goal posts down and have a bit of consideration for some of those who are trying to play!) But it was very hard to get angry with a boy with such enormous saucer blue eyes and golden ringlets half-way down his back. (Excuse me. Why are all these branches and leaves lying about in the penalty area? One of these days, Pickering, I'm going to come down on you like a ton of bricks. Aaaaaaaargh! An elephant trap, they've done for me again!)

NARRATOR: From Trouser Lodge he went, inevitably, to Borstal, and thence to Eton. Harold Euston recalls:

HAROLD EUSTON: I think it was untrue to say, as many did subsequently, that Basil was a nonentity. He was, in those days, on the fringe of that brilliant circle who called themselves Les Trois Mousquetaires, and which included Battersby Wyndham-Smith, Walter, later Enid, Fitznaughton, Lord Arthur Sibthorpe, Graham Brown, Wilfred Plunket-There, Oliver Grimshaw and the Master of Egg. Together they produced an Eton ephemeral magazine, which was to have been called the *Daily Express*, but one of the more enlightened house-masters pointed out to them that another publication of a similar name already existed, and the project collapsed before it had gathered wind.

NARRATOR: Basil left Eton at the, in those days, unusually early age of thirteen, for reasons of health. He was lucky enough, on his first day away from Eton, to strike up an acquaintance in a backstreet in Soho with the distinguished American collector, Ambrose Brahms, who, after only a few moments' acquaintance, invited Basil to join him in his villa on the slopes of Mount Etna—with its breathtaking view of the bay of Naples. Godfrey Wheems, the devoted companion of Brahms's last days, continues the saga.

GODFREY WHEEMS: The Villa dei Puovi was a camping ground, if one may use the expression, for itinerant aesthetes from all over Europe. At the time of Basil's arrival, Brahms was already well advanced in years, but his considerable powers showed no signs of waning. He was as active in the swimming pool as he ever had been. I remember he had just acquired a very, very early Picasso, formerly in the possession of Gertrude Stein, and Basil Vacuum was foolish enough, during the course of a rather *déclenché* evening, to put his foot through it. Turning on Brahms with that look of vacuous innocence mingled with demonic bestiality which only he knew how to assume, he snarled 'Sorry, ducky, I'll get you a new one next time I'm in Harrods.' Brahms's wrath knew no bounds, and had it not been for the sudden and disastrous eruption of the volcano which was to destroy the Villa and its environs for ever and to inspire the last chapter of St John Wardleigh's unpublished novel *Twilight at Rimini*, things might have turned very nasty indeed.

NARRATOR: After the languid days at the Villa dei Puovi, Oxford must have seemed to the young Basil Vacuum like a blast of hot water.

SIR RAY GAMAGE: The generation which came up after the First World War went down again three years later. A reaction against the horrors of the trenches was inevitable. It has been said, to my mind unfairly, that they were snobs. This was quite untrue. The fact is that they had a perfectly under-standable predilection for those of a higher social class than that to which they themselves belonged. Naturally, the atmosphere of a large country house at the weekend, with its intermittent and dilatory conversation on trivial topics—the way in which the trees changed colour with the passing seasons, the whereabouts of the *Times* newspaper, the boredom of life in general—was preferable to the company of saloon bar rowdies in the *Cat and Wicket*. I do not remember Vacuum myself, but I have been assured by those who do, that the sight of his carrot red hair and flashing green eyes as he gave a dressing down to some unfortunate waiter for failing to squeeze arrowroot on his *petit pot de chocolat*, was indeed unforgettable.

NARRATOR: Basil Vacuum's name was, in fact, not Basil Vacuum. His father was a middle-European onion vendor who fled to England during the Berlin Potato Famine. Basil, or Henry as his real name was, referred to him simply as Alf, and his sur-name appears to have been either Galoch or von Beetmann-Hohlbein, though he confused the issue himself by taking out Dutch citizenship under the name of George Robey. What-ever the facts may be, his name, or rather his names, became synonymous with the Gay Young Thing Movement of the Twenties. One whose parties later became a legend was the Viennese eccentric Hector Mackevoy Beamish. A man who would prefer to remain anonymous takes up the tale.

MR X: (No sugar thank you, the old ticker you know.) The fact that there were very few girls at Oxford in those days gave rise to a number of somewhat bizarre situations. (No fairy cakes, thank you, I'm trying to give them up.) It is not true to describe Basil Vacuum as a homosexual. It was simply that *mutatis mutandis* he preferred to appear at such parties in a stunning floor-sweeping ball gown and a small velvet handbag studded with emeralds. Few who danced with him, as I did, will forget the pebble spectacles, the large cigar, the mobile black eyebrows and painted moustache, which undoubtedly inspired the portrait of Lady Capstan-Weatherhead in Graham Trimble's *Exodus*.

NARRATOR: Few knew Basil so well as Murray Buckle, then President of the Oxford University Experimental Badger Hunting Club.

MURRAY BUCKLE: Oh those parties! What fun we all had! There were parties in drains, parties under water, parties up telegraph poles, and one particular party in Oxford Prison. The scene: one o'clock in the morning. The time: under an Oxford Railway Bridge, or it could have been the red ballroom at Blenheim Palace. Enter a man of less than usual stature, to all intents and purposes a dwarf. I will not mention his name. Suffice it to say that he is now Chairman of the House of Lords' Darts Team. Enter another, plainly the worse for wear for inhaling benzendrine out of an old nose pump. Enter Osbert, Evelyn, Harold, Maurice and Johnny B. on this occasion dressed as the Archbishop of Canterbury's mother. Oh how we laughed! (Is that enough? Perhaps I could have it in cash. Temporarily embarrassed, wine merchant hammering on the door and so forth, I expect you know the form.)

NARRATOR: Basil also took a keen interest in the politics of the day: surprisingly, for one of his leanings, he was among the first to become aware of the menace of Fascism in Europe. A practising Member of Parliament takes up the story.

M P: I remember it was at a party given by the old Lady Astor, or Lady Cunard as she then was, or it may have been one of Chips Channon's soirées—one's memory of those days is inevitably confused—and Basil, or it could have been Guy Burgess or Arthur Askey, suddenly rounded on the wife of the military attaché at the Serbo-Croatian Embassy: 'I don't think much of this little tit Hitler, do you, ducky?' he said. We all laughed at the time, but few of us realised how true these words were, and how much courage it took to say them.

Twelve years later the war was upon us, I joined the Women's Land Army and lost touch with Basil for ever.

NARRATOR: With the coming of the war, Basil was recruited into the ranks of the top secret operation that was called, in order to deceive the enemy as to its true purpose, the Top Secret Operations Executive. Brigadier Sammy Standfast recalls those days.

BRIGADIER STANDFAST: In the early days of the Phoney War, some pretty odd characters turned up at our secret head-quarters at Number 17b, Belgrave Square, and we had little idea who we had on our books, as the entire records went up in smoke as a result of the chief of the Middle East Section lighting his pipe in an unguarded moment. It was some months before we discovered Mr Gruff, a trained chimpanzee from the London Zoo, working in the cipher section. Basil Vacuum came to us with the strongest possible recommendation of having been at Trouser Lodge with Kim Philby. He was immediately put in charge of the Entire European War Effort.

NARRATOR: Basil's career as CIMQ6 was to be short-lived. Colonel Wimsley Gort, who knew him at the time, tells why.

COL. WIMSLEY GORT: I was in the Gargoyle Club at about three o'clock one morning. Guy was there, Kim, George Blake, Klaus Fuchs, Patience Strong and Dylan Thomas. Suddenly—and I think he always came into the room suddenly—Basil burst in, dressed in a transparent nylon nightie—they were very hard to come by in those days—and a huge picture hat. 'Hullo, duckies,' he said, 'guess what I'm doing. I've been made head of the Entire European War Effort, so bloody well watch it, that's all!' With this, he picked up a bottle of Montrachet Père et Fils that Osbert had smuggled in from Greece, and poured it over Dylan's head. Dylan's reaction was immediate. He gave a low growl, and sank his teeth into Basil's leg. The resulting wound caused him to be invalided out of the Secret Service and to be transferred to what was described as a 'cushy number' with the Commandos. He often told me that MI6 had been his spiritual home. We were very sorry to see him go.

NARRATOR: Little is known of the wartime dangers to which Basil constantly exposed himself. Sir Arnold Grimsdyke, now first secretary and typist in Tel Aviv, saw Basil at his lowest at the height of the Blitz.

SIR ARNOLD GRIMSDYKE: I suppose everyone remembers the day a bomb fell on the old Mauve Carnation Club. The carnage was appalling. Everyone was in bed at the time—it was about three o'clock in the afternoon, I suppose—and the present Shadow Minister emerged from the Blue Powder Room wearing only a feather boa and a pair of Edwardian corsets. As the smoke cleared it was apparent that many members were trapped under the collapsed Tiepolo ceiling, though luckily Buffoni's tiny plaster figure of a boy playing the euphonium was miraculously unscathed. (They're not going to war again are they? Tel Aviv is absolute murder in wartime. Oh no, it's only the Tel Aviv Police Band. I wonder, could we have the window closed. Thank you.) As the ARP moved about their grisly tasks, probing the wreckage for possible survivors, a cry of ecstatic delight was heard from beneath the rubble. 'Whoops, ducky!' came a familiar voice, 'watch what you're doing with that walking stick, if you don't mind!' And a moment later the unclothed Basil—he had been playing billiards when the bomb dropped—emerged unabashed from the wreckage to pursue a dumbfounded warden out into Old Compton Street and down into Piccadilly.

NARRATOR: Perhaps one of the most disastrous effects of the Blitz was that it gave Basil slight headaches, which may have been responsible for his increasing reliance on alcohol. Never a light drinker, he now seemed to be turning more and more to seek that Lethe which his sensitive nature required to protect it from the outside world.

HECTOR BABCOCK-HYTHE: It would be wrong to describe Brian Tedium as an alcoholic. He just tended to consume a good deal more drink than anyone else. He would think nothing of consuming two bottles of brandy before breakfast. Breakfast would consist of a tumbler containing a unique mixture of rum, sherry, absinthe, strychnine and artificial colouring matter. He would then fall asleep, often in the most unusual places, until dinner time. Sooner or later it was bound to catch up with him; and he began to see things. I remember the evening we were sitting hand in hand in the Library at Droppings, and a number of pink dogs happened to be sitting by the fire playing picquet. 'Do you know, ducky', said Basil, 'it's an extraordinary thing, but there's a green snake crawling up my trouser leg: what do you think it wants?' Of course there wasn't any snake, he was imagining it. But the funny thing was, as I pointed out afterwards, that he couldn't see the dogs at all.

NARRATOR: As night descended, Basil's sexual predilections became more and more of a mystery to his friends.

DAME IRENE THIMBLE: It wasn't true, as was so often said, that Basil only liked men. One evening I remember in particular when his infectious charm bubbled over like a burst watermain. It was the night of the Coronation in 1953, and we were celebrating with a bottle of champagne we had saved up since the end of the war. Having nowhere to go, we repaired to Basil's flat on the Victoria Embankment. I suppose there were about a hundred of us. We found him very down in the mouth. 'Oh dear, ducky,' he said, as he was borne back on the tide of incoming merrymakers. 'A joke's a joke, but give me Margate on a Sunday afternoon any day of the week.' Later, when I cornered him in a clothes closet during an impromptu game of 'Sardines', he became most affectionate in the darkness, asking me for some reason to kiss him goodnight and calling me Sergeant-Major.

NARRATOR: His last years were clouded with melancholy. The rudeness which had been the hallmark of his earlier years now erupted in unexpected outbursts of violence. Had it not been for Sid, the retired heavyweight violinist, who became his gentleman's gentleman and devoted companion in the dark days the end might have come sooner than it did. Jeremy Wisbech concludes:

JEREMY WISBECH: The last time I saw him was in the Arpeggio. Osbert, Evelyn, Maurice, Johnny B., Harold, Dylan Thomas, Guy Burgess and Patience Strong had just returned from a football match and were in merry mood. Basil, dressed in a muslin shift and knee-length silver boots, looked devastating in false eyelashes and a *fin de siècle* tutu. For a moment he eyed them through his lorgnette, and then with a flash of the old wit he cried 'You're drunk, duckies, and I am too, too drearily sober.' Ten years later he was dead.

NARRATOR: The circumstances of Basil's death remain a mystery to this day. As far as we can tell, he decided to leap from the deck of Socrates Mollasses's yacht, then anchored in Monte Carlo harbour, partly because he found the party on board, in his own words, 'too, too dreary' and partly because his eye had been taken by a party of matelots on their day out, gliding under the hull in a catamaran. His body was never found, and the chaplet of wilted pansies floating on the surface of the Mediterranean was his only memorial. Bore? Drunk? Layabout? Dilettante and degenerate? An untalented parasite? Was he anything more? The answer must inevitably be no.

Harold Pinter

MAC

Harold Pinter is one of the most renowned of post-war English playwrights: among his plays are *The Caretaker* and *Landscape*. He began his life in the theatre as an actor, and here he recalls a man who was very important to him at that time, the Irish actor-manager Anew McMaster.

'I've BEEN THE toast of twelve continents and eight hemispheres!' Mac said from his hotel bed. 'I'll see none of my admirers before noon. Marjorie, where are my teeth?' His teeth were brought to him. 'None before noon,' he said, and looked out of the window. 'If the clergy call say I'm studying King Lear and am not to be disturbed.' 'How long have you been studying King Lear, Mac?' 'Since I was a boy. I can play the part. It's the lines I can't learn. That's the problem. The part I can do. I think. What do you think? Do you think I can do it? I wonder if I'm wise to want to do it, or unwise? But I will do it. I'll do it next season. Don't forget I was acclaimed for my performance in *Paddy The Next Best Thing*. Never forget that. Should I take *Othello* to the Embassy, Swiss Cottage? Did you know Godfrey Tearle left out the fit? He didn't do the fit. I'm older than Godfrey Tearle. But I do the fit. Don't I? At least I don't leave it out. What's your advice? Should I take *Othello* to the Embassy, Swiss Cottage? Look out the window at this town. What a stinking diseased abandoned God-forgotten bag. What am I playing tonight, Marjorie? *The Taming of the Shrew*? But you see one thing the Irish peasantry really appreciate is style, grace and wit. You have a lovely company, someone said to me the other day, a lovely company, all the boys is like girls. Joe, are the posters up? Will we pack out? I was just driving into this town and I had to brake at a dung heap. A cow looked in through the window. No autographs today, I said. Let's have a drop of whiskey, for Jesus' sake.'

Pat Magee phoned me from Ireland to tell me Mac was dead. I decided to go to the funeral. At London Airport the plane was very late leaving. I hadn't been in Ireland for ten years. The taxi raced through Dublin. We passed the Sinn Fein Hall, where we used to rehearse five plays in two weeks. But I knew I was too late for the funeral. The cemetery was empty. I saw no one I knew. I didn't know Mrs Mac's address. I knew no one any more in Dublin. I couldn't find Mac's grave.

I toured Ireland with Mac for about two years in the early 1950s. He advertised in *The Stage* for actors for a Shakespearian tour of the country. I sent him a photograph and went to see him in a flat near Willesden Junction. At the time Willesden Junction seemed to me as likely a place as any to meet a manager from whom you might get work. But after I knew Mac our first meeting place became more difficult to accept or understand. I still wonder what he was doing interviewing actors at Willesden Junction. But I never asked him. He offered me six pounds a week, said I could get digs for 25 shillings at the most, told me how cheap cigarettes were and that I could play Horatio, Bassanio and Cassio. It was my first job proper on the stage.

'Those two? It must be like two skeletons copulating on a bed of corrugated iron.' (The actor and actress Mac was talking about were very thin.) 'He undercuts me,' he said, 'he keeps coming in under me. I'm the one who should come under. I'm playing Hamlet. But how can I play Hamlet if he keeps coming under me all the time? The more under I go the more under he goes. Nobody in the audience can hear a word. The bugger wants to play Hamlet himself, that's what it is. But he bloodywell won't while I'm alive. When I die I hope I die quickly. I couldn't face months of bedpans. Sheer hell. Days and months of bedpans.

Do you think we'll go to heaven? I mean me. Do you think I'll go to heaven? You never saw me play the Cardinal. My cloak was superb, the length of the stage, crimson. I had six boys from the village to carry it. They used to kiss my ring every night before we made our entrance. When I made my tour of Australia and the southern hemisphere we were the guests of honour at a city banquet. The Mayor stood up. He said: "We are honoured today to welcome to our city one of the most famous actors in the world, an actor who has given tremendous pleasure to people all over the world, to worldwide acclaim. It is my great privilege to introduce to you—Andrew MacPherson!" '

Joe Nolan, the business manager, came in one day and said: 'Mac, all the cinemas in Limerick are on strike. What shall I do?' 'Book Limerick!' Mac said. 'At once! We'll open on Monday.' There was no theatre in the town. We opened on the Monday in a 2,000-seater cinema, with *Othello*. There was no stage and no wingspace. It was St Patrick's night. The curtain was supposed to rise at nine o'clock. But the house wasn't full until 11.30, so the play didn't begin until then.

It was well past two in the morning before the curtain came down. Everyone of the 2,000 people in the audience was drunk. Apart from that, they weren't accustomed to Shakespeare. For the first half of the play, up to 'I am your own for ever,' we couldn't hear ourselves speak, couldn't hear our cues. The cast was alarmed. We expected the audience on stage at any moment. We kept our hands on our swords. I was playing Iago at the time. I came offstage with Mac at the interval and gasped. 'Don't worry,' Mac said, 'don't worry.' After the interval he began to move. When he walked on to the stage for the 'Naked in bed, Iago, and not mean harm' scene (his great body hunched, his voice low with grit), they silenced. He tore into the fit. He made the play his and the place his. By the time he had reached

> 'It is the very error of the moon;
> She comes more near the earth than she was wont.
> And makes men mad'

(the word 'mad' suddenly cauterised, ugly, shocking) the audience was quite still. And sober. I congratulated Mac. 'Not bad,' he said, 'was it? Not bad. Godfrey Tearle never did the fit, you know.'

Mac gave about half a dozen magnificent performances of *Othello* while I was with him. Even when, on the other occasions, he conserved his energies in the role, he always gave the patrons their money'sworth. At his best his was the finest Othello I have seen. His age was always a mystery, but I would think he was in his sixties at the time. Sometimes, late at night, after the show, he looked very old. But on stage in *Othello* he stood, well over six foot, naked to the waist, his gestures complete, final, nothing jagged, his movement of the utmost fluidity and yet of the utmost precision: stood there, dead in the centre of the role, and the great sweeping symphonic playing would begin, the rare tension and release within him, the arrest, the swoop, the savagery, the majesty and repose. His voice was unique: in my experience of an unequalled range. A bass of extraordinary echo, resonance and gut, and remarkable sweep up into tenor, when the note would hit the back of the gallery and come straight back, a brilliant, stunning sound. I remember his delivery of this line: 'Methinks [bass] it should be now a huge [bass] eclipse [tenor] of sun and moon [baritone] and that th'affrighted globe [bass] Should yawn [very deep, the abyss] at alteration.' We all watched him from the wings.

He was capable, of course, of many indifferent and offhand performances. On these occasions an edgy depression and fatigue hung over him. He would gabble his way through the part, his movement fussed, his voice acting outside him, the man himself detached from its acrobatics. At such times his eyes would fix upon the other actors, appraising them coldly, emanating a grim dissatisfaction with himself and his company. Afterwards, over a drink, he would confide: 'I was bad tonight, wasn't I, really awful, but the damn cast was even worse. What a lot.'

He was never a good Hamlet and for some reason or other rarely bothered to play Macbeth. He was obsessed with the lighting in *Macbeth* and more often than not spent half his time on stage glaring at the spot bar. Yet there was plenty of Macbeth in him. I believe his dislike of the play was so intense he couldn't bring himself to play it.

It was consistent with him that after many months of coasting through Shylock he suddenly lashed full-fired into the role at an obscure matinée in a one-horse village; a frightening performance. Afterwards he said to me: 'What did I do? Did you notice? I did something different. What did you think of it? What was it I did?' He never did it again. Not quite like that. Who saw it?

In the trial scene in *The Merchant of Venice* one night I said to him (as Bassanio) instead of 'For thy three thousand ducats here is six', quite involuntarily, 'For thy three thousand *buckets* here is six.' He replied quietly and with emphasis: 'If every *bucket* in six thousand *buckets* were in six parts, and every part a *bucket* I would not draw them—I would have my bond.' I couldn't continue. The other members of the court scene and I turned upstage. Some walked into the wings. But Mac stood, remorseless, grave, like an eagle, waiting for my reply.

Sometimes after a matinée of *Macbeth* and an evening of *Othello* we all stayed on stage, he'd get someone to put on a record of Faust, disappear behind a curtain, reappear in a long golden wig, without his teeth, mime Marguerite weaving, mime Faust and Mephistopheles, deliver at full tilt the aria from Verdi's *Othello* '*Era la notte e Cassio dormia*', while the caretaker swept the dust up, and then in a bar talk for hours of Sarah and Mrs Pat Campbell, with relish, malice and devotion. I think he would still be talking about them now, if he wasn't dead, because they did something he knew about.

In order to present *Oedipus* the company had to recruit extras from the town or village we were in. One night in Dundalk Mac was building up to his blind climax when one of the extras had an epileptic fit on stage and collapsed. He was dragged to the wings where various women attended to him. The sounds of their ministrations seeped on to the stage. Mac stopped, turned to the wings and shouted: 'For God's sake, can't you see I'm trying to act!'

His concentration was always complete in *Oedipus*. He was at his best in the part. He acted with acute 'underness' and tenacity. And he never used his vocal powers to greater or truer effect. He acted along the spine of the role and never deviated from it. As in his two other great roles, Othello and Lear, he understood and expressed totally the final tender clarity which is under the storm, the blindness, the anguish. For me his acting at these times embodied the idea of Yeats's lines:

'They know that Hamlet and Lear are gay,
Gaiety transfiguring all that dread'.

Mac entered into this tragic gaiety naturally and inevitably.

He did Lear eventually. First performance somewhere in County Clare, Ennis, I think. Knew most of the lines. *Was* the old man, tetchy, appalled, feverish. Wanted the storm louder. All of us banged the thundersheets. 'No, they can still hear me. Hit it, hit it.' He got above the noise. I played Edgar in *Lear* only a few times with him before I left the company. At the centre of his performance was a terrible loss, desolation, silence. He didn't think about doing it, he just got there. He did it and got there.

His wife, Marjorie, was his structure and support. She organised the tours, supervised all business arrangements, sat in the box office, kept the cast in order, ran the wardrobe, sewed, looked after Mac, was his dresser, gave him his whiskey. She was tough, critical, cultivated, devoted. Her spirit and belief constituted the backbone of the company. There would have been no company without her.

Ireland wasn't golden always, but it was golden sometimes and in 1950 it was, all in all, a golden age for me and for others.

The people came down to see him. Mac travelled by car, and sometimes some of us did too. But other times we went on the lorry with the flats and props, and going into Bandon or Cloughjordan would find the town empty, asleep, men sitting upright in dark bars, cowpads, mud, smell of peat, wood, old clothes. We'd find digs, wash-basin and jug, tea, black pudding, and off to the hall, set up a stage on trestle tables, a few rostrums, a few drapes, costumes out of the hampers, set up shop, and at night play, not always but mostly, to a packed house (where had they come from?); people who listened, and who waited to see him, having seen him before, and been brought up on him.

Mac wasn't any kind of dreamer. He was remote from the Celtic Twilight. He kept a close eye on the box-office receipts. He was sharp about money, was as depressed as anyone else when business was bad. Where there was any kind of company disagreement he proved elusive. He distanced himself easily from unwelcome problems. Mrs Mac dealt with those. Mac was never 'a darling actor of the old school'. He was a working man. He respected his occupation and never stopped learning about it, from himself and from others.

For those who cared for him and admired him there must remain one great regret; that for reasons I do not understand, he last played in England, at Stratford, in 1933. The English theatre can never know the depth of its loss.

Mac wasn't 'childlike' in temperament, as some have said. He was evasive, proud, affectionate, mischievous, shrewd, merry, cynical, sad, and could be callous. But he was never sour or self-pitying. His life was the stage. Life with a big L came a bad second. He had no patience with what he considered a world of petty sufferings, however important they might seem to the bearer. He was completely unsentimental. Gossip delighted him, and particularly sexual gossip. He moved with great flexibility and amusement through Catholic Ireland, greatly attracted by the ritual of the church. He loved to speak of the mummy of the Blessed Oliver Plunkett in Drogheda 'with a lovely amber spot on its face'. He mixed freely with priests and nuns, went to Mass, sometimes, but despised the religious atrophy, rigidity and complacency with which he was confronted. He mixed with the priests partly because he enjoyed their company, partly because his livelihood depended upon them. He was a realist. But he possessed a true liberality of spirit. He was humble. He was a devout anti-puritan. He was a very great pisstaker. He was a great actor and we who worked with him were the luckiest people in the world and loved him.

Robert Skidelsky

SIR OSWALD MOSLEY

Robert Skidelsky is a Research Fellow of the British Academy. He is the author of *Politicians and the Slump*, and *Progressive Schools*.

SIR OSWALD MOSLEY is the most fascinating, perplexing, disturbing phenomenon in modern English politics. He is far too considerable a figure to be written off as a crackpot extremist of a particularly repellent kind, or even, more charitably, as a promising young man who went astray. His own account of his career deserves to rank, if fairly considered, as one of the most distinguished political testaments of our time. There's something else, too, which marks him out from the common run of fascist leaders this century, big or small. Of all of them, he's virtually the only one who had a real chance of coming to the top through the normal political system. In 1930 he had the political world at his feet, and might easily have become prime minister of either a Labour or a Conservative Government. The late John Strachey, one of his early associates, told me shortly before he died that Mosley would have been a difficult, but a very great, prime minister.

What then went wrong? Why was the British political system unable to utilise a man of Sir Oswald's brilliant and varied gifts? Was it his fault? Or was it the system's?

The answer is a bit of both. It is easy enough to pinpoint the failures of character and judgment that destroyed him, and I shall do so in a minute. But it must not be supposed that these failures furnish the sole explanation of his downfall. His good qualities frightened the English political establishment almost as much as his bad ones—his dynamism, his creativity, his political courage—'unequalled in anyone I have known' as Lord Boothby has said —almost as much as his fascism and anti-semitism.

His success in these circumstances becomes more problematic. Whether he would ever have succeeded in capturing one of the main party machines for his particular brand of strenuous, Gaullist-type leadership, is doubtful. The exclusion of both Lloyd George and Churchill at the height of their powers suggests that the political establishment generally favours the quiet life—at least in peacetime—and Mosley was cast if anything for the role of a great peacetime leader—an English Franklin Roosevelt. Even the world depression of 1929-33 failed to dislodge mediocrity from the driving seat. There seems to be no permanent place for a Lloyd George, a Churchill, or even a 'good' Mosley in the modern English political system. All three, in their very different ways, seem to us obsolete—atavistic almost, in their crude and explosive energy. Whether this is a tribute to our gentler civilisation, or merely a mark of our decline, history alone will finally decide.

The starting point in any explanation of Mosley's failure must be his own background and personality. Lady Violet Bonham Carter has written of Winston Churchill that 'politics were his natural and inevitable vocation'. People like the Churchills or the great aristocratic families like the Cecils had been bred in the central traditions of English political life—the traditions of compromise and adaptation that had enabled them to stave off the revolutions which had engulfed most other European nations. Mosley by contrast entered politics as a complete outsider, as a lone wolf. He sprang neither from the Whig-Conservative political establishment, nor from the politically conscious sections of the working-class.

Instead he came from the ranks of the county squirearchy, from a wealthy Staffordshire family that had hibernated quietly for some hundreds of years, remote from the political changes that had gone on all around it. These backwoodsmen still emerge occasionally and briefly to deliver a great blast of the trumpet against some progressive reform before retreating once again to their country fastnesses. A flavour of life at Rolleston, the Mosley seat, is conveyed by the bare-fisted family boxing matches which occasionally used to take place in the ancestral hall. Sir Oswald's grandfather knocked out his son with a 'single right to the jaw'; Sir Oswald fought his own father in the same tradition, though without the same result: the bout was terminated with a 'merry handshake' before any damage was done. The externals of wealth and spaciousness concealed a life little refined from the crudeness of Elizabethan times. It was almost as if the rise of middle-class, liberal England had passed unnoticed, leaving the top and bottom of the social spectrum united in a feudal ethic of chivalry and toughness.

The two great middle-class training grounds for politics have been the ancient universities and the Bar: Mosley's training-grounds were Sandhurst and the trenches in the First World War. Admittedly he went to Winchester, but his arrogance was not of the well-known Wykehamist kind: of intellectual interests he had at this time none. He never showed much aptitude for team-games, but excelled at fencing and boxing; the Fascist blackshirt followed the design of a fencing jacket. At Sandhurst he was involved in numerous fights, both with authority and with his fellow cadets: already his personality divided, rather than united, people. Nevertheless, the army left its mark. It was an instrument designed for action. The objective was given and definite: discussion was limited to means. This was the model he favoured for politics. At most times he believed that there was one clear political priority—whether it was curing unemployment in the 1920s, avoiding war with Germany in the 1930s, or getting into Europe in the 1950s. Political discussion should be directed towards discovering the best method of achieving these objectives. There was little room for compromise in this model. A strategy based on a series of internal compromises would almost certainly fail to achieve its declared objectives.

His war record from 1914–17 was brave and honourable. The slaughter of the trenches turned his mind towards politics. The sacrifice of the flower of England, indeed of Europe, imposed on post-war politicians two main duties: the prevention of war in the future, and the construction in England of a land fit for heroes. His motive for going into politics was thus directly linked to his wartime experiences. He often spoke of himself as a representative of the war generation.

These, then, were the objectives imposed by history and sacrifice. As to method, he had before him the model of the wartime, interventionist state. The wartime state is a combination of big business and military attitudes. The party struggle is suspended, ideologies thrown out of the window because everyone is concentrating on national survival. The best men are appointed to positions of leadership and given the tools to do the job. Full employment and high wages are necessary to keep up national morale. Individual selfishness is subordinated to the national good. This, Mosley concluded, is how the state ought to be run in peacetime. Given certain overriding political objectives, the sole problem is one of method and organisation. Those bred in the central traditions of English politics know that this kind of state is an exception. For Mosley, fresh to politics, it came to be the norm.

If his background and experience disqualified him from playing the part of a politician's politician, certain features of his personality contributed even more to that result. Although he constantly spoke of the need for national union, his own temperament seemed destined for ever to divide men into enthusiastic supporters and implacable foes. He was an inspiring public speaker, yet from his earliest days in politics his meetings were marked by rowdiness, often provoked by an over-reaction on the speaker's part to criticism or heckling. Wherever Mosley stood or spoke, despite his repeated assertion that it was issues, not personalities, that were at stake, it was his own personality and methods that provoked the constant storms in which he found himself.

An example is his speech in a Cambridge Union debate in 1920 on the Indian Amritsar massacre. Mosley was on a good liberal wicket, condemning General Dyer. Yet his speech provoked a furious controversy that went on for weeks in the undergraduate journals. Not content with attacking General Dyer for over-zealousness, or even panic, Mosley in a 'fanatical fulmination' blamed the massacre on the British feeling of 'race superiority': General Dyer regarded the Indian as a 'fungus on the white man's soul, to be shot down and destroyed'; his methods were those of 'Prussian frightfulness'. 'So ended', in the words of the under-graduate reporter of the *New Cambridge*, 'the most deplorable speech it has been our misfortune to hear at the Union Society ... a speech which deliberately attempted to arouse the worse passions of racial hatred.' Today, this undergraduate righteousness seems rather misplaced; and certainly the speech was well received, and subsequently defended, by the Indian students. Nevertheless, the furore was not untypical of the reactions which Mosley aroused. It was not so much the substance, as the method, which gave rise to complaint: the stridency, the use of invective, the inflaming of passions, the polarisation into extremes of enthusiasm and resentment—so different from the characteristic English method of 'reducing the temperature', taking the heat out of controversy.

In mitigation one should perhaps plead his youth and back-ground: he entered Parliament at 22, and was even then only 23. Indeed his whole conventional political career was crowded into an extraordinarily short span of years: by the time he was 34 he was already outside the mainstream of English politics. These, moreover, were years of the most dazzling success. It was not so important then to be a good party man, as parties themselves were in constant convulsions, and Mosley's switches from Coalition Unionist, to Independent, to Labour, didn't seem particularly extraordinary. He was taken up by the established giants: Lord Robert Cecil, Lloyd George, Churchill, Birkenhead, Ramsay MacDonald. He was constantly in the news, whether it was marrying Lord Curzon's daughter in the presence of two Kings and Queens, exposing the Black and Tans, fighting tempestuous elections, conducting public controversies with his father, devising new economic policies, resigning, or capturing headlines with some startling speech or phrase. These successes fed an already formidable arrogance and conceit. In the cartoons of the 1920s he is depicted with his nose held high in the air, as if to avoid the bad smells of the surrounding political countryside. The late Herbert Morrison told me that Mosley used to speak to him 'like a land-lord addressing his tenantry'. His success also bred a sense of his own infallibility. His economic policies were superlatively good, but he showed less than flexibility in adapting them to new circumstances. Nor did he do anything to disarm the suspicions and jealousies which his successes and brilliance produced. He was always a great teaser, and his early career is littered with rather heartless practical jokes and unkind remarks which certainly didn't endear him even to those who admired him and would gladly have worked with him.

He was an example of a particular type of delayed adolescence. It would have been disastrous to have given the early Mosley supreme power. Characters like his should be given a chance to grow up before they are allowed a sniff of real power: but para-doxically their early excesses put them out of the running for it in later life when they are better equipped to exercise it. In a sense Mosley is right when he claims that he has gone on improving like a good wine: he would be better in power today than in 1931, though the risks would still be considerable.

How then did he manage to get so far? The answer is that he had a brilliant mind and a compulsive dynamism. These qualities were focused in the late 1920s on exactly the right issue: the conquest of mass unemployment, the great blight of the inter-war years. If one can rewrite history for a moment, the ideal combina-tion in government in the late 1920s and early 1930s would have been Lloyd George as Prime Minister to provide an overall and continuing dynamism, Mosley and Ernest Bevin in joint charge of economic affairs, and Stanley Baldwin to apply the brake. Instead Mosley was consigned to complete futility in a Labour

administration baffled by events which it never began to understand, and lacking even the will to protect the interests of its own
supporters. Sheer frustration drove Mosley and many other
M.P.s of his generation to the verge of madness. In political
terms he went over the edge: most of the others just held back in
time.

Could that ideal political combination have come about if
Mosley or Lloyd George or the various other actors in this
tragedy had played their cards differently? I believe the answer to
be 'No', and for one very clear reason, namely, that the political
battle at that time was constructed round personalities and issues
which had almost nothing to do with the burning question of the
hour. This political battle was bound to place in power personalities like MacDonald and Baldwin and their henchmen who were
quite incapable of coping with the problems which they faced,
and what is more, who were encumbered by ideologies and
interests which would have prevented them from dealing with the
problems on their merits even had they had the will or capacity
to do so. Mass unemployment continuing for 20 years was the
price England had to pay for this long drawn-out struggle between
Socialism and *laissez-faire* capitalism, and for the inability of the
English political system to focus on the relevant problems.

Once this central fact is recognised, then much of the indictment
of Mosley for leaving the old parties and starting up a movement
of his own falls to the ground. Of course, in political terms, it was
extremely foolish. 'The English hate new parties', wrote Sir Colin
Coote the other day. Foolish and reckless it may have been: add,
too, Mosley's own youth, arrogance, absolute conviction in his
own rectitude, supreme contempt for the conventional practi-
tioners of the political game. But I wouldn't have thought that
the formation of the New Party or even the British Union of
Fascists could be called dishonourable. In fact those who coun-
selled Mosley to hold back—Beaverbrook, Bernard Shaw,
Macmillan, Keynes, Boothby and many others—didn't do so on
the grounds that what he was attempting was morally wrong.

They considered it to be imprudent. They said: 'Stay on, try to work within the system, learn to compromise.'

After Mosley's parliamentary defeat in 1931 he told Harold Nicolson that he was tempted to retire, spend a few years studying and broadening his mind and then return. A real political genius like De Gaulle would have done just that. Even had he abandoned British Fascism after a couple of years, Mosley's political career could have been salvaged. But unlike the General, Mosley was incapable of withdrawing to await a more favourable moment to strike back. He pressed indefatigably on to disaster.

In fairness, the choices of the time were incredibly difficult. Who, after all, was right in the 1930s? The National Government which brought England to the verge of disaster in 1939? The Communists who had to acquiesce in the atrocities of Stalinism? The Labour Party, floundering as much as everyone else? In the upshot, history vindicated the handful of men round Winston Churchill who saw with a terrible prescience the coming struggle with Germany. But even Churchill was written off as wildly irresponsible in that myopic decade. Few emerge with credit, and when the final accounts are drawn up, Mosley's part may come to be viewed more kindly. 1539443

Does his career have any lesson to offer for today, beyond the awful warning that o'erweening vanity can destroy the most brilliant gifts? I believe it does. A country which is faced with the grave and difficult choices facing Britain today needs men with the kind of qualities which Mosley brought to politics, though it needs just as importantly to protect itself against them. Had Mosley been given his chance in a subordinate position in the early 1930s he would have been no danger and might have been of great use. His career, in short, challenges us to examine afresh our political traditions, to devise some way of enabling the best to serve the community, without at the same time making the community their servant.

Chaim Raphael

THE PAST INSIDE US

Chaim Raphael was Head of the Information Division at
the Treasury from 1957 to 1968, and has recently become a
Research Fellow in history at the University of Sussex.
His books include *The Walls of Jerusalem* and (under the
pseudonym Jocelyn Davey) a series of detective novels.

AUTHORS ALWAYS HAVE the greatest fun, and the greatest
anguish, in deciding on titles for their books, especially when they
feel that they want to suggest something subtle and poetic on top
of the book's obvious character. In this situation, the best advice
to an author is probably: 'Watch out!' The more poetic the title,
the harder it is for someone to remember when he goes into a
bookshop.

Perhaps I should have borne this in mind in choosing the title
for the book I called *The Walls of Jerusalem*. The book is about
Jerusalem, so that part of the title is fair enough. And it even deals
at one point with the walls. The underlying subject is the destruction of Jerusalem by the Romans in A.D. 70, and I explain, *en
passant*, how it came about that one wall—now called 'The
Wailing Wall'—was left standing.

But I have to confess that—against my own advice—I was also
trying to express something deeper by this title. What I had in
mind really was not the physical city but the 'Jerusalem' that
every Jew carries inside him—his folk memory, and his personal
links with his people's past. In writing this book, I was trying as a
Jew to get inside the walls of this personal Jerusalem.

To feel strongly about the past inside you is mostly a matter of temperament. Even those who seem to start off against the same background—brothers and sisters, or people long established in the same village—draw on their past quite differently. I myself feel it all strongly. I even claim, as an English Jew, to have more than one past, in potent form, inside me. I have a long English past and a long Jewish past to draw on. This may sound slightly comic, since my English past, in factual terms, is pretty brief: my father and mother came from Russia to live in England in the 1890s. But if you are born and brought up here, the past comes pouring in. English history has flowed into my personal life from periods long before my family became English. I won't say that I have the proper reaction to everything Anglo-Saxon in the air around me. I was never able, for example, to respond as an English child no doubt should to *Puck of Pook's Hill*. But I have always been stirred, in a curiously intimate way, by essentially English writers like Chaucer or Cobbett. Or to take a really extreme case —just to confront the issue head on—if I stand, say, in the ruins of Fountains Abbey, I feel that this is a world from which some part of me sprang.

If I feel able to say this for the English past inside me, how much more so for my Jewish past. Here, the first element is the force of direct memory: family memory; my parents' childhood in small Russian-Jewish towns; the stories they told us as children, some sad, some nostalgically happy. Their past entered my life also through the festivals and Jewish ceremonies which were observed by them in a timeless spirit as if they had been carried on un-changed—not always true—since the days of Moses.

For many Jews it is this direct but *vague* connection with a long traditional past which is the dominant Jewish influence in their lives. In my own case, my curiosity about history has intensified my feelings. As a result I have grown into my past—or it has grown into me—in what is almost an eerie way. It's not that I have developed some metaphysical feeling about Jewish history and its place in human history; it's rather that the work of the scholars and their new discoveries have given me a chance to make

37

connections—not mechanically, but with a constant sense of self-recognition and self-awareness. I'll give a few examples in a minute of what I mean.

But I'd like to make the point first that this digging of oneself out of the past is by no means a Jewish prerogative. I have to say this—though it might seem obvious—because I might otherwise be thought to be basing it all on the fact that a Jew draws on a particularly ancient past. We Jews may be a special case, but there are plenty of other people with long interior memories.

One writer I think of in this regard is Jacquetta Hawkes, who talked about this whole subject in her wonderful book *A Land*. In that book she dealt with the most ancient aspects of man's existence, but constantly turned geology and archaeology into a direct connection with things she felt deeply about in her own life—the ploughlands of Norfolk, the cliffs of Dorset, the sculpture of Henry Moore. She has done the same in her new book *The Dawn of the Gods*, bringing the earliest civilisations of Knossos and Mycenae into the personal poetry of her own life as a scholar—and as a woman.

This approach is very sympathetic to me, because it echoes my own reaction to so many different aspects of my Jewish past. It's never a simple process. I don't feel that Jewish history is a steady unfolding story from the remote and perplexing to the modern and comprehensible. The really ancient past is often more understandable and personally moving than levels, old and new, where my own nature, and the things I have learnt, seem to offer some personal insights and satisfactions.

This is what I was writing about in *The Walls of Jerusalem*. I gave quite a few examples there of the way in which as a boy, I found my Jewish background constantly illuminated by discoveries from other worlds. Often it was by accident. I happened to spend my early years in a small north-eastern town. When I was a child, my father used to read me rabbinic stories about a period full of anguish for us—when the Temple at Jerusalem was destroyed by the Romans. One set of stories was about a subsequent revolt by the Jews, which was put down by a wicked

Emperor called Hadrian. This man's cruelty was so great that the rabbis, telling the story, always accompanied his name with a curse: 'Hadrian, may his bones be crushed!' One day I went on a school picnic to a tumble-down ruin near our town, and was told that this was called 'Hadrian's Wall'. It took me quite a time to understand that this was the same Hadrian: that my private Jewish world could be related in this way to the world outside. From then on, as I stumbled through Caesar at school, my ancestors were always in the background, holding their own, or —if defeated—going down fighting.

This part of my Jewish past came to life for me in an even more sensational way about 15 years ago, in relation to a mythical Jewish hero of that same revolt, known in the stories as 'Bar Kokhbah'. For nearly 2,000 years Bar Kokhbah had the status in Jewish legend of King Arthur or Robin Hood. Imagine what the people of Nottingham would feel if some documents about Robin Hood were suddenly discovered in Sherwood Forest. This, in fact, is what has happened with Bar Kokhbah. In the early 1950s, archaeologists working in the Holy Land let it be known—though it was all shrouded in mystery for a while—that they had discovered letters actually written by Bar Kokhbah to his soldiers at various camps, and in the identical tone of the legends—a mixture of military instructions and bravado. The first discoveries led to more. The Israeli archaeologist Yadin, discoverer of Masada, launched a search in the caves of the desert and found not only more letters but hoards of other contemporary documents, giving countless illustrations of the social background of a period known until then only in the pages of the Jewish Talmud. Suddenly it was all given reality.

The response is rather different for more modern times, though here too the unfolding of the past constantly brings the unexpected together, with shafts of personal involvement. Let me spell out an example. My father's name was David, and his father's Sabbathai. I knew this as a small child (though I never met my grandfather) because when my father was called to the reading of the Law in synagogue, the cantor would cry out in Hebrew:

'Arise, David son of Sabbathai!' The name was otherwise unknown to me, until I read in the history books about a vast
upheaval that swept through the Jewish world in the 17th century
at the news that a man called Sabbathai Zevi had appeared in
Turkey and was about to lead the whole of the Jewish people back
to Palestine. Feeling personally involved, I read everything I could
about this strange episode; but the greatest delight was to find an
entry about it in Pepys's Diary. Pepys is describing a visit to his
bookseller's in St Paul's Churchyard on 19 February 1666, and
this is what he says: 'I am told for certain, what I have heard once
or twice already, of a Jew in town that does offer to give any man
£10 to be paid £100 if a certain person now resident in Smyrna
be within these two years owned by all the Princes of the East as
the King of the world, and that this man is the true Messiah. One
named a friend of his that received ten pieces of gold upon this
score and says that the Jew hath disposed of £1,100 in this manner, which is very strange.'

One can always count on Pepys: and it's nice to know also that
this early Jewish settler had so quickly absorbed the British habit
of being willing to bet on anything.

It's not difficult to feel at home with the wandering Jews of
European times. What seems at first much stranger is how the
scholars have opened up contacts with the Jews who seemed really
remote—the patriarchs who wandered over Palestine nearly 4,000
years ago, or the writers of the Psalms who go back to well on
to 3,000 thousand years. Perhaps in one sense it's not strange,
since all of us—Christians as well as Jews—are already so familiar
with the Bible. The adventures of Abraham, Isaac and Jacob in the
Bible have made them very real as characters: the imagery of the
Psalms, in Hebrew or the English of the Authorised Version, is
woven into our language and thought. In what way, then, has it
all become real and intimate in any new sense?

If I say 'through the discoveries of archaeology', I don't mean
that archaeology has proved 'the truth' of the Bible. The Bible
stories, the poetry of the Psalms, the thundering of the Prophets,
exercised their drama on us long before the first archaeologist

began to dig. The Bible can never be more 'true' than it has been in this way, through the centuries.

Nor do I mean that archaeology has now made it more convincing to Jews that this is where their history began: that these are our ancestors. We could never doubt this. Of course we can never prove that all Jews today are the descendants of the Patriarchs. There has been much erosion and mingling since those days. Despite this, we have always been confident of the link, and proud of our ancestry. And this is because each generation of Jews was born into a self-contained tradition—a story that had come down in fragments but was filled out by an act of imagination.

What has happened now is that the fragments no longer stand on their own; and anyone—particularly any Jew—who has already accepted this past inside him may well feel a burning curiosity to follow the clues which have now emerged about that ancient world.

Perhaps the most illuminating are those which relate to the patriarchal world of Abraham. Whereas once we read the detailed but mysterious stories of his adventures in Genesis as part of a figure of myth, the scholars can now describe the period for us— say about 1800 B.C.—from a variety of discoveries mostly made only in the last 40 years or so. These sources not only document the social, economic and legal background lying behind the archaic Genesis stories, but even provide countless parallels to the names of the ancient chieftains with whom Abraham was always tangling. The scholars are, of course, still arguing—and will go on arguing—on how to add it all up. I feel drawn myself to the picture which emerges in the work of the archaeologist William Albright, who tells us that the Hebrews were the 'Abiru' or 'Apiru' who came in successive waves from Mesopotamia, travelling over Palestine not as wandering shepherds but as traders. And when circumstances called for it, as raiders or mercenaries. Their caravans of donkeys, not camels, moved up and down from Syria to Egypt, carrying spices and metals, wines and perhaps textiles. Nor is this all of merely social interest. With evidence now available that details given in Genesis really go back to stories surviving from the patriarchal age itself, Albright argues that the same is true for the emergence of monotheism. This is startling—but rather comforting—for our feeling about the past. Many scholars used to argue that monotheism could not have arisen so far back. It had emerged, they said, in the period of the Israel monarchy nearly a thousand years later, and had been grafted on to the patriarchs as an anachronism. But Albright now tells us that Hebrew law and belief can be put back firmly where they belong —with the old Father Abraham himself.

Most of this has come to light, as I said, in not much more than the last 40 years. Two major sources for the patriarchal period, both from Iraq, are the archives of Nuzi, found in 1925, and those from Mari, emerging in 1933. For the poetry of the Bible, the outstanding discovery was in 1929, a hoard of writings unearthed at Ugarit on the north coast of Syria. Included are stories of the Canaanite gods—the mighty god Baal and all the others, Dagon, Reshef, Ashera and so on—whose worship was so fiercely condemned by the Hebrew prophets. Now one reads their story as an epic, and in language which often sounds like the Psalms, and helps us to understand its rhythms. Here are four typical lines:

> The skies rain oil,
> The wastes run with honey,
> For Baal the Mighty is alive,
> The Prince of Earth exists.

Sometimes the interest lies in the actual god-names, which we can now see were swept into Hebrew as poetry but adapted miraculously to the praise of *one* God—the God of Israel first, and later the God of all men. Always one is astonished to see how the religion which was just then emerging among the Hebrews—a fierce monotheism linked to a moral attitude to life—could take over so decisively against the barbarous fertility cults—including temple prostitution and child sacrifice—that the Hebrews found around them in the whole of the Middle East.

I said earlier that one is sometimes closer to the faraway past than to the immediate past. Certainly it is true that there is a peculiar satisfaction for a Jew in being able to see his Middle East ancestors in the round. In this sense, a Jew's feelings always flow back to the source.

I found this thought expressed very movingly in a recent poem by Nigel Dennis, describing a burial which he witnessed in the Jewish graveyard of Malta. All around him were the names of Jews—from all manner of countries—whom Fate had brought for their last moments to Malta. The poem ends with these lines:

Strangely you have travelled! How happy I feel
To discover you here! The ground you are in is
Never cold, as Lodz was; the wind here is never
Sharp as it was in Vienna. You are all returned to
The Middle Sea of your forefathers, the world of
Stone, dust and olive. Welcome a thousand times!
Shalom! Shalom!

H. Harvey Wood

OLD POSSUM AND LANCER COLLINS

H. Harvey Wood has been the British Council Representative in Edinburgh, Paris and Rome. He is the author of
many studies in Scots literature, of which the most recent is
Two Scots Chaucerians.

W HEN THE FIRST volume of my edition of the plays of John
Marston appeared in 1934, I waited eagerly, as all young writers
do, for the reviews. In due course they appeared, in all kinds of
publications, learned and not-so-learned, British, French and
American. Some were favourable and some were not, some were
fair, some were unfair, and some were just plain ignorant. One
that gave me immense pleasure, not so much for what it said as
for where it was, occupied the whole of the front page of the
Times Literary Supplement, and carried over on to the next page.
This, I thought, was glory; although the reviewer seemed to me
to have rather peculiar opinions about Marston as an Elizabethan
playwright. In the same year, T. S. Eliot's *Elizabethan Essays*
appeared, and there was the review, set out as an essay, and I
realised that to the honour of the place of my review I had to add
the ineffable honour of its authorship. In spite of all this, and in
spite of the authority of a Faber imprint, I still found some of Mr
Eliot's dicta a little puzzling, to say the least of it. He singled out
Sophonisba as Marston's best play, as 'the most nearly adequate
expression of his distorted and obstructed genius'. That any man
who had read all Marston's plays should have come to this
conclusion was sufficiently odd: that T. S. Eliot, in particular,

44

should have done so was astounding to me. And so in the introduction to the third and last volume of the plays, I adverted to
Eliot's review, and suggested that there was matter in *The
Insatiate Countess* which might have been expected to appeal to the
sometimes obstructed genius of Mr Eliot—that lines like:

> A bastard, a bastard, a bastard:
> I might have liv'd like a gentleman,
> And now I must die like a Hanger on:
> Shew trickes upon a woodden horse,
> And runne through an Alphabet of scurvie faces

might have made some appeal to the author of:

> Then how should I begin
> To spit out all the butt-ends of my days and ways?

Rogero in Marston's play spoke, I suggested, with the authentic
accent of Mr Prufrock, with the uneasy embarrassment of a
superior person trapped in inferior circumstances. All this time,
I had not met Mr Eliot. It seemed to me as unlikely a meeting as
one with Edward Lear ('How pleasant to meet Mr Lear')—as
unlikely as that of my ever seeing Shelley plain. That I should, in
about ten years' time, be called upon to review T. S. Eliot, and
T. S. Eliot *as a dramatist*, would have seemed a wildly improbable
prospect at that time.

But the year after I finished the Marston, the war broke out,
and in 1940 I found myself no longer a University lecturer, but
the British Council's Representative in Scotland, dealing, not
with students, but with thousands of Polish men, women and
children, the crews of Dutch and Norwegian vessels, Free French
units, lumberjacks from Newfoundland, and so on. 1944 found
me in London, where I met Rudolf Bing, and our meeting in
London led to a series of meetings and consultations in Edinburgh,
out of which the Edinburgh Festival was born. To my duties as
the British Council's Representative in Scotland was now added

the additional responsibility of presiding over the Festival's Programme Committee, and early in the Festival that Committee approved, with some trepidation, the inclusion in the drama programme of a new play by T. S. Eliot, called *The Cocktail Party*. The trepidation was not as ridiculous as would now appear. The play was still being written, we were told that it was based on a classical myth (we were not told which, but the news did nothing to encourage us) and at the same time we were told that it was to be presented in the manner of West End drawing-room comedy. *Murder in the Cathedral* was one thing, the Committee thought, but a cocktail-party play with Greek implications was another. I must admit that I had grave doubts about the ability of Eliot to construct a play in a modern idiom that would hold and entertain a Festival public. The names of Alec Guinness and Martin Browne were reassuring, however, and in due course the play came to Edinburgh, and Eliot came with it. He attended rehearsals just like a real dramatist, and in the intervals between rehearsals we met. I had met a number of poets before, but never one who in appearance and demeanour suggested rather a bank manager or insurance agent than a literary man. The first night is now a matter of history. It was a tumultous success; a theatre audience had found that it was possible to be entertained by Mr Eliot; and at the end of the performance I was rushed to the BBC to review the play. I do not pretend to remember what I said; but I am sure it must have been pretty trivial and wide of the mark—but not, I make bold to say, any more so than Eliot's comments on Marston. He, unlike me, had had the opportunity of reading the texts of the plays he was criticising, and all the critical comment of scholars of three centuries. I had not even been given advance notice of what Harold Hobson was going to say. But I tackled Eliot while he was in Edinburgh about his curious choice of *Sophonisba* as Marston's greatest play. His reply was modest enough, but a little surprising: 'Oh, I expect it was the only play of Marston's I had read at the time.'

In 1950, I moved to Paris, to represent the British Council in France, and during my four years there, I saw quite a bit of Eliot.

He opened a magnificent exhibition of British books, *Le Livre Anglais* in the Bibliothèque Nationale, and he received an honorary doctorate from the University of Paris. The degree ceremony was a matter of an hour or two, but Eliot stayed happily in Paris for several days, and became very much at home in our house. My younger daughter, Alison, began to be a little bored by the frequent appearances of this elderly stranger, until she discovered that he was the author of *Old Possum's Book of Practical Cats;* whereupon she climbed on to his knee, and the two of them exchanged catty gossip for the rest of the afternoon. When Eliot got back to London, instead of sending my wife an ordinary bread-and-butter letter, he sent Alison an additional cat poem (the Cat Morgan one) in his own abominable typing. It was in the nature of an invitation to Alison to pay him a return visit, and the invitation was issued in the name of the Commissionaire Cat, Sir Henry Morgan, Buccaneer. He explained how Cat Morgan, having retired from the Barbary Coast, was now taking his ease in Bloomsbury Square: it described the dainties to which, in retirement, he was partial, and it finished up with a piece of practical advice:

> So if you 'ave business with Faber—or Faber—
> I'll give you this tip, and it's worth a lot more:
> You'll save yourself time, and you'll spare yourself labour,
> If just you make friends with this Cat on the Door.

And just to make it quite plain that the invitation was officially authorised, the typescript was neatly signed 'O. Possum'. Alison has successfully resisted all bids, however tempting, for the typescript, and is still its proud possessor.

But it was while he was in Paris that the poet met Lancer Collins. Collins was the senior British Council driver, and had held this post ever since the Liberation. At the outbreak of World War One, Collins was with his regiment in India, and in no time at all found himself in France fighting the kind of war he had been least prepared for. But he survived four years of trench warfare, married a Frenchwoman, and took her home proudly to his native Devon. Madame Collins took one shuddering look around, and promptly marched her husband back to Paris, where he remained until the Germans marched in in 1940. By now he was not only a French *mari*, but a French *père* and *grandpère* into the bargain; but he had retained his British nationality, and so the Germans interned him. His position was realised to be an odd one, however, and so he was visited almost daily in his cell by a German officer, who invited him to sign a document accepting French nationality, in return for which he could be reunited with his loved ones. Collins treated the offer with the contempt it deserved, and sat out his imprisonment until the end of the war, when he emerged, straight-backed, wax-moustached, and still defiantly British—surely the most admirably stupid man ever to have served the British Council. When I first met him, he had spent 36 years in France, as husband, father and grandfather, without having learned anything that could have been defined (except by an indulgent philologist) as French, while having almost entirely forgotten his English. This was very useful when Collins (who must have been one of the worst drivers in Paris) was pulled up by the police. Then, without effort, he gave a splendid impersonation of a clueless British chauffeur; but every now and then he was bowled out by an *agent* who remembered seeing him around for the last 30 years. Long before Mon Général had thought of it, Collins had invented Franglais. I remember telling him to park in a particular place, and getting the memorable reply; 'But, msoo, if I was to gare the voiture there, I wouldn't be able to sort.'

Collins took Eliot under his wing from the moment of his arrival, drove him everywhere, waited long hours for him at the Sorbonne, and when the enthusiasm of French students threatened to become embarrassing, conspired with Eliot over side-door exits and quick get-aways. He delivered the great man at our front door in the manner of one who has safely accomplished a mission of great moment and danger; and it was both touching and amusing to see the understanding that developed between the two men. The time came for Eliot's last meal with us, after which Collins was to drive us to the station. We were all sorry to see him go—even Alison, although only Eliot's tact averted a nasty last-minute situation. Both Old Possum and Alison were fairly hearty potato-eaters, and there came a nasty moment when the poet's hand was outstretched to take the last potato. By the grace of God, he looked across the table, and found himself transfixed by the cold critical eye of the rival potato-client. Nothing in Eliot's life ever became him more than the speed with which he sized up the situation, smiled at Alison, and suggested that they should share the potato—a suggestion that was accepted with dignity.

When we had seen Eliot off, Collins relaxed a little, and beamed with pleasure when I thanked him for all the extra hours of duty he had devoted to our guest. 'Oh,' he said, 'I became quite fond of the old gentleman. I don't think he'd 've managed without me.' I broke it gently to Collins that he and the old gentleman were precisely the same age; but it had to be admitted that Collins' ramrod back, quick movements, and misleadingly alert manner gave him the appearance of a man 20 years Eliot's junior.

Later, when I was stationed in London and met Eliot, we talked over his Paris visit, and the only member of my establishment he asked about was Collins, about whom he inquired with great particularity and obvious affection. But Collins, alas, was retired from his British Council service. The roads of France were that much safer for it; but for Collins himself it must have felt as though the Union Jack had been lowered on him. He retired to his huge French family, and died, not long after, among foreigners.

Gerard Fiennes

LOST PROPERTY

Gerard Fiennes worked for the railways from 1928 to 1967.
He rose from an assistant yardmaster to Chairman of a
British Railways Region earning £130 million a year, and
spending somewhat less. As a result of writing his book
I Tried to Run a Railway he was, he says, 'invited to retire'.

WHEN I WAS a railway manager—and that wasn't very long
ago—I always thought that the decisions of a manager should be
taken in the light of the purest logic.

And of course it was this process which led me to be in the
corridor of this train carrying in my hand a napkin and in that
napkin was a set of false teeth, upper and lower and I was trying
to find the owner. It was my habit, when I was a manager, to mark
in my diary three days in each month in letters of fire 'KEEP CLEAR.'
And on those days I used to go around the railway doing what the
then chairman of British Railways Board used to describe with
dreadful scorn as 'swanning around'. These were agreeable occasions. I went out just to talk and be talked to, to see and to be
seen and on the whole if there is one thing that railwaymen like
more than an unexpected productivity payment, it is chat.

This habit of swanning around led to some unexpected events.
I remember one day at Paddington. I went down to South
Wales and I was travelling with one of the Assistant General
Managers, James Flynn. We'd worked fairly solidly, leaving
Paddington, about as far as Swindon, and one of the things which
we'd been working on was punctuality. I'd been complaining a

good deal about the running, the loco performance was not good, the men were just getting a new series of diesels, reliability wasn't all that hot. The men were driving in notch four instead of top notch for fear of the nuts and bolts falling off. And they had a point. Anyway on this trip as we went through Swindon the rush and clatter was pretty impressive so I looked up and then looked at my watch and found that we were about eleven minutes before time. So when we got to Newport I said to James: 'I'm going to get on this footplate, tell this driver what a good guy he is.' So I did just that, got out of the compartment, walked along the platform, climbed up the two steps into the diesel, just flashed an engine pass at him and stood attentively at his side. He let it go until he'd actually left Newport station, he ran through the tunnel, past the rather difficult signal—difficult to see—at the outlet from the tunnel and then he turned to me. And he said, 'They tell me the new General Manager's in the train', and I said, 'Well, he was but he got out at Newport.' 'Dio-o!' he said, 'he should have gone on to Cardiff, I wonder where the silly bastard's got to.' So I said 'Here' flat and being a Welshman of course he collapsed with laughter and no doubt has dined out on that story as often as I have.

I never thought that this sort of thing did me much harm as a manager. In fact, I think on the whole managers should be figures of fun rather than very important persons. They certainly shouldn't be very self-important persons. And I did get one reward in this way. There was a passenger guard at Liverpool Street, Bill Moss, with whom I used to ride many years ago and our brake van on our commuter train in the mornings was always crowded with commuters. Not because they couldn't get seats in the train because they could, but they wanted to hear Bill Moss telling me how to run the railways and they wanted to hear me telling Bill Moss how to get his train along the road. And the upshot was that Bill retired a month or two before I did and when my terrible disgrace fell on me Bill wrote, he was I think the first person to write and he started his letter, 'I always knew you would come to a bad end because of your terrible ways.'

The aura of a General Manager never surrounded me in quite the same way as it did Sir Herbert Walker, Sir Felix Pole, Milne or Keith Grand. Nevertheless it was on the Western Region where you were regarded as nearest to God. I remember one day walking from Reading on one of those swanning around days and going south-westwards. And eventually I came to Southcot Junction signal box which has since gone as part of the Reading re-signalling and I walked up the steps to the signal box and opened the door. 'Fiennes, General Manager Paddington.' The usual reaction for the signalman was to wipe his hand on the seat of his trousers and then come forward and shake mine. This bloke looked at me with utter disbelief. He said, 'You can't be'. And I said, 'Well, I am', took my gold pass out of my pocket and showed him. "Why?' 'General Managers don't walk', he said.

Now this is the kind of thing you run in to when you go out incognito, when you take everything that is coming to you. Nevertheless the story that I am going to relate was a surprise even in that category.

I had started in the Lost Property Office at Paddington where there were thousands of bicycles, there were hundreds of umbrellas, there were scores of wigs and wedding rings being sold to rows of incurious East End dealers. But there was nothing of particular interest there, nothing nearly so spectacular as an occasion at King's Cross.

I went some years ago to the Lost Property Office at King's Cross to congratulate the chief of it on his birthday. Now there is a most complicated procedure for getting into the Lost Property Office at King's Cross. You arrive at a kind of wicket and you're inspected very severely through it and after a time the door is released and you go in. And during this time when I was being subjected to this scrutiny there were sounds of high revelry within, and when the door was eventually opened there in the middle of the floor was a sailing dinghy, mainsail and jib set, at the helm was birthday boy. On the middle thwart were two porters each with an oar out singing sea shanties and rowing him presumably from Putney to Mortlake brewery. Now Paddington contained nothing as spectacular as this so off I walked across to the station and got on the first train which was going which happened to be bound North and West. After a little while I went along to the dining car, I sat down in a seat and lifted the napkin and under the napkin neatly superimposed one upon the other was a set of false teeth—upper and lower. I laid the napkin slowly down.

I looked at the false teeth, they looked back at me, clenched and uncommunicative. Just at the moment—enter the dining car conductor. 'Sir', he said, 'Guvnor—' and words failed him. 'Not mine,' I said and bared my own at him. Whose then? There seemed no immediate answer to this. And we looked at the teeth and the teeth looked back at us. At that moment the train took Twyford station at perhaps some miles an hour more than the then permitted 75. It was indeed this event which led to the line being straightened at that point. As I say, we went round that curve at slightly more than the permitted 75. The teeth rolled, the upper jaw bounced once upon the table and then bounded to the feet of the travelling ticket collector who had just come through the swing door. Now travelling ticket collectors are trained to show no surprise so this man of iron picked up the teeth and handed them back to me with every circumstance of respect for his General Manager and a certain sense of suppressed glee. 'Not mine,' I said and showed him again. Whose then? And then we went into conference. It was fairly clear that nobody had left these teeth and then got out of the train because there had been no stops since Paddington. It was fairly clear that it was not a suicide because what suicide would take out his teeth first? The most plausible explanation was that it was a seat reservation. Somebody wishing to have lunch had taken this very logical step to reserve his place. But if so, why hide them under the napkin? All these things fell to the ground and it seemed quite obvious that some-body, somewhere on this train was without his teeth. And I've only known one instance where being without your teeth was a positive advantage. That was at my first wife's home, Llangollen, where the local vicar was reproving the local reprobate. 'Martha,' he said, 'you will be cast out where there is weeping and wailing and gnashing of teeth.' 'Vicar,' she replied 'let them as 'as 'em, gnash 'em.' So we didn't come to a conclusion. And I proceeded to instant management. 'Bob,' I said to the conductor, 'when you go along the train, calling First Service, you will bear these on a salver and call them with First Service, or alternatively you, Snapper, will go along the train and as you clip tickets you will get every passenger into conversation and peer anxiously into his mouth.' Now one of the things about this kind of instant management is that you must never allow the managed a choice. It's like Denis Compton calling for a run—it's an invitation to debate and so it proved here. And the second thing is of course that railways are now a democracy and there is a procedure of consultation whereby management lays its proposals before the staff and the staff discuss them, with management, and make proposals for the decisions to be improved. Snapper said, 'Seems to me these 'ere are Lost Property and that's the guard's job' and here we were in a demarcation dispute. Reluctantly I wrapped these teeth in the napkin and set off for the guard. And when I got to the guard I recognised that here was no solution because this guard was one of those towering, resplendent, former Great Western guards. He was about seven feet high, he was about five feet wide, you used to see him in the days before nationalisation in the finest broadcloth and with a small sort of Turkish fez on the top which had a button on it. It was very largely due to employing people like this, who called Peers of the Realm and Lords Lieutenant by name, that the Great Western earned their towering reputation for public service. I didn't even unwrap the napkin and show him the teeth. If I had his reaction would have been quite simple. He would have taken them, thanked me politely, gone to Worcester or Hereford which he was going to, he would then have returned to Paddington and when we got to Paddington he would have alighted on the platform and shouted 'Boy' and three or four would have leapt to his command, he would have handed them to them—to one of them—to be taken to the Lost Property office where three months later they would have been sold to those same rows of East End incurious dealers. No, this was no answer. I stayed with him gossiping for a few minutes. I told him a small story. Some relations of mine who lived near Banbury, a cousin Hersey, one got into a—this is really very unlike her—she got into a Ladies Only compartment at the rear end of a train and just as the train was moving out a man leapt on the footboard, opened the door and swung himself in. And one of the battle-axes growled at him, 'Sir, can't you see that this is a Ladies Only' and the man swept a withering glance round the compartment and replied, 'Madam, its appearance will so preserve it' and fell headlong on the platform. And this guard was not amused. So I took the napkin with the teeth in it and I started back disconsolately along the corridor and as I did so a figure came out of a lavatory, tall, grey, spectacled, drooping on his stem and bumped into me. 'I'm so sorry,' he said 'I've lost my spectacles.' 'Sir,' I said, proceeding to instant management, 'Your spectacles are on your nose, but here are your teeth.' Upper and lower snapped into place. 'Thank you so much,' he said, 'I can't see to eat without them.' At that moment the brakes went on, the train slowed, it came to a stand. It was Oxford, naturally, and if across the space of years that don, for so he must have been, will satisfy my curiosity about the questions which are still unanswered, then my address is Dartmouth, Aldeburgh, Suffolk.

Michell Raper

AN INVESTIGATION

Michell Raper produces talks and features on BBC
Radio. His poetry has appeared in many magazines and
anthologies.

I WAS LIVING IN Richmond at the time. One day I walked into
a second-hand book shop and got talking to the proprietor, a man
named Eric. He had a pinkish rather scholarly face and a manner
that veered between the affable and the abrupt. Rather a character,
I thought. A week or so later, after I'd been in the shop a few more
times—I was looking for some out-of-the-way Victorian mem-
oirs—he said suddenly, 'You must come to supper. You must
meet Irene,' as if it was something we had already settled.

They lived in a large rambling flat in Battersea. Irene, his wife,
was small, attractive, dark-haired and she had a way of swooping
on arguments she disagreed with and bearing them off in triumph
like a bird with a twig in its beak. I remember it was an exhilarat-
ing, if somewhat exhausting, evening I spent—one in which I
seemed to be carrying on three conversations at the same time.
It was late in the evening when Irene said to her husband, 'We
must tell him about our walk,' and then suddenly—to me—'Do
you believe in the supernatural?'

'That depends . . .' I said.

'Well, see what you make of this.' And they told me.

It had happened in the summer of 1954. Irene had decided to do
something about Oscar Wilde's old house in Chelsea. 'Doing
something' meant campaigning to get the GLC to put up a blue

plaque on the wall of the house in Tite Street where Wilde had lived with his family until his arrest in 1895. It had been an exhausting business, both mentally and physically. Quite apart from the organisation involved—there was to be an unveiling ceremony attended by most of the theatre's aristocracy—she came across odd lingering hostilities, a suggestion here and there that no one ought to put up a plaque or anything else to the memory of a man like Oscar Wilde.

Towards the end of July, with the preparations still not complete, they suddenly felt they both needed a complete break from the whole thing. Why not a day in the country? Eric suggested visiting the Rookery—a famous old house near Dorking in Surrey. They could go to Dorking and from there catch a bus to the Rookery, have a picnic lunch and spend the afternoon walking in the Surrey hills. Accordingly, a few days later, Eric left his bookshop in the care of an assistant and he and Irene set off for Dorking on the morning train. The day was fine and sunny. Everything seemed set for a pleasant day. It was only afterwards that they discovered that both of them had felt an odd unwillingness about the whole trip. A sense of depression which neither of them had mentioned for fear of spoiling it for the other.

Things began to go wrong quite early. They got to Dorking all right and caught the bus to the Rookery, but somehow or other they managed to get off the bus at the wrong stop—a village called Wolton Hatch. What should they do—hang around and wait for another bus, or stay in Wolton and make the best of a bad job? They decided to stay.

Across the road at the end of a path lay the village church. They spent a short while looking round it and then came out into the porch. It was midday. The afternoon stretched emptily ahead of them. How should they spend it?

On their right leading directly out of the churchyard lay a small path. They decided to follow it. Perhaps they had expected a long cool walk through the woods. If so, they were disappointed. Almost at once the path started to climb and after a few minutes they found themselves in open country again. On their left was a small clearing, backed by trees and scrub. On their right, as they turned, was a grassy slope, with more trees at the bottom.

Fourteen years later they can still remember not only what the scene looked like, but the sounds which floated up from the woods below—bird song, a dog barking, and a man hidden by the trees chopping wood. The only other thing to be seen was a wooden bench which faced the slope on their right.

Irene said: 'Let's sit here and eat our sandwiches. We've wasted enough time. Let's eat and then start walking.'

But once they were sitting down she found her appetite had gone. 'I felt an awful depression,' she told me 'I could still hear the dog barking and the man chopping wood and I got a sort of comfort from it because they were human sort of sounds, I just sat there crumbling the bread and throwing the bits to the birds. Everything seemed to stop and go dead. I said to Eric, "Has it gone cold?" and he said, "No" and I said, "Feel my arm" and he did.'

Eric confirmed this point. 'Her arm was icy.'

A moment before she had felt isolated—cut off from everything. But now she realised that she was not alone. Three men had appeared in the clearing behind her, and were standing watching her. Whether they had stepped out of the bushes or not she could not say. All she knew was that they were suddenly *there*.

They were an odd-looking group, dressed in black with hats which partly shaded their faces. The two on the outside were holding or supporting the one in the middle whose face bore an expression of pleading as if asking for help. As for his companions, what she remembered about them chiefly was their eyes which were fixed on her with extraordinary intensity.

'Were you frightened?' I asked.

'Petrified. It was the sort of fear that locks the limbs. A concentration of evil. I half turned to get a better look at them and then I realised that I could see them *without* turning round—through the back of my head, in fact. I just whispered to Eric "Let's go".'

They fled. That is, they hurried away along the path, followed

58

it as it swung right over a narrow bridge crossing the railway line, then they lay down on the grass and went to sleep. Above her, as she dozed, Irene heard the drone of a passing aircraft. It sounded —like everything else that afternoon—ominous and filled with a kind of heavy dread.

Neither of them knows when they woke. The first thing they can remember is travelling back in the train to London.

In the compartment, Irene said 'Something happened back there,' and Eric agreed—something most certainly had. It was the first time they had spoken since they left the clearing. For a long time they kept off the subject. It was frightening and at the same time almost embarrassing.

'When did you first talk about it?' I asked.

'Oh, a lot later,' Irene said. 'I picked up a magazine in the shop and there was an article in it to do with psychic research. It said that people who had these experiences were often too embarrassed to talk about them. That was the first time it occurred to me that there'd been anything odd about what happened to *us*.'

Confirmation of a totally unexpected sort came in a letter. Someone wrote to Irene asking for details of the Oscar Wilde plaque. But in this case the someone was the landowner on whose estate they'd been walking that afternoon in July. Struck by the coincidence Irene wrote to him telling him about their experience in the clearing. Could he throw any light? He could and he couldn't. That is to say—so ran his answer—the scene of their odd encounter was near the spot where a certain Bishop Wilberforce had been killed by a fall from his horse in the summer of 1871. Irene's description of the man in the middle sounded a little like him. And did she know—but of course she didn't—that there was some suggestion of mystery about the Bishop's death? He invited her to come down and visit him. It was to his family home he explained, that Wilberforce had been riding on the afternoon of his death. She didn't go. Slowly an idea was forming in her head. There was only one way to get rid of the memory of this disturbing vision.

Without telling Eric, she set off one morning, took the train to Dorking and from there caught the bus to the village where they had stopped that July afternoon. It was a day like the last time she had been there. The sun shone, the birds sang, there was an atmosphere of peace. She walked up the church path and into the church. The plan was simple. She must retrace every step of her previous journey—but this time alone. It was not so much an exorcism as a challenge. She was defying whoever the men in black might be to show themselves again.

She walked round the church and out into the porch, every detail of the previous visit still clear in her mind's eye. The next part was easy. You took a few steps forward and there was the path on your right. Only now she found that she had remembered it wrongly. There was no path. She tried again. Still no path.

This time she didn't go back into the church but started on a step by step examination of the churchyard, looking for any kind of opening which might turn out to be the missing path. But there was nothing.

Totally bewildered she returned home and told Eric what happened. A few days later he made the same experiment with the same result. Only this time he found evidence—if evidence was needed—that the path really had gone. In the churchyard he met a man who worked on the estate. Without going into a detailed explanation Eric asked to be directed to the path which led out of the churchyard to the fields. The man looked blank. Eric persisted. It led to a clearing, he explained, with a wooden bench and a view of trees at the bottom of a slope. The workman assured him that there was no such bench, no such clearing and in fact no stretch of country answering to that description anywhere on the estate. Of course, if the gentleman would like to ask his foreman who had lived in these parts all his life. But already, Eric said, the man was beginning to look at him askance 'as at one who has taken leave of his senses'. So—like Irene—he went home, leaving the mystery unsolved.

Unsolved it remained. The path had gone, so had the clearing, so—if indeed they had ever existed—had the men in black. But if they had gone, where had they come from in the first place?

And what was the connection, if any, between the men in black and the late lamented Bishop Wilberforce?

Ever since my two friends told me this story it had stayed, nagging, at the back of my mind. Anyway, after a time I decided to make my own investigation into the mystery. The first step was to find out as much as possible about the Bishop—his character, his reputation, and above all his death.

A biography written shortly after he died gave all the facts. Samuel Wilberforce, third son of the great William Wilberforce. Born 1805. Died 1873. Bishop of Oxford and late of Winchester. Wilberforce was something new in bishops—thrusting, ambitious energetic—the first of the modern bishops his admireres said. Those who did *not* admire him called him 'Soapy Sam'. He turned the nickname to his own advantage: 'Always in hot water and always getting out again with my hands clean' he told the House of Lords, where he was a familiar and controversial figure.

The face—the biography included a photograph taken late in life—was square-jawed, pugnacious, with shrewd eyes. The mouth was broad and humorous, but with a slight downward turn to it which gave a touch of grumpiness to the final impression. Was this the face seen in the clearing? And if so—why the expression of pleading? And who were the two stern companions?

I continued with my researches. Everything about Soapy Sam, it appeared, was on the grand scale—his congregations, his emotions, his friendships, his quarrels. When he died, Mr Gladstone said that a great void had opened. Carlyle, who also knew him, commented simply, 'Oh, happy accident!'

Were there, I wondered, others who not only welcomed Soapy's death but were even prepared to assist it? On the day he died Soapy was riding in the country with a groom and Lord Granville with whom he was spending the weekend. Earlier he had been depressed but no sooner was he in the saddle than he became like a boy, galloping up and down the hills and laughing and talking incessantly. Granville was surprised. Did the Bishop never get tired? Never on such a horse as this, was the Bishop's reply. They began to canter, Granville and the groom first, Soapy

Sam following some distance behind. Granville remembered hearing a thud, and, on riding back, found the Bishop lying on the grass perfectly still. Later, he wrote: 'From the groom's account it appeared that the horse, probably a little tired, had put his foot in a gutter of turf and stumbled without coming down. The Bishop must have turned a complete somersault, his feet were in the direction in which we were going, his arms straight by his side—the position was absolutely monumental. I took off the Bishop's boots and handneckerchief. I remember my despair at not knowing whether there was anything I could do which would be of use. For some time I could feel no pulse, but at last I could feel the beating distinctly. However I was afterwards told by the doctor that these were my own pulsations and not those of what, alas! was a corpse!'

Three points struck me about this account as being a little odd. At first it appeared that the groom had seen Wilberforce fall. But then come the words 'the Bishop must have turned a complete somersault', which rather implied that they were both guessing at what happened by the Bishop's position on the ground.

Secondly, the position itself: 'absolutely monumental' as Granville put it. Does a man, who has been thrown violently into the air come down again with his arms neatly at his side?

And finally, could the jolt of his horse stumbling in the turf have been enough to throw a solidly-built man into the air with such spectacular force?

There was no reason to suppose that Granville and the groom were not telling the truth, as they saw it. But how much *had* they seen? Supposing they had seen nothing. Suppose, for instance, they were riding on ahead, with Soapy following alone and out of sight. The Bishop's horse suddenly stops, frightened by something the Bishop hasn't seen. Out of the bushes step two men. The Bishop smiles in greeting, taking them to be two members of his flock who have come out to salute him. The two men move closer, not returning his smile.

It is all over in a minute. One of them seizes the horse's bridle, the other drags Soapy from the saddle and sets about him. The

Bishop is about to cry out for help but is silenced by a blow from a stick.

Granville, riding on ahead, hears nothing. It isn't till he turns to make a remark about the scenery that he finds he and the groom are alone. Puzzled, but not alarmed, he rides back. There on the grass lies Soapy Sam, his horse whinnying with fright beside him.

Well, that was one possibility—a lightning attack by two unknown assailants who vanished directly afterwards never to be seen or heard of again. . . . Not very promising.

I spent another afternoon with Eric and Irene checking their stories and going over the account of Wilberforce's death as given by Lord Granville. Looked at coldly, the theory of the unknown assailants seemed improbable—or rather as probable or improbable as a dozen others. The photograph of Wilberforce which I took with me struck no particular chord with Irene. It might conceivably have belonged to the man she had seen. There again it might not. The only other piece of information she could give me was the comment that they had 'taken it with them that day', meaning the sense of depression and heaviness which had hung over them from the moment they left Battersea.

I went home disheartened. It really looked as if at long last the trail had dried up. But if it hadn't been Soapy Sam, then who was it Irene had seen in the clearing? Lying in bed that night I tried to go over the whole episode step by step. But instead I found two thoughts—apparently disconnected—floating through my head. One of them was Irene's remark about 'taking it with them'. That made sense in a way. It could mean that the first landscape had been some sort of waking dream—an hallucination—and, as the estate workman confirmed, had nothing to do with the 'real' or physical landscape round the village church which they had found on their second visit. But a joint hallucination—was that possible? Well, yes and no. I'd been struck all along by the fact that it was Irene who had had the stronger—more intense—experience. Wasn't it possible that the hallucination—or vision—had been hers, but that—like a spirit medium at a seance—she had been able to pass it on to someone close to her?

But that was only half the story. The whole episode of the vanishing landscape had been like a frame for the focal point—the appearance of the three men in the clearing. Again from nowhere came some words, this time three lines of verse:

'He staggered, and, terrible-eyed,
He brushed past the palms on the landing
And was helped to a hansom outside'.

John Betjeman had written that about—surely—about Oscar Wilde . . . the arrest of Oscar Wilde to be precise. And wasn't it the whole business of the Wilde plaque and the associations it had conjured up which had sent both her and Eric, nervous and exhausted, on their country expedition?

What had the men in the clearing looked like? She had seen them clearly, yet what had been suggested to me was an almost symbolic tableau—a desperate and pleading man between two implacable guardians. A man who staggered, terrible-eyed, begging, at the back of her mind, for comfort and understanding.

If you can call it a theory, that is mine, and it satisfies me. I'm not suggesting that it explains anything. How can anyone explain how two rational intelligent adults can walk through a landscape which isn't there when they go back to it?

Certainly, I doubt if the theory will satisfy Irene herself. She has already been back to the church on at least one more occasion and will probably go again. I sympathise, but in a way I feel she is wasting her time. The ghosts—or whatever they are—the ghosts of the three men and the landscape which framed their brief appearance have already been exorcised. The man in the middle had needed help. But has she not already given him help in the only way she can—by helping posterity to honour his name?

About that, at least, there is indisputable evidence. It is on the wall of No. 16 Tite Street, London S.W.3.

II
PROBLEMS

Sir Isaiah Berlin

THE ROLE OF THE INTELLIGENTSIA

Sir Isaiah Berlin was formerly Chichele Professor of Social
and Political Theory at Oxford University, and is now
President of Wolfson College, Oxford. His books include
The Hedgehog and the Fox and *Two Concepts of Liberty*.

THE WORD 'INTELLIGENTSIA', like the concept, is of Russian
origin and was invented sometime in the 1860s and 1870s. It did
not mean simply educated persons. It certainly did not mean
merely intellectuals as such.

Russian society in the 19th century was, to use a contemporary
term, underdeveloped. It was a backward society, consisting to a
vast extent of a mass of illiterate, semi-starved peasants, a certain
number of bureaucrats holding them down with various degrees
of efficiency, and a small class of persons who had received sufficient education either to be officials, administrators or clerks, or
to form that minimum number of lawyers, doctors, land sur-
veyors and teachers without which even so backward a mass as the
Russians could scarcely be expected to get on. There was a very
oligarchical, not to say despotic, regime at the top, and a Church
with no central tradition of scholasticism or rational argument—
with many saints and martyrs and visionaries but with none of
the intellectual discipline which formed the Church of Rome;
knowledge and learning were scarce. The small minority of
persons who had access to the civilisation of the West and freely
read foreign languages felt relatively cut off from the mass of the
people; they felt they were almost foreigners in their own land—

what is nowadays called 'alienated' from society. Those among them with sensitive consciences were acutely aware of a natural obligation to help their fellows who were less happy or less advanced than themselves.

These people gradually became a group, who held that to speak in public, to write, to lecture, imposed on them a direct and peculiar moral obligation. If you lived in Paris in the Thirties or Forties of the 19th century, you lived in a world in which a great many ideas circulated and collided: faiths, ideologies, theories, movements clashed with each other and created a general 'climate of opinion'. But no given ideology, no given set of concepts, so dominated that society as to create a fanatical ascendancy. In a country like Russia, cut off from the West in the first place by the great medieval religious schism, into which few ideas from outside were allowed to penetrate, in which literacy was very low, almost any idea which came in from the West—provided that it possessed any degree of initial attractiveness—fell upon marvellously rich and virgin soil, and was taken up with a passion hardly imaginable in the West. If there is a large vacuum, and a very fresh and untutored people, many of them eager for light, then almost any idea—no matter how fanciful or obsolete—is likely to find some ready response somewhere. This was the position in Russia in the second quarter of the last century. Hence the immense addiction to theories and doctrines—not merely as something of intellectual interest, not merely as something to while away an idle hour, but to some a source of salvation, something which, if believed in and acted upon, might lead people to a better life, like that which some of them fondly imagined was being led in the West.

These young men were pro-Western if only because they groaned under a yoke which prevented them from obtaining that minimum degree of normal education which, it was imagined, was becoming more and more open to the inhabitants of the West. Consequently, they idealised the West. Like the enlightened thinkers of an earlier day in France and Germany, they believed that only by the critical use of reason could the reign of superstition, prejudice, tradition, dogma, blind obedience, arbitrary rules and servility be arrested. They believed in modern science and in human progress. They discovered that certain Western thinkers—in particular after the failure of the French Revolution—had turned away from reason and science back to non-rational sources, religious and aesthetic, dogmatic and intuitive. Some of the Russians were influenced by this too, but most of those who drank at Western sources in the end regarded this as a false path: a betrayal of the present to the past. Burke and Maistre made relatively little headway among them. The Russian intelligentsia—because it was small and consumed by a sense of moral responsibility for their brothers who lived in darkness—grew to be a dedicated order, bound by a sense of solidarity and kinship. Isolated and divided by the tangled forest of a society impenetrable to rational organisation, they called out to each other in order to preserve contact. They were citizens of a state within the state, soldiers in an army dedicated to progress, surrounded on all sides by reaction.

This is the kind of phenomenon which, it seems to me, tends to occur in large, socially and economically backward communities, run by an incompetent government and an ignorant and oppressive Church. In this sense, there can be said to have been an intelligentsia in Spain in the 19th century; perhaps in the Balkans and in certain countries of Latin America and Asia. It did not happen to such an extent even in France, where the notion of the intelligentsia as such, as an independent social formation, did not arise. Still less was it the case in England. I am not concerned—nor competent—to examine the social and economic roots of this phenomenon: I only wish to say something about its most obvious characteristics.

If you were a French or even an English writer in the 19th century, you might very well have taken the view that you were a purveyor like any other kind of purveyor. This was the attitude of some of the French writers who believed in art for art's sake, who believed that their business was simply to write in language which was as lucid or as expressive or as beautiful as they could make it, and who saw themselves simply as craftsmen, as persons who produce an object and wish to be judged by that object alone. If a man makes a silver bowl, provided the silver bowl is beautiful, that is all that can be expected of him. His private life, convictions, behaviour was none of the public's—or the critics'—business. This point of view was rejected with ferocity by the Russians of whom I speak. The idea that a man plays roles—that if he is a goldsmith you should judge him *qua* goldsmith, and that his private life has nothing to do with it, that if he is a writer you judge him solely by the merit of his novel or poem—was rejected by the best-known Russian men of letters, because they believed that man was one, that any form of compartmentalisation was a maiming of human beings and a distortion of the truth. This fundamental point of difference is what distinguishes the general attitude of most of those whom we consider typical Russian writers from a good many writers in the West. And it is central to the Russian concept of the intelligentsia.

I don't mean to say that all important Russian writers thought this. Those who were born in the 18th century—Pushkin and his contemporaries—for the most part cannot be regarded as belonging to the intelligentsia. Writers like Gogol and Tolstoy—different as they were—rejected the very idea of it. Their view of human beings was quite different from, say, that of Belinsky or the young Herzen, or, in some moods, Turgenev. They did not believe in reason, in science, in the West; they looked with contempt upon those deluded imitators of 'Europe' who did not understand the inner life of man, which had nothing to do with progress or science or reason. This is also to a great extent true of Chekhov, even, at times, of Gorky. Turgenev stood betwixt and between. Sometimes he inclined to one side, sometimes to the other. He oscillated comfortably between qualified support and critical irony. The real members of the intelligentsia were the political pamphleteers, the civic-minded poets, the forerunners of the Russian Revolution—mainly journalists and political thinkers who quite consciously used literature, sometimes very poor examples of it, as vehicles for social protest.

Given that this is the central concept of the intelligentsia, let me now move to the West. Professor Northrop Frye, in a suggestive contribution to a recent collection of lectures, makes an important point. He says that, broadly speaking, the tendency of Western thinkers had been to take science as the paradigm; and because science is objective and factual and means freedom from personal or subjective influences, and in particular from value judgments, there has been a tendency among intellectuals to prize and over-prize objectivity and scientific methods, even to the point where such objectivity becomes detachment—detachment of the kind which is normally ascribed to those engaged in the natural sciences, which makes an atomic physicist shrug off inquiries about his social responsibility with a certain degree of irritation; he says that he is simply engaged in the discovery of the truth; the application of his discoveries are no more his business than that of any other citizen of the state, however it is governed. People engaged in psychological or physiological research are sometimes equally reluctant to admit their responsibility, though their experiments may lead to all kinds of astonishing transformations of human beings and may give to certain individuals dangerous powers of conditioning people, of altering their responses. This is called the detachment or objectivity of science; and Frye thinks that it can go too far, that scientists engaged upon work which has obvious social implications cannot simply opt out of responsibility in these matters, although he does not, in the end, tell us how much responsibility these persons bear, or what they should do about it. He also says that social concern, such as I have attributed to the Russian intelligentsia, can go too far.

Such social concern can easily, in moments of crisis, become a kind of hysteria, as it does in the case of those who seek to protect our societies against real or imagined perversion, and this is responsible for all kinds of censorships, intellectual crusades, attempts to organise writers or artists to defend their nation, against communism or against fascism or against atheism or against religion. The organisation of artists and writers can become a danger. The attempt to cling to some existing order and to rationalise the defence of this order as some kind of intellectual duty—if I don't misinterpret Frye—becomes a form of intolerance, a suppression of freedom of speech and of freedom itself. Between these two poles the unfortunate dealers in ideas and other forms of human communication are compelled to live and find some kind of acceptable equilibrium.

These are the dangers of the West. But in the land in which the intelligentsia was born, it was founded, broadly speaking, on the idea of a permanent rational opposition to a status quo which was regarded as in constant danger of becoming ossified, a block to human thought and human progress. This is the historic role of the intelligentsia as seen by itself, then and now. It does not just mean intellectuals or artists as such; and it certainly does not mean educated persons as such. The educated can be reactionary, just as the uneducated can. So can intellectuals. So can artists. We know this very well in our day. It is a melancholy phenomenon which has happened on both sides of the Iron Curtain. Nor does it mean sheer opposition to the Establishment as such. Protesters and marchers, people who oppose the use of atomic energy for destructive purposes, or the Vietnam war, no matter how sympathetic their moral position, or admirable their sense of social responsibility, are not members of the intelligentsia simply because they are protesting against the behaviour of their government. These persons do not necessarily believe in the power of reason or the beneficent role of science, still less in the inevitability, or even the desirability, of human progress, conceived in secular and rational terms. Some of them may appeal to irrational faiths, or wish to escape from industrial society into some simpler, but wholly utopian world.

Sheer protest, whether justified or unjustified, does not qualify one to be a member of the intelligentsia as such. What does do so is a combination of belief in reason and progress with a profound moral concern for society. And this, of course, is much more likely to occur in countries where the opposition is deepest and blackest; and least likely to occur in loose, democratic, relatively open societies, where the sort of persons who might be made

72

indignant in the more reactionary societies are apt to bend their
energies to ordinary pursuits—to being a doctor, lawyer, professor of literature—without any oppressive sense that in doing so
so they are somehow failing in their duty, that in not taking part
in some kind of collective civic indignation they are indulging
private desires and deserting their civic post. The *intelligentsia
militant*—and this is what the original intelligentsia was, and it is
part of its essence—is generated by truly oppressive regimes. There
are, no doubt, many despotisms: but to look on England, of all
countries, as despotically ruled seems perverse. There are many
other things wrong, socially and economically; but a country in
which the government needs to make up to a wide electorate,
however it does this, and is in danger of being turned out, is,
whatever else it may be, not a despotism. To say, therefore, that
British society stands in need of this kind of ferocious, unsurren-
dering, well-organised revolutionary intelligentsia seems to me an
exaggeration. Others may think quite differently.

To the old 19th-century intelligentsia the very notion of a class
of persons involved in intellectual pursuits—such as professors,
doctors, engineers, experts, writers, who in other respects live
ordinary bourgeois lives, and hold conventional views, and who
play golf or even cricket—this notion would have been absolutely
horrifying. If a man was a professor in late 19th-century Russia,
then the mere fact of his involvement with ideas made him an
implacable opponent of the regime in which he lived; if it did not,
he was, in the eyes of the militant, a traitor, a man who had sold
out, a coward or a ninny.

No doubt it is the duty of those who deal in ideas to be rational
and to suit the action to the word, to live integrated lives, not to
divorce their thoughts from their actions (the kind of thing of
which Goethe was accused by Russian critics), not to say to
themselves that to be a professor or an artist is a profession like
that of a blacksmith or an accountant, which does not impose
special social responsibilities. But it does not follow that awareness
of one's intellectual responsibilities must in any modern Western
society turn one into a permanent subversive, into someone

systematically opposed to the status quo, on the grounds that those who are comfortable in it, and and those whose lives it penetrates, are automatically enemies of progress and of mankind. And that is why one cannot, if the valuable use of the term is not to be hopelessly diluted, really speak of an English intelligentsia. One can speak of English intellectuals; one can speak of persons who like ideas and those who do not; of levels of education; of progressives and reactionaries, rationalists and sceptics; one can talk about the duties of literacy. But if you said to someone who was educated, and fascinated by, or at least at home with, ideas (for example, to some politically inactive first-generation Bloomsbury figure, or a follower of, say, André Gide in France), that for him not to be politically rebellious was a moral abandonment of his social post, an acceptance of cowardly ideological illusions, he could answer: 'This is only true on certain assumptions.' For example, on Marxist assumptions, which entail that one necessarily belongs to one's class, which is engaged in class warfare; either to the class which is fighting or to the class which is fighting back; either to the class which is progressive or to the class which needs to be destroyed. But if you do not accept these assumptions, then such obligations do not necessarily follow. It is one thing to be critical, to take part voluntarily in controversy; it is another thing to assume that since there are very few such people, they constitute a kind of standing *force de frappe*: ready to fight and die in a resistance which never lets up, always at the barricades.

The two things are not identical. In Russia they were, for the particular historical reasons which I have tried to indicate. Something of the sort was and is also true in certain other countries; it is true of some of the children of East European immigrants in America or Israel; it may be true in much of Asia and Africa today; but there is a complacency about the direct and automatic application of this notion to essentially less repressive forms of government. America is at present possessed by discussion and doubts on this very subject, and is in a peculiar position. Huge, dark forces have arisen—and are being justly resisted there. But for whatever reasons, the enemies of enlightenment do not seem to me to be so powerful and so sinister in England today, and neither hippies nor militant students, neither war resisters nor Americanophobes, whatever view one may take of their acts or goals, resemble the old intelligentsia in its heyday, save to the degree to which it stood (and stands) for human decency against cruelty, hypocrisy, injustice and inequality. The same is true of every progressive movement in history—yet early Christianity was not the revolt of an intelligentsia, nor is Buddhism. This is not a pedantic, verbal point. Central notions, even labels, which have played a part in human history have some claim to have their integrity respected.

Alasdair MacIntyre

DEATH AND THE ENGLISH

Alasdair MacIntyre teaches and has taught philosophy and sociology at various universities in England and America. He is the author of *A Short History of Ethics* and of *Secularisation and Moral Change*.

THE ENGLISH HAVE a great and traditional gift for misplaced moral feeling. The transplant of a lung in Edinburgh, and the news of the most recent of the heart transplant operations, have made it impossible to avoid noticing that a large general issue has been raised by the new surgery. For some time it had been clear that surgical innovations and skill were, like other technologies of modern society, capable of being developed without apparent limit. But during this period there was almost complete silence on the moral issues involved. Now, however, transplant surgery has arrived as decisively as did the mini-skirt and with something of the same tele-visual, colour-supplement aura; and the performance of a variety of transplant operations seems to have become to some nations what the possession of their own nuclear weapons is to others. As with nuclear weapons, all too characteristically, now that the development has occurred and is clearly irreversible, we have at last begun to talk about the moral issues. But it's not only that it is a moral tradition of our society to react in this way after the event; it's also following a tradition to react with the philistinism of *The Times* leading article on heart transplants, or the philistinism which supposes that we can deal with moral issues of this sort by calling conferences about them.

The Times said, for example, of those religious feelings that are to some degree affronted by transplant surgery that we must recognise that they exist, even if they do not stand up too well to rational scrutiny. The suggestion plainly is that such affronted feelings are, and can only be, an irrational survival from the past.

It was in *The Times* also that it was asserted that the pages devoted to moral considerations by Mr Donald Longmore in his excellent book, *Spare-Part Surgery*, may come to be considered the classical statement of the ethical case for transplant operations. I call Mr Longmore's book excellent because of its quality as a lucid and enlightening account of the new surgery for the layman. But it is perhaps significant that after 170 pages devoted to science and technique, Mr Longmore feels able to dispose of moral matters in another brisk four pages. He's able to do so because it is to him apparently self-evident that the case for these innovations is the 'humanitarian' or 'philanthropic' one, and that resistance to such innovations must be irrational.

Mr Longmore is more illuminating on the real content of the moral standpoint which he is defending, however, when he makes a swift transition from ethical to economic considerations. For he admits that the costs of the new surgery are going to be such that even if doctors do not have to decide on the relative economic worth of those whose lives they are considering saving, medical policy-makers almost certainly will have to make such decisions. A climate will be created which will clearly involve treating the bodies of those dead from whom heart or lung or whatever it is are to be taken as a store of more or less scarce natural resources. To suppose that we can dispose with a few swift knock-down observations of the moral issues involved in viewing our dead like this is surely a species of moral philistinism. I speak of philistinism because of the deep insensitivity which a view like this betrays to the intimate relationship that must hold between the ways in which men treat the bodies of their dead and the feelings bound up with such treatment, on the one hand, and the general condition of their culture on the other. When we study alien societies we are often wise to take their funerary rites to be an important clue to that whole complex set of attitudes and behaviour which expresses their view of human life and of the cosmos. Why should it be otherwise with our own society?

It is not necessarily easy to decipher the meanings of the rites performed and the attitudes exhibited to death. We have to place them in the context of other important rites and attitudes. But perhaps if we note some large differences in this respect between some of the societies which anthropologists have studied and our own, we may get important clues. One such difference is the extent to which death has become a private matter in our society. Certainly we occasionally hold memorial services and express a collective acknowledgment of death in this and other ways. But the standard funeral seems to gather only a small group of relatives. This is not so much a sign that the community does not recognise death, as that no community exists in the sense in which it did and does in those small-scale societies in which the death of one person is recognised as a diminution of the whole. Nobody's death is as likely to diminish anyone else in an individualist society in which every man is to some degree an island: consequently, the bodies of the dead become less meaningful objects, and are the more easily regarded as useful stores of tissues and organs, as natural resources to be exploited to the full. For the contrast with our own society we do not have to leave the British Isles. A Highland funeral or one in rural Ireland—remember Synge's *Riders to the Sea*—may still be the community recognising in the death of one of its number not simply a loss to it, but also a connection with a larger community—that of the past dead— which the newly dead has now rejoined. And the dead man's body is a real and symbolic object of importance, in no way available to be used or exploited.

A second contrast between our own modern society and some others—for example, certain African societies—has been pointed out by the anthropologist Mary Douglas. It is that we have no concept, or at best an increasingly vague one, of the proper length for a human life. In some societies there is an age by which it is recognised that a man must have achieved what he has to achieve.

If he dies after this he dies as a man who has had the opportunity of doing what he had to do. If he dies before this, the incompleteness of his life would have to be marked by others in some way. But in our society, we lack any real idea of what would constitute a completed life, and hence also, any clear idea of what would constitute a satisfactory death. I have been told by psychoanalysts of patients whose neurotic anxiety about death is due to the fact that they cannot recognise any point at which they would be content to die. Nothing would count as fulfilment for them, and hence the fear of death cannot be exorcised. The horizon of life recedes indefinitely for such people. We can surely recognise a resemblance between this neurotic fear and the spirit in which transplant surgery is being received. It seems to have become an unquestioned assumption that life should be extended as far as medical science will allow, and to this it may be retorted that my argument is inconsistent with the fact that doctors now sometimes let patients die when their life could be extended. This is true, but the inconsistency is only apparent, not real. Behind both the extension of life by transplant surgery and the leaving to die of the patient who will never emerge from a coma lies the same belief that it is medical criteria which are the appropriate criteria for judging whether a life should be extended or terminated. Life is taken as having a physical terminus, but no social or moral limit.

On these two points, the privatisation of death, and the loss of any sense of an appropriate length of life, I have contrasted contemporary English society with alien cultures—Celtic or African. But, of course, we could equally well contrast contemporary English society with its own past. To do so would bring out the point that those rites in which a collective attitude to death was expressed in this society and its concept of an appropriate length for a human life—threescore years and ten—were both drawn from the Christian religion. It's almost too obvious to say that the changed attitude to death in our culture is closely linked to secularisation. But it's not too obvious to point out that the precise nature of this relationship is by no means clear. For the Christian Churches exhibit to a striking degree attitudes not very dissimilar to those of the rest of society. In the case of the Churches, the notable thing is how little death is now talked about. Modern preachers and theologians are for the most part notably reticent upon all those great questions which involve death. They're apt to insist upon the symbolic character of references to eternal fire or eternal happiness. But these references were always understood to be in some sense symbolic—only this fact was not used by theologians in former ages to purvey what too often appears as agnosticism about what happens after death and about the significance of death. Thus, if our inability to cope with the fact of death is part of a general secularisation process, then that process has eroded the life of the Churches too.

Someone may object that I've been talking too parochially about English society. They may say that the phenomena which I have been trying to describe are characteristic of all or of most advanced industrial societies, and ought therefore to be explained, if they can be explained, in terms of the general characteristics of such societies rather than in terms of any specific characteristics of English society. There's obviously a large degree of truth in this. In its almost completely uncritical acceptance of the advance and expansion of technology, whether computer or weapons or medical technology, British society is no different from West German or Russian or American. and in so far as transplant surgery means that we now feel able to regard the bodies of the dead as available to serve any technique which pushes back the limits of death, we're certainly no different from other industrial societies. But there remain crucial differences between such societies. Evelyn Waugh in *The Loved One* and Jessica Mitford in *The American Way of Death* have commented sharply on the lavish and expensive funeral rites of the United States. In England, death is not—as it is in America—an occasion for conspicuous consumption in the form of conspicuous cremation. The morticians' decking out of the dead so that they may be as lifelike as possible is too easily depicted from an English standpoint, with the aid of Mr Waugh's acids, as merely vulgar. But it is in fact revelatory of a quite distinctive attitude to death, one in which death is obtruded but disguised, in which the rites seem to express a determined assertion that death is not going to be allowed to make a difference. There is a relationship here to the similar cosmetic attempts to conceal ageing, the blue rinses and the painted nails, and the dances at which senior citizens behave like infirm teenagers. Or note again the existence of those housing projects for the old where hospital facilities are not allowed, and where if you become at all seriously ill you have to leave. All these are devices designed to banish death from consciousness. Of course, American culture is far from being all of a piece, and this is only one among the attitudes to death exhibited.

But it is distinctively American, and it is not an attitude usually found in England. Yet this American attitude is at least well-defined, whereas the impression I have of England is that the practices of the English in the face of death reveal that they do not know what to think about it or how to react to it. I do not mean at all by this that the national attitude is one of intelligent agnosticism, but rather that nothing has taken the place of the lost religious attitudes to death. Bewilderment and incomprehension mark our griefs. One indication of this is the way in which a surprisingly high proportion of those who do not attend church, or hear or use religious language at any other time, resort to the church when they are bereaved. What must be largely meaningless phrases, unconnected with the real feelings of the bereaved, still hold their place because there are no other words to use. If I am right about this, then our willingness to see life extended indefinitely by medical innovation is connected, not with a wish to obliterate the fact of death from our consciousness, as is the case with the rituals of Forest Lawns and the American morticians, but rather with an inability either to confront death or to turn away from it, with a confusion rather than with any well-articulated set of beliefs.

This inability, this confusion, is not simply characteristic of the English attitude to death: as in other societies, the attitudes to death seem to be closely linked with the rest of the culture. I have two reasons for asserting this. The first is that it's not only death that we do not know how to celebrate. We are also confused about birth, about what it is to become an adult, and about marriage. But even more important is another connection between our confusions about death and our general scheme of values. I remarked earlier that we have no sense of what is an appropriate length for life, and also that this is not just a question of the age at which a man may be taken to have completed his life, but also a matter of what the completeness of life may be thought to consist in. One of our embarrassments about the lately dead is that we are no longer clear about what it is to have fared well in life, and what it is to have fared badly. We do not have any socially established concept of the good life, of that life after which a man ought to be content to die and to make what has been called 'a good death'.

Clearly, the development of this moral confusion has a very long history, and a history that has not yet been written. But when that history does come to be written, the First World War will have an important place in it. The rituals of Armistice Day, of the two minutes' silence of the Last Post, of the recitation of 'They shall not grow old as we that are left grow old', have all the pathos of an attempt to respond to the omnipresence of death which was bound to fail. For it was the very same moral scheme which had allowed all these young men to be sent to their deaths that was bound to deprive men of any adequate sensitivity to death itself. You cannot treat death as lightly as the English leadership did during that war and expect death still to be taken seriously after it. At that point in our history, the gap between rhetoric and reality was bound to become too plain, and the Burkean vision of the society in which we are indissolubly linked with the past and to the dead was finally dissolved, in part because too many people were allowed to die in that war without point or purpose.

This last point recalls me sharply to the point from which I set out. The moral confusion involved in our attitudes to war deaths may be the same moral confusion which surrounds the discussion in would-be humanitarian terms of such enterprises as transplant surgery. I hope that it will not be supposed that I'm advocating any specific policy in this area. I am merely trying to observe and to diagnose crucial changes in our culture. But it is worth drawing one practical moral. In a society where moral confusion is as endemic as it seems to be in ours, it is those who are most self-confident in their moralising, and most assertive in their opinion that their own moral beliefs are necessarily humane ones, who are most likely to fall flat on their faces.

Margaret Drabble

FOSTER-PARENTS

Margaret Drabble's latest novel is *The Waterfall*: other well-known novels by her are *The Garrick Year* and *Jerusalem the Golden*. She is writing a biography of Arnold Bennett.

WHEN SOLOMON SUGGESTED that the baby be cut in half, it was relinquished by its natural mother, who preferred to lose a whole live baby rather than possess half a dead one. Brecht, writing some thousands of years later, restates the problem, but he tips the balance away from the natural mother, who in his version is totally neglectful, to the naturally motherly—to, in fact, the foster mother. And in doing this he is stating the attitude that prevails emotionally today—that children belong, not to those who give birth to them, but to those who rear them and have their welfare most at heart. A survey of newspaper cuttings over the past few years reveals a large number of cases in which foster children have become the victims of a tug-of-war between foster parents and either natural parents or local authorities, and in all these cases, public sympathy has been overwhelmingly with those in actual, not legal, possession of the child. In a recent leader *The Times* states that the case for amending the law is now overwhelming, and this is generally recognised to be so. Proposals were put forward some time ago, by Mr Leo Abse and the Camden Council, suggesting among other things that the local authority should be able to assume the rights of a parent for any child who has been in care continuously for three years or more, or for an aggregate of three years out of five.

Although it's clear that some alteration of this kind needs to be made, and probably will be made, the whole background of the subject is so complex, and emotionally so charged, that it is very difficult indeed to decide on the rights and wrongs of any particular case, let alone to decide on legislation that will cover fairly a majority of cases. One of the most powerful influences governing the present state of feeling about the matter is the research of John Bowlby, whose work on maternal care and mental health helped to alter the whole emphasis of child welfare. He demonstrated, and few would attempt or wish to dispute his conclusions, that institutional life is seriously and irremediably harmful to children; that they need above all a constant parent or parent substitute and that untold damage can be done to a child by removing it from that parent substitute in the early months of life.

This evidence, while it has undoubtedly done a great deal for the welfare and rights of children, has also created a whole host of new problems—and its effect has been so powerful that there is now a whole generation of mothers like myself who feel that they are depriving a baby of maternal care if they leave it with grandma for a couple of hours while they go to the post-natal clinic at the hospital. More seriously, it has altered the official attitude to the treatment of children in care. Since 1946 there has been a vast increase in the number of children boarded out rather than kept in institutions, although the percentage still varies enormously from council to council. But fostering, too, has its problems, and a distressingly high failure rate—as high as 50 per cent—was reported by Dr Parker in a book published in 1966. It's not surprising that the failure rate is high—fostering is an extremely difficult job, in which those fostering are expected to act as parents and to give love and security to a probably difficult child, while they themselves are required to withhold any claim over the child, and any expectation of security in their future relationship with him. Not surprisingly, many people find themselves quite unable to do it. They are being asked to achieve a relationship, and are at the same time denied the wherewithal to do it—commitment, expectation, and all the bonds that make legal parenthood possible and worth while. How can a mother be expected to achieve a relaxed attitude towards a child when she knows that it can at any moment be reclaimed at the whim of a natural parent, towards whom she may, in any case, cherish hostile feelings on the child's behalf? How can she, as such mothers are expected to do, welcome the attentions of the intruding natural parent, and encourage the child to love and remember with affection someone whom she herself can often view merely as an unwanted and disturbing rival for the child's trust? Comments made by foster parents about natural parents often reveal hostility and even contempt. Remarks about the natural mother are often charged with social disapproval.

Perhaps the whole concept of fostering is contradictory, though this would be a sad conclusion, because for so many children it's the only possible hope of love and happiness—quite apart from the fact that it is much the least expensive way of accommodating a child in care. It's odd, in a sense, that evacuation, that project which has come under such heavy fire recently, should have contributed so much to the practice of and faith in fostering; and it's interesting that it's only now that we're hearing the voices of the evacuees raised in protest and bewilderment. It was, of course a two-sided problem—evacuees were boarded out rather than put in institutions, as Bowlby would have approved—but, on the other hand, they were wrenched not even from mother substitutes but from mothers.

The real crux of the whole thing is, of course, the right of the natural parents over the child. When the child is relinquished for adoption there is no problem: if the baby is considered adoptable, it is adopted, as there are more adoptive parents than children to go round. The decisions that are sometimes made concerning adoptability and the tortuous processes that both sets of parents have to endure, I won't go into, as they're a different subject. But if the natural parent refuses to give up her rights in the child, or vacillates about them, it is then that the problem arises. Who should have the right to decide the child's future? Is there such a thing as a blood tie? What is best for the child, and when? As I said, public opinion is strongly opposed to the mother who won't let her child remain with foster parents who have proved themselves loving and devoted, and it's a depressing fact that some mothers only feel the urge to claim their child if they're sparked off by the foster mother's natural urge to adopt. A kind of rivalry develops, dormant feelings of possession are stirred up, and the child becomes the victim of a sordid scene of competition, sometimes sadly marked by the ability of one side to buy more bicycles.

The question of social class often rears its head. There was a case taken up by the late Robert Pitman in which a child was abruptly removed from one set of foster parents by a lady whom Pitman described as a spinsterly middle-aged social worker, on the grounds that they were too high-class, socially and intellectually, for the particular child to whom they happened to have taken a strong liking. A great deal of sense and nonsense was talked about the influence of environment as opposed to the concept of inborn intelligence, but most people ignored the very real problems involved in shuttling children available for fostering but not for adoption backwards and forwards between very different kinds of home—as, in fact, in the evacuation affair—and possibly thereby cutting them off from any hope of being happily reunited with their real family—a hope which, at present, child-care officers are supposed to put first.

It's natural that people feel for the foster parents, but this doesn't mean that there aren't cases in which the mother's or even the father's right to the child shouldn't perhaps be upheld. There have recently been two celebrated disputes, one of which went one way and one the other. One court has decided, to general approval and legal apprehension, that a child of Spanish parents should remain in its English middle-class foster home, despite the Spanish family's desire for its return. This too was complicated by the class issue, for the Spanish parents at the time of handing the child over had been very hard up, but had worked to achieve a secure home for their family in their own country—and there were murmurs that the judges had decided in favour of a middle-class, rather than a respectable working-class, home. Whereas in fact they had decided, as they should have done, with the child in mind and not the parents, and most people would have approved the decision on those grounds despite the admittedly complex legal aspects.

On the other hand, there was the so-called blood-tie case, in which a natural father claimed his small boy from would-be adoptive parents and won his case, on the grounds that he was able to offer him a good home and that the child would feel the tie of blood between himself and his father, and would benefit from being brought up by his own flesh and blood. This case aroused an enormous amount of criticism, some of it very violent and outspoken: sympathy with the child torn from its adoptive parents was expressed in the most passionate terms, the judges were criticised as having no insight into family problems and for ignoring expert Bowlby-orientated advice, and so on—and on balance, I personally feel the decision was wrong. But to pretend that it wasn't a difficult decision, that it was a cut-and-dried issue, was ludicrous. It was a painfully difficult decision. There was no question of the father's good faith—the only point that justly received a great deal of attention was the disastrous delay before the proceedings were heard, a delay which, measured in months in the life of a small baby, is highly significant. It was hardly the father's fault that it took so long to deal with his application: it was the fault of an inappropriate system. But what I think I took exception to most of all was those people who wrote to the newspapers claiming that there is no such thing as a tie of blood, and, more perniciously, that a father has no right in his child, that he cannot feel as a mother feels and that his emotions with regard to his own flesh and blood are irrelevant. This cannot be so. It is more rare, perhaps, for a father to be desperately concerned about his own illegitimate child, but it is by no means unknown: fathers have adopted and provided homes for these children and it is a grotesque injustice to say that this never happens or that it shouldn't happen.

As for the question of whether a child needs to know who his natural parents are, or has any real benefit from being brought up by them rather than by adoptive parents, when the issue is in dispute—this again is not a simple matter. It seems to me that possibly our society has gone too far in denying the natural— emotionally, not legally, of course—and to suggest that a child has no interest in his natural parents, even if he is adopted as a baby, is simply not true. Adopted children want to know who their natural parents are, and the older they get, the more they want to know. Under Scottish law they have a right to find out, but here they have not, and inevitably the uncertainty is distressing—as it is, we are told, for the Negroes in the United States who are denied information about their slave ancestry. Access to the information can, of course, cause terrible pain and distress for mothers who have made new lives for themselves, and one can sympathise with the plight of a respectable married matron who suddenly finds a neurotic 20-year-old on her doorstep saying: 'Mother, here I am.' But the inquiry after identity is a natural one nevertheless. In fact, the search for the unidentified parent is archetypal: Theseus travelling through danger to a discovery of his true descent, Tom Jones travelling through more comic mishaps to his. All children in adolescence spin fantasies about their real parents, imagining themselves the foundlings of multi-millionaires and film stars, but for the adopted these fantasies must be unbearably acute, unless handled carefully by understanding parents. What about Emma's fantasies on behalf of the unfortunate Harriet Smith in Jane Austen's *Emma*?

The truth is that very little is known about what happens to adopted children. Very little research and follow-up work is done, though there is evidence that there is a high incidence of psychiatric disturbance. Surely more should be known about this, so that the authorities could decide on a child's future with more information? It is possible that research might provide evidence which would prove that it is as disturbing for a child to be denied possible contact with, or knowledge of, a natural parent as it is for him to be torn from adoptive parents at a susceptible age. The fact is that we do not know. Nobody knows. Such investigations are obviously difficult to pursue and many would object to them on the grounds that prying into vulnerable situations simply makes those situations more vulnerable; but they ought nevertheless to be made. Otherwise we are talking about unknown factors and arriving at legal decisions on unknown evidence. If the child's welfare is truly our preoccupation, and not the welfare and wholly admirable emotions of distressed foster and would-be adoptive parents, then we ought to find out. I myself wrote a novel which, although I didn't realise it at the time, contains a passionate defence of the importance of a blood relationship, so this is clearly something on which I feel deeply, and research done in the United States by R. J. Isaac supports the view that children who are adopted become haunted at some point in their lives by the knowledge—not the feeling, but, let's face it, the knowledge— that they were rejected, for whatever reason, by their natural parents.

I hope I don't appear to be presenting an argument that attacks adoption and fostering as ways of caring for children in need of care. Obviously adoption is the best and only happy solution for children whose parents genuinely wish them to be adopted, or who abandon them, and many adoptive parents deal with the problems with remarkable understanding and success. But I do think public feeling can be whipped up all too easily on the subject of children. What, for instance, would be the public attitude towards the attempts of Cathy—in some sequel to *Cathy Come Home*—to reclaim those fictitious infants from devoted foster care? What blame would be attached, what rights assigned to her?

However, when all is said, the fact remains that something must and will be done about these children who are at the mercy of the arbitrary decisions of vacillating and often cruelly neglectful parents, and who are at the moment, as *The Times* said, in a position of maximum uncertainty. The local authorities, as the

London borough of Camden points out in the report of its Children's Committee, are in an extremely difficult position: they aim, wherever possible, to reunite a child in care with its own family, but sometimes this can mean that a child is in and out of care repeatedly, to its obvious detriment. Should parental rights be taken away from such families as are intermittently unable, even though willing, to provide security and continuity? And what security can be offered to children in the care of foster parents who are eager and willing to care for a child throughout its childhood, but who couldn't take the steps of legal adoption anyway, even were it available, because they need the financial support of the fostering allowance? These points have all been raised and are being considered, and some decisions need to be made, as numerous examples bear witness. But, as ever, what we want is not more heat but more light. Not enough is known about the consequences —the long-term consequences—of adoption and fostering. Children aren't children for ever, they grow into adults; and it is the right of a child to grow up in the best possible way, not the rights of parents, either foster or natural parents, that should be protected.

John Holloway

THE LAND OF MORE

John Holloway is Reader in Modern English at Cambridge
University, and a Fellow of Queen's College, Cambridge.
His books include *The Victorian Sage* and *Shakespeare's
Tragedies.*

W HEN PEOPLE BEGAN to use DDT for a variety of sensible
everyday purposes, no one thought that before many years they
would be worrying that it had turned up in the fatty tissues of
Antarctic penguins; but they are beginning to worry about
now, and it's a typical, almost a symbolic case. Recently some
American biologists discovered that certain similar substances,
equally poisonous, though not used as killers but simply in plastics
and lubricating oils, have found their way into the tissues of many
kinds of wild life in the United States. This probably holds good
in Europe as well. Does it matter? A quarter of a million British
sea-birds die every year from oil-slick. The European Inland
Fisheries Commission has reported that discharges of warm or hot
water from industry, and especially from nuclear power stations,
are becoming a major threat to fresh-water fish. Does that matter?
Recently, the Suffolk Executive Committee of the National
Farmers Union expressed concern that no research was being done
about fluoridation of water and long-term risk to livestock. That's
a bit nearer the knuckle. Some local authorities now recommend
that infants be given only purified bottled water, because of the
risk that ordinary supplies, running off highly fertilised land, can

lead to nitrate poisoning in the very young. That matters all right.

Recently, also, a branch of the National Union of Agricultural Workers called for the total prohibition of aerial crop-spraying within two miles of any village. When I read this, I remembered seeing the stuff come down in clouds about two years ago from a low-flying helicopter—I'd whisked up the windows of the car. So those penguins did matter after all. I link all these facts with others, where the hidden costs of progress and its hidden risks also begin to show, once you look. The new Greater London Council's plan for urban motorways will mean that 45,000 people will have to be rehoused—and how many more will find life miserable? Blackheath Village, Chelsea's Cheyne Walk, and a lot more fine architectural areas will be wrecked. Two of our remaining presentable towns in Southern England, Chipping Norton and Godalming, are also threatened, or worse than threatened, by new roads. The Ministry of Housing has just announced that if more stringent measures are not taken, every single scheduled private building will disappear within the foreseeable future. Meanwhile, in London alone, 7,000 children are killed or injured by traffic every year. Tens of thousands of people dump rubbish in the countryside every month: the relics of our new luxury—cars, old television sets, washing-machines. Ten thousand miles of hedgerow are uprooted every year: partly to help cars on corners; partly—as the report put it—to allow every inch of land to be cultivated. The AA has started a tree-planting programme to make up. Some 50,000 acres of land are lost every year to roads, buildings and reservoirs.

The Ministry of Technology is starting a series of little explosions near to 12 English cathedrals, to see how cathedrals will stand up to sonic bangs; and it has paid £4,000 on 500-odd claims for compensation after 11 supersonic test-flights. A major gas leak 25 miles out to sea and a full mile down has just been successfully plugged. The *Wall Street Journal* says that billions of tons of sewage on the bed of Lake Erie may suddenly be going to rise towards the top—from the affluent to the effluent society.

Glasgow University has just announced a research programme to see how more privacy could be got in—guess where—private homes.

One feels like asking, in the end, how crazy can the world get? Rational men would never come to conduct the affairs of their society along these lines, if they really had a free and open choice. They might, of course, do so if they had to take over a state of chaos and had no choice, save to struggle to stave off difficulties, one after another, as these became intolerably grave. But no rational men would actually set up conditions in which their very food and water and air were constantly polluted, their children killed and injured, and their whole environment rendered fouler all the time to ear, eye and nose—not through their failures, but through their very efforts and so-called advances.

Imagine you kept knocking your own children down because you always ran to the bottom of the garden to get started on the weekend digging. You'd walk. Imagine you found you were fertilising your cabbage patch so heavily you were polluting your own water supply. You wouldn't set up a research programme to see how to cancel out the danger; you'd fertilise less, have fewer cabbages and put your feet up more. How on earth have we got ourselves into the position of feeling obliged to squeeze every last ounce of productivity out of land and air and sea, and under the sea, and spend untold millions saving every minute of time, and then more millions and the best of our intelligence and energy staving off all the impoverishments of life which these desperate efforts themselves bring?

One could say something of how this has happened, but first, I think, one should take stock of how it's clearly happened unawares. And one should take stock of how this unawareness has become almost a characteristic feature of our political life. Our major problems now regularly grow up one by one and become serious while in politics we seem to preoccupy ourselves with something else and feel bursting with a sense of how important that something else is. I remember one midnight in the late 1940s when all the locomotives suddenly began hooting and blowing for all they were worth: the railways were nationalised. Some thought it was the end of our troubles and others the end of the world. The debate on nationalisation raged throughout the Fifties. Now it seems to have mattered less than we thought. Then, in the next decade, our political life centred on things like Cyprus, Egyptian bases, Persian oil; but in the background lay the matters of international trade, roads and traffic, immigration and maybe automation. These things really mattered far more and we thought about them far less. In the Sixties we've tied ourselves in knots to 'save the pound', as it's called, and twice over to get into EEC. And suddenly it seems as if we'd been taken up by a craze—especially over saving the pound—as much as by a major issue.

Meanwhile, a bigger matter than any of them has been coming from right off stage. This is population. Population trends are notoriously difficult to predict. In the late Thirties, a most distinguished demographer gave one possible figure for the population of the UK in the year 2000 as four million. They are also extremely difficult to reverse once they get under way. In terms of human happiness, no one could possibly see the recent great decline in infant mortality as other than perhaps our greatest recent success; but, at the same time, a government which wishes to limit the size of families has the hardest of tasks. My personal view is that there are no religious arguments which relate to government policy here, because if a state uses fiscal means to discourage large families, it simply presents some of its citizens with the choice between not having more children or accepting a financial disadvantage. It brings no pressure to bear on them to adopt one of these courses rather than the other, and of course it says absolutely nothing about implementing either choice by one means rather than another.

But there are some other virtually decisive objections to the use of fiscal policy for this purpose. First of all, for an obvious reason it's most unlikely to be really effective. Second, if intelligence is inherited, then fiscal deterrents probably deter least where we should probably like to deter most. Third, and most important, such a policy would be likely to inflict suffering, material or perhaps not material alone, on the children themselves. So, all in all, a steadily rising population, which is extraordinarily difficult to control, has been developing in the background, while our public life has engrossed itself with lesser matters. Full employment over two decades helped to conceal the problem, because it encouraged us to think about over-population in narrowly economic terms, in terms of productivity. Now, speaking broadly in social terms, it's here and probably to stay; 20 years, even ten years ago, we might just possibly have met it with a large-scale, long-term emigration programme. Now, short of a holocaust, we're probably doomed for generations to be a crowded country, eager to squeeze out the last drop of productivity everywhere, constantly making inroads in the name of welfare on the amenity of our environment, and striving to cope with new and ever more sophisticated problems as they emerge all the time, by ever more sophisticated remedies.

But this life-at-the-margin pattern can't be seen as just a problem in economics and productivity. It's something else too—something vital, though obscure, about the quality of our existence. Recently, there's been controversy among behavioural scientists about aggression in animals and the possibility, or otherwise, of man's being himself innately aggressive. But whatever the experts decide to tell us about innate aggression, they seem to agree on two environmental factors which cause aggressive behaviour: sudden changes in the structure of groups, so that the individual's position becomes fluid or uncertain, and overcrowding. At how many points might these be relevant to the social context of today? Does the way drivers behave on overcrowded roads, for example, come into the picture? All the time one seems to come back to multifarious but little understood ways, many more than I need catalogue, in which a high population density helps to press us up against the margin and to force us into an almost frenetic rhythm, where life is to wrestle with a problem, watch the solution create a new problem, wrestle again, and so on for ever.

But, intractable as it may be, dense population doesn't yet

compel us to this pattern by itself. There has to be comething else as well, and that something is why I called this article 'The Land of More.' How deeply the philosophy of more and more has become ingrained in our society by now! We often hear the word 'materialism', but it's not that alone. In part, it's also the contrary of materialism which has given us our assumptions. For example, for two or three centuries it was easy—and I believe it was right, too—to see our unparalleled commercial expansion as not only profit but also service to the common good of mankind. The same combination of self-interest and altruism was valid for our colonial and even our exterior imperial expansion. For a long time, enthusiasm for reform and improvement had been limited only by the opposition of those who didn't share the enthusiasm. It has not been limited—as today it increasingly is limited—by being up against the margin of the possible. This is why today we find ourselves asking for more new towns and more country parks and more home-grown food all at once; or for more cars on the road, able to go at more speed—and for more people unhurt by road accidents all the same. And in universities we want more people coming out with more adequate knowledge and expertise and more time spent in participation meetings as well.

But although this deep ingraining of the creed of more and more in part has a background in altruism, we're going to deceive ourselves if we think that's the full story, or even the main part of the story. The main part of that creed is of another kind. It hasn't been concerned with public amenity, or disseminating the benefits of civilisation, or cultural advance, but with something very simple indeed: with simple greed for more things to have and less work to get them. Without this deeply ingrained habit of mind, no doubt we could combine high population with a rational life instead of a scramble, and it is ingrained because in the past there has not been greed so much as easily realised prosperity, and real, or even desperate, need.

Heaven knows there's poverty enough in Britain today, but only 60 years ago nine-tenths of us badly needed more and today the picture is at least not that. Yet the conviction that life means to work for more and to press for more is as deep as ever, until it has perhaps become the great irrationality of our time. For me this shows most clearly in the obsession for more speed, until a national newspaper can speak of the 'quite staggering improvement' of flying to New York in three hours, not seven. No doubt everything staggers someone, but consider this, not in technical terms, but as human happiness and fulfilment, and it's perhaps rather more than a triviality and that's all you can say. But everyone knows that if we have to press on with the Concorde aircraft, it's not for the wonder of saving those hours at all: it's because we feel we've got to be able to sell planes so as to get money, so as to buy something else, for always more people, expecting always more things.

Those today who claim to be revolutionaries strike me as unaware of what revolutions bring, and perhaps this is no harm, because they also seem no good at bringing revolutions about. Moreover, their demands are often much too much in the image of the very Land of More that they think they despise. All the same, some of them have hold of a certain great thing that the rest of us evade. They have a sense, even if a confused one, that our world is not a case for tinkering, because in part it is a gigantic folly; and through population combined with a creed of more it's almost trapped into making that folly its inalienable and always less rewarding rule of life.

Grimm has a tale of a poor fisherman who caught a magic talking fish, but threw it back. The fisherman's wife was a devotee of the creed of more and more. Over and over, she sent her husband down to the shore to beg from the magic fish: first a fine house, then a manor, a castle, a palace. 'Go back,' the fish used to say genially, 'she's there already.' But each time the weather by the shore was worse than before. The last time, the water was black, and—I understand this story better now—that black was released sewage from the lake bottom. The sky was black, and that was the trails of filth from jet aircraft. And the fisherman said, 'Now my wife wants to rule the Moon', and the fish said: 'Go back, but your palace has gone. Go back to your hovel.'

Brian Harrison

DRINK AND THE VICTORIANS

Brian Harrison is a Fellow of Corpus Christi College,
Oxford, where he teaches history and politics. A book by
him on *Drink and the Victorians* will be published in due
course.

IN THE 1860s Englishmen drank three times as much spirits and
twice as much beer per head as they do now, and there were three
times as many pubs per head of population. These figures show
how strikingly drinking habits have changed in the last 100 years.
I think the contrast is important for two reasons: first, it takes us
right into the heart of recent British social history. But second, it
warns us against misinterpreting Dr Edward Smith's survey of
working-class diets in 1863.

Smith took his sample from what he called 'for the most part
persons of fairly thrifty habits'. His objective was to discover, he
said, 'upon how small an income a large family may live and yet
maintain a fair amount of health'; he was *not* trying to describe
the typical working-class diet of the period. Later in the century
Seebohm Rowntree drew attention to what he called 'secondary'
poverty—that is, poverty which springs from unwise expenditure
rather than from insufficient income. I suppose that, in matters of
diet, the most striking apparent irrationality of the Victorian poor
was the fact that, when they were forced by poverty to choose
between food and alcoholic drink, they tended to choose the
drink. There were a few teetotal families in most working-class
communities, but they were always outnumbered by the drinkers.

The conflict between these two styles of life—between the 'rough' and the 'respectable' working man—is one of the major themes of 19th-century social history. But if you look more closely at social conditions in England at the time when Smith made his survey, you can see that the Victorians often had good reason for the heavy drinking which now, at first sight, seems so irrational—reasons wider and deeper than the fairly obvious one of escape from bad conditions.

In the 1860s, alcoholic drinks were widely used as straight-forward thirst-quenchers. Before modern systems of water-supply were developed, drinking-water was often scarce and polluted. Milk was equally dangerous, and the soft-drink trade had hardly begun. There were hot drinks, of course: tea and coffee had become much cheaper in recent years. But they were troublesome to make, and tea and coffee-shops were few and far between, especially in country areas. And, anyhow, working people preferred alcoholic drinks to relatively expensive non-intoxicating drinks like these. In the 1840s Londoners could get a pint of strong beer for only twopence-halfpenny, but a cup of tea cost them twopence and a cup of cocoa fourpence.

Of course, alcoholic drinks were popular for other reasons. Beer was an evocative drink which aroused plenty of patriotic senti-ments—John Bull with his foaming tankard, agricultural pros-perity, contempt for the wine-drinking, frog-eating French and so on. In the 1860s, drink taxes contributed over a third of all public revenue, whereas now—although there's been an absolute increase in their amount—they contribute only one-fifteenth. A similar alignment—between wine and patriotism—exists in France to this day. Pubs were the natural focus for late-Victorian imperialism: a lot of them helped to recruit the armed services, and one Thames-side publican in London gained a great deal of favour with the government during the Crimean War by going about in a small steamer with music playing and streamers flying, recruiting sailors for the Fleet. Sydney Smith asked rhetorically in 1923: 'What two ideas are more inseparable than Beer and Britannia!'

Alcoholic drinks were thought to strengthen you for any kind of hard work. Fat red-faced men were considered models of good health. A rowdy Lancaster audience trundled a fat brewer in front of Joseph Livesey, who was lecturing there on teetotalism in 1834, and shouted: 'Show us a specimen like this with your water-drinking!' Joseph Barker, the Methodist minister, wrote of his pledge-signing in the 1830s: 'I cannot describe the solemn terror with which I ventured for the first time to reject my customary allowance of porter, ale, or wine.' Farmers thought they'd never get the harvest in if they didn't first fortify their labourers with 'harvest beer'. Soldiers and sailors prized their rum-rations as a way of keeping out the cold. Rum also helped banish fear; an Indian sepoy commented on the heavy drinking among British troops there:

I hardly know what white soldiers loved fighting so much for, unless it be for grog; they would fight ten battles running for one lata full of *daroo*. Their pay is nothing; it cannot be for that. They also love plunder, but I have seen white soldiers give a cap full of rupees for one bottle of brandy. There is something very extraordinary in it, I am certain, because I know European soldiers worship it, give their lives for it, and lose their lives by it.

Alcoholic drinks were important as painkillers, too. Criminals about to be flogged, patients being prepared for an operation or for tooth-extraction, pregnant women entering upon labour, babies unable to sleep—alcohol kept them all quiet. Doctors even administered alcoholic drinks as medicines: the zealous Dr Todd prescribed six pints of brandy in 72 hours for Charles Hindley, MP for Ashton; Hindley did not recover. No wonder the gout-rest formed part of the furniture of every West End club till the end of the century. And, needless to say, alcohol could also moderate pain of a less physical kind: gin was a godsend in the miserable social conditions of Early Victorian England. In Carlyle's words it was 'the black throat into which wretchedness of every sort, consummating itself by calling on delirium to help it, whirls down liquid Madness sold at tenpence the quartern.'

In the 1860s alcoholic drinks were used frequently on any kind of social occasion. In fact, in these years, work and play still weren't aspects of life that were clearly separated. 'Drinkings' often occurred at the work-bench when craftsmen welcomed a newcomer, or behind the counter when shopkeepers entertained a customer. Nothing caused more trouble to early factory-owners than the drinking habits of the people they employed. Many bargains were clinched over a drink—for many goods and services, drink was actually part of the payment. Pubs drove a roaring trade at the fairs, where so much business was transacted in those days. Cigarettes hadn't yet been introduced: all the more reason, then, for offering an acquaintance a drink. There was lavish drinking at funerals: Lord Ashley, as a schoolboy at Harrow, was inspired to undertake his life's work as defender of the poor by seeing some drunken bearers drop a pauper's coffin and expose its contents. Religious festivals were often drunken occasions, and when Samuel Wilberforce, the formidable Bishop of Oxford, tried to reform them in the 1850s, one leading inn-keeper actually petitioned for compensation. The drunken clergyman and minister were quite familiar figures in Victorian England. In view of all this, it's hardly surprising that the pioneer teetotallers in the 1830s were regarded as slightly mad. Peter Phillips clutched at his friend Richard Mee, who was about to sign the teetotal pledge at Warrington in 1834, and exclaimed: 'Thee mustn't, Richard, thee'll die.'

But the high level of drinking can't be blamed solely on attitudes to drink: it must be attributed also to the publicans' extensive social role. In 1872 Sir William Harcourt, the prominent Liberal politician, claimed that 'as much of the history of England has been brought about in public-houses as in the House of Commons'. Until 1872 there was no legislation to prevent public-houses outside London from opening all night every week-day, and there were special drinking places for all classes: the aristocracy had their great roadside inns just as the labourers had their sordid back-street beerhouses. So drink-sellers filled two roles which have now largely been taken over by other institutions: they presided over the local recreation centre, and over the local meeting-place.

The working man's home was often cold, uncomfortable and noisy, and he naturally felt the need to get away from it. In fact, the poorer and the larger his family, the more likely it was that he'd spend his evening in his specially reserved seat at the pub. And so we have the familiar Victorian scene—the wife struggling for her share of the pay-packet, sometimes pleading for it out in the street, sometimes literally fighting for it in the home. Victorian sentimentality oversimplified such scenes, of course: you can deduce that much from the many music-hall songs which stress the Victorian male's fear of the landlady and 'the missus'. Pubs offered communally many comforts which working men could never afford to buy for themselves—light, heat, cooking facilities, furniture, newspapers and companionship. Drink-sellers even remembered the need for public lavatories at a time when jerrybuilders and parsimonious local authorities often forgot them. The lavish baroque façade of the Victorian pub, its brilliant blaze of light, its extravagant fittings, gained effectiveness from the drabness of its slummy surroundings. The drink-seller was never the parasitic villain portrayed in the temperance tract: he was a popular and respected provider of recreation to a world which would have been intolerably dull without him. In a poor climate, and in cities which hadn't many open spaces, the tavern was a vital source of fun.

In a society starved of recreation, publicans pioneered commercial entertainment. For many years, travelling actors and circuses had performed at inns, and for a long time publicans had been sponsoring cruel sports. London pubs were often run by retired prizefighters, who followed their clients with tents and booths to the Epsom races and other sporting events. And the public-house played a crucially important role in the life of the prostitute. A witness before a Parliamentary inquiry in 1868 described a 'notorious house' in Aldershot: 'We at length reached a long room, furnished with chairs, forms, and narrow tables, and where, among some 200 soldiers, there were probably about 35 or 40 women. At our end a fiddler was playing on his instrument a lively tune, to which a few couples were dancing a merry accompaniment. Three or four persons, acting as waiters, were briskly engaged in seeking and attending to orders, bringing in beer etc, which was shared by the soldiers with their female companions, who either sat by their sides, or, as was more frequently the case, on their knees.'

Nobody was more inventive than the early Victorian publican in catering for popular recreational needs. In 1852 Charles Morton, the future impresario, opened the Canterbury Hall beside his London pub—the first of the many London music halls to evolve out of the less formal public-house entertainment which had hitherto been found in the 'free-and-easy'. Some publicans rivalled the chapel by promoting hymn-singing on Sunday evenings. So to abandon the pub was a really formidable decision for a mid-Victorian working man to take, and often required him to form a completely new set of friendships. Mrs Wightman, the Shrewsbury temperance reformer, wrote of a working man taking the pledge in 1858: 'I saw the hard struggle to give up all, for I knew not till then, that, with the working man, signing the pledge involves nearly everything included in the world, the flesh, the devil.'

The pub dominated the transport system. Trade unions had a network of 'houses of call' throughout the country, where their members could lodge and look for work. Inevitably the drinking-place became the centre for oral and written news. Some publicans hired out newspapers for a penny an hour, and others paid special newsreaders to keep their illiterate customers up to the minute. In the publicans' 'large rooms', local political parties and societies held their meetings free of charge. London working men's debating-halls were almost always attached to drinking-premises—with interruptions at the end of each speech, from waiters calling for 'orders'.

Again, the publican—with his easy access to small change and his personal interest in holding on to his customers—was the ideal treasurer for local friendly societies and savings-clubs. And at a time when merchandise was often carried around on the trades-man's back, public-houses were also trading-centres in their own right. Public auctions usually took place there, and in the 1830s Holderness farmers were still tramping up and down the stairs of the Hildyard Arms with their corn samples, for lack of a public corn-exchange. We also have to remember that in a relatively uncomplex society, and before the rise of the welfare state, there were few specialised public buildings: many people went to the drinking-place—as to the chapel—simply because there was nowhere else.

None the less, by the 1860s several influences were already diminishing the social importance of drink. Non-intoxicating drinks were getting cheaper, more palatable and more accessible. The old drinking patterns were incompatible with modern industrial processes—with the precision and regularity required from the factory's work force. From the 1870s onwards, Dr B. W. Richardson began to turn doctors away from alcoholic pres-cription. And from the 1840s onwards, the railway pushed the publican out of his central position in the transport system. The Duke of Wellington told Miss Burdett-Coutts in 1847 that 'before the steam invention' he had stopped six or eight times every summer at the Fountain in Canterbury, but that since using the railway he'd never been there. The decline of the fair and the growth of retail shops pushed the publican out of his crucial role in economic exchange. Restaurants and coffee-houses sprang up as alternative places for getting cooked food, and increased affluence weakened the publican's recreational role by improving the comfort of the working man's home. Increased state inter-vention, by covering the country with public buildings, created so many types of public house that the original public-house acquired a specialised meaning and a hyphen. Lord Avebury, the champion of public libraries, said in 1903 that there were now public houses all over the country, 'not for the sale of beer, but for the free use of books'. Improved recreations siphoned off the masses into football stadiums, theatres and later into cinemas. Accelerating all these changes, of course, was the ideology of 'self-help': the idealisation of independence, sobriety and respectability—as embodied in the temperance movement.

By the mid-Victorian period, a sustained campaign had been launched to discredit the publican—a campaign from which he is only now recovering. Public drinking gradually ceased to be respectable. As early as 1852 G. R. Porter, the statistician, could claim that 'no person, above the rank of a labouring man or artisan, would venture to go into a public-house to purchase anything to drink'. Drinking hours were progressively restricted, children were excluded, the police became more vigilant. Perhaps one of the most dramatic incidents in this campaign was the conversion to temperance work of the brewer's son, F. N. Charrington. One evening in 1873, he was walking from the family brewery in Mile End to the ragged school where he taught: he saw a man come out of a tavern and knock his wife, who was pleading for money, into the gutter. Charrington looked up, saw his own name in huge gilt letters above the tavern, and realised in a moment the hypocrisy involved in all his family's pious pretensions. From then on he abandoned all income from the family brewery and worked for the poor in the East End.

Per capita consumption figures responded only slowly to all this, but during World War One they took a plunge, and public-houses have been closing down ever since. It would be wrong to speak as though all these changes constituted progress. Today drug-taking revives many of the problems confronted by Victorian temperance reformers. And it is questionable whether the mass entertainment which has superseded Victorian pub recreations really possesses their warmth, colour and sociability. But these are different questions. The major point I want to make is the striking contrast between the roles of drink and of drink-sellers then and now. A modern dietary survey based only on information from sober families would be far more accurate as a guide to national habits than Edward Smith's survey was 100 years ago.

W. D. M. Paton, F.R.S.

DRUG DEPENDENCE

Brian Harrison's talk ended with the thought 'Today
drug-taking revives many of the problems confronted by
Victorian temperance reformers'. W. D. M. Paton, the
Professor of Pharmacology at Oxford, here contributes an
important study of those contemporary problems.

I MUST BEGIN BY clearing the field. Some drug dependences
arise from medical causes—the diabetic who must have insulin, or
the cretinous child who must have thyroid hormone for the rest
of his life—but for such the dependence only arises for a patho-
logical reason. What we are concerned with here is dependence
on drugs arising *without* such medical cause. But this group too is
extraordinarily heterogeneous. People can become dependent on
aspirin or purgatives or stomach powders or on almost any item
in the Pharmacopoeia which they believe at one time or another
has helped them. This too I do not want to discuss, although we
shall perhaps throw a little light on it. What I want to deal with
is the epidemic of dependence on drugs of the type of heroin,
cocaine, amphetamines and cannabis. For there is what one can
describe as a true epidemic, particularly for the first of these,
beginning around 1959–60, the number of heroin addicts slightly
more than doubling every two years. The fact that it has arisen
particularly among the young is an especially alarming feature.
Such events lead one to think very hard about the causes and
results of drug-taking. I shall say little about alcohol and barbiturates: not because these are unimportant—far from it—they all

have their associated social cost and mortality. But that mortality hits, by and large, in middle age. What I have chosen to concentrate on are the drug dependences which take their toll of the adolescent, who has not yet even had a shot at adult life.

A second necessary clarification is to get away from the words 'addict' and 'addiction'. Although these words are themselves perfectly good (they simply refer to an individual being bound in some way, and I shall use them in this sense), they have become nearly inextricably tried to drugs such as morphine. This leads to futile discussions, for instance, as to whether a drug produces a 'true' addiction, when on the one hand it undoubtedly traps its victims, yet on the other does not produce morphine-like withdrawal symptoms or tolerance. As we shall see, withdrawal symptoms and tolerance are not essential to the dependent state. A new nomenclature is needed, and a World Health Organisation committee has in fact proposed, wisely to my mind, that one should think in terms of the *dependence* of an individual on drugs, and distinguish that dependence according to whether it has physical or psychic features. (The Brain Committee in its second report accepted this approach and defined an addict as 'a person who, as a result of repeated administration, has become dependent upon a drug controlled under the Dangerous Drugs Act and has an overpowering desire for its continuance, but does not require it for the relief of organic disease'.)

The value of the word 'dependence' I think goes further than this. Let us start by defining drug dependence as occurring when 'the administration of a drug brings into play forces which predispose to its continued administration'. This way of putting it means that we do no ask, for instance, 'Is there true dependence present here or not?', but more usefully *describe* each dependence by separating out and characterising (1) the forces brought into play, (2) their intensity, and (3) the social cost for each dependence. This approach is helpful too in bringing drug dependence into line with our ordinary everyday life. For instance, I like Kellogg's cornflakes in the morning, and if I don't get it I feel slightly aggrieved. This is a slight, very slight, dependence. Life is in fact built up of such dependences. Any habit represents one: some dependences are trivial, some benign and pleasurable, some not so benign: some, such as dependences on friends and family and work, are part of what makes you what you are.

Now if we turn to drug dependence, what forces lead to a drug, once given, to tend to be given again? I think there are four main forces which one can recognise. The first is that they can produce what one could term *'primary pleasurable rewards'*. Sometimes this is a very intense, pleasurable sensation, comparable with that of sexual orgasm. I shall call it 'orgasmic', even though this may be something of an over-simplification. Further, some drugs, primarily the opiates, are analgesics relieving discomfort. Getting rid of any aches or pains can be positively pleasurable, though in a different way. Another primary reward provided by all the drugs we shall consider is an escape of some sort from the unpleasantness of personal situations by (a) blurring the fact of their existence, or (b) changing one's sensory state so that one is distracted by interesting sensory changes or (c) simply by inducing an exhilarated, or a pleasant, detached, dreamy state. All such pleasurable sensations will predispose to re-administration when the effect of the drug has worn off.

There is a second, rather more subtle, major *secondary reinforcing influence*: namely the whole context in which drugs are taken, which psychologically comes to be associated with the primary rewards of drug-taking and to share their force. As a trivial analogy, it is a little bit as though at about 7 o'clock in the evening you happened to be walking along a rather pleasant street in Soho where there is a restaurant you are accustomed to visit. The mere fact that you are in that street, that you are seeing the familiar awnings and familiar faces, smelling the familiar smells, all these, quite apart from hunger, increase the chance that you may turn into that restaurant. And if you do, then the *next* time you are in that vicinity, the chance that you turn into that restaurant is further increased. It is the same with any recurrent personal problem. Whether you face it, or dodge it, increases the chance of facing or dodging it next time. So, too, when you come to consider the fate of a morphine addict discharged from hospital, it is not surprising that although he may be nominally cured during his period in hospital, when he goes back to the old environment, the old problems, the old rooms and buildings, the old company, which, with drug-taking, had made up his life, he should move again in his old pattern: small wonder that the relapse rate is high. This social environmental aspect, of course, has to some extent been dignified by the recent description of the 'sub-cultures' involved in drug-taking and other activities. The term seems to me grandiose: 'sub-' I would agree with, but 'culture' seems to me as yet too strong a word to apply to a social activity which has still to display any stability of structure or consistency of attitude. But the term is appropriate in stressing that there is a social environment which can reinforce the process of drug-taking.

There are two other possible reinforcing factors to drug dependence, more famous, though perhaps less important than those I have mentioned.

The first is *the withdrawal syndrome*, made familiar from descriptions of the physical effects of Morphine and heroin withdrawal. They can indeed be dramatic—cramps, sweating, gooseflesh and the like: but psychiatrists have found that quite a number of those who are addicted to heroin don't take enough of it to get these withdrawal symptoms; and yet they are firmly dependent on the drug. Other drugs (including cocaine) have no such withdrawal symptoms at all. One needs to be a little subtler in assessing withdrawal effects. For instance, the feeling of after-depression, of 'let-down', as it can be called, after a dose of cannabis or amphetamine, although hardly detectable physically and only reportable by the addict, is evidently a factor rather effective in reinforcing dependence, putting into mind directly the idea of re-administration of the drug. The withdrawal reaction, therefore, includes not only the dramatic 'cold turkey', but also the loss of the pleasurable sensation, and the after-depression. I think it is probably true that, in this sort of sense, withdrawal symptoms always occur.

Finally, there is the question of *tolerance*, again made famous with the opiates, but almost negligible with some drugs. In itself there is no reason to suppose that the development of tolerance induces dependence; but clearly it accentuates the problem of supply and focuses attention on re-administration. It will also accentuate the intensity of withdrawal symptoms, intensifying *that* reinforcement of the dependence.

Armed with this approach, of dependence induced and maintained by primary reward, by social reinforcement, and possibly also by withdrawal symptoms and tolerance, we can now consider particular drugs, and ask in turn about them what can be said about the intensity of the dependence, the factors generating it and the cost of that dependence to the individual and to society.

The opiates are so called from their pharmacological relationship to opium, and include morphine, heroin, pethidine and many synthetic analogues. Opium dependence is probably very old, but did not become intense until the introduction of the hypodermic syringe, which allowed a higher concentration of the pure material to reach the brain in a shorter time than can be achieved by mouth. The next step was, instead of merely injecting the drug subcutaneously, to inject directly into a blood vessel, so that in only a few seconds it hits the brain with maximum intensity. It is with this intravenous route of administration that the most intense pleasurable sensation is obtained as well as the most intense dependence; and it is this sensation which has been compared by addicts to that of sexual orgasm. To this must be added, as we noted earlier, two other pleasurable features: the removal of any physical discomfort; and apart from the orgasmic effect, the induction of a pleasant, detached, day-dreamy state. All these three elements, of course, represent an escape from life's problems, and all will predispose to taking the drug again. In addition, we know that with the opiates both withdrawal symptoms and tolerance *can* be intense. Add to this the influence of the social environment of heroin-taking, and it is obvious that for intravenous heroin all the factors are there to develop a very profound dependence indeed. One can roughly measure this dependence by what the dependent individual will do to get the drug; and it is well known that there is almost no limit to the measures the deeply dependent heroin addict will take.

What can one say of the cost to the individual and to society of such a dependence? This question needs to be considered carefully. I would argue that my dependence on Kellogg's cornflakes, or yours on (say) porridge, implies no cost to society. Thus, it is theoretically possible that heroin-dependence would be equally harmless. But the theoretically possible is not endorsed by experience. One has to point first to a *death rate* in the young heroin addict 20 times greater than normal, as Dr James and his colleagues recently showed (achieving in a year or two of heroin addiction an effect comparable to a life of heavy smoking). Second, there has appeared what is nearly a set of *new diseases*: a fulminating pneumonia, a bacterial endocarditis due to neglect of sterile precautions, skin abscesses and thrombosed veins, and an abnormally high incidence of jaundice in young people probably due to the carriage of the jaundice virus by dirty syringes shared between addicts. Such a medical outcome is perfectly reasonable, because the drug characteristically makes you 'care-less', for instance as to aseptic precautions. Third are the simple social misery and *social loss* of young talent which accompanies the addicition. Lastly—a fairly new and important point—there is *infectiousness* of the condition which carries the cost beyond that of the addict himself; for instance, in one study 40 cases of heroin addiction were traced to a single addict.

We have to say, therefore, that the social and personal cost of opiate addiction is appallingly heavy; and that with current incidence of *new* cases of heroin addiction of 500 to 600 a year, one is truly dealing with a major medical emergency.

This cost might be mitigated if the condition could be readily cured; but it is an unhappy fact that the cure rate is bad. Many procedures have been tried, and reports follow a pattern common in therapeutics. A new procedure is introduced by a doctor full of enthusiasm, and for a while his patients do well. Then as the procedure becomes more familiar, the initial flush of enthusiasm passes over into practice of a new fairly well worked out routine, and the success rate dwindles. There is in fact a question as to whether there is any one therapeutic procedure which can be unanimously agreed to be better than any other. An interesting method is to give the drug methadone, which is like morphine or heroin and is itself a drug of addiction, although with less euphoric effect. It also has the capacity to block heroin or morphine's action; so that the craving is removed and if heroin is tried, no effect is produced. At the cost possibly of a life led under this drug, the heroin dependence can be removed, to be replaced by a controlled methadone dependence. Some success has been claimed, and it may represent an approach which, with new drugs, could be further developed. But of course it also raises the question of the merits and safety of what may have to be a life-long therapy. Notice, too, that even at its best, such drug treatment does nothing for the personal problems which led to the addiction, nor about the reinforcing environment.

The second drug to consider is cocaine, now often taken together with heroin, cocaine intensifying the euphoria and heroin serving in part to dampen down some of the strong stimulant effects which cocaine produces. What are the forces inducing dependence here? Just as with the opiates, there is an orgasmic pleasure associated. Again the great euphoria and excitement provides an escape from the environment. But it is remarkable that while dependence on cocaine can become very strong indeed, yet, if it is to cocaine alone, there is little tolerance developed, and there are no withdrawal symptoms of the morphine type. The main withdrawal symptom is essentially an exhaustion and after-depression, as well as symptoms of chronic intoxication. Some recent important work on cocaine needs mention, the experiments by an American Dr G. A. Deneau, in monkeys, using a self-injection technique. Here the monkey, free to move in a cage but with a cradle on its shoulder carrying the apparatus for hypodermic administration, was able to give itself a suitable dose of cocaine every time it pushed a lever. The monkey was left to discover that pushing the lever had this effect, which in due course it did, and found it 'liked' the results. Deneau then found that these animals, of their own volition, would give themselves up to a regime of dosage of cocaine repeated as the effects of successive doses wore off, carrying themselves to a state of malnutrition, into a state of convulsions and finally coma. The most extraordinary and pathetic feature was that as these monkeys recovered from their coma, the first thing they did was to stretch out a hand for a lever to receive another dose of cocaine. These are remarkable, and in some ways horrible, experiments, but not more horrible than the case-histories of drug addiction. I think they show unequivocally that there is in cocaine something which, independent of the complexities of human psychology or of physical well-being, independent, too, of tolerance or withdrawal symptoms, can nevertheless lead to its continued administration.

Third come the amphetamines. Amphetamine (trade name Benzedrine) is the parent substance, which has spawned a plentiful progeny. Some of them have been used, I think wrongly and on far too large a scale, as slimming aids. A more valid therapeutic use is to treat mildly depressed states or to neutralise the depressant effect of some other drug. The possibility of abuse has been known for at least 25 years, since I was a medical student, when people occasionally emptied the contents of a Benzedrine inhaler into their coffee. But it is only recently that widespread abuse of the amphetamines, either alone or with barbiturates, has spread among the young, and, worse still, the giving of amphetamine-like substances by the intravenous route. With the intravenous amphetamines one has to say that the intensity of the 'lift' that can be produced has an orgasmic quality as a dominant part of its action. The amphetamines also have some effect on the heart and circulation which limits the dose to begin with; but with continued administration tolerance develops both to the central and to the peripheral effects, and relatively enormous doses can eventually be taken. On withdrawal of the drug there is no withdrawal symptom such as is seen with the opiates, but there can be quite a distinct 'let-down'. Japan has had a major epidemic of amphetamine-taking and Newcastle too. There has been a severe outbreak of its intravenous use in Stockholm, with the formation of a colony of youngsters in the criminal districts just living, under poor conditions, giving each other intravenous doses of the amphetamine-like substance, Preludin.

The Swedes have made the comment that they feel that this intravenous amphetamine abuse is the most infectious of the addictions, raising again the question of addict-to-adict spread which we noted with heroin. This concept deserves far more attention. There has been a tendency to think of the addict as an atom, in isolation (as indeed psychically he may be). But at least socially for heroin, cocaine, amphetamine, cannabis and the like, this is false. It is an important fact: addicts infect other addicts.

Having considered these three sets of drugs, the opiates, cocaine and the amphetamines, I think one should pause and consider them together. They all have the property, not shared by other drugs, of generating an intensely pleasurable sensation; this is not their only action, and the change of mood and detachment from surroundings is also important. But I suspect that it is the orgasmic character of these drugs which makes them 'hard'. Can one say anything about the nature of this particular action? At the fundamental level, the pharmacological action of the drugs, I think the evidence all suggests that these drugs interact with the neurohumoral transmission between neurones. The cells of the brain are believed to communicate with each other by releasing from their nerve endings, where one neurone impinges on another, chemical substances of the type of acetylcholine, noradrenaline, or hydroxytryptamine, to mention three of the more important candidates. Consequently if a drug can interfere with the release of these transmitters, or can antagonise them, or can increase their action, or otherwise modify the chemical transmission process, any of these procedures will be expected to interfere with neuronal activity. One can show, in certain test situations, that morphine and the other opiates, cocaine and the amphetamines can inhibit the release of acetylcholine and probably also that of noradrenaline. Cocaine can, in addition, interfere with the disposal of noradrenaline, and amphetamine can release it. I used to think one could build a useful theory on this basis: the drug stops transmitter release, and as a result, stocks of transmitter in the nerve terminations pile up and could break through the block, giving rise to tolerance. Withdraw the drug, and now the nerve-endings are able to pour out an abnormally large amount of transmitter, since the restraint by the drug is removed, to produce an exaggerated effect, the withdrawal response. But tolerance and withdrawal are not crucial to dependence, so that the usefulness of such an approach seems less clear. In any case this is not a very helpful level for our present discussion, because we cannot tie the statements down to particular neurones.

A more useful comment which one could make on the action of these drugs is to draw attention to some work of a neuro-physiological kind by Dr J. Olds in America. He has shown that there exist in the brain of rats specific, sharply localised centres whose excitation electrically by implanted electrodes seems to be a source of intense 'satisfaction' to the rat. The experiment consists of arranging that the stimulation is done, not by the investigator, but by the rat, by learning to press a lever. Positions of the electrodes can be found, particularly in the hypothalamus, whereby the life of the rat is then given over largely to self-stimulation. The satisfaction achieved is such that it takes dominance over almost any other activity of the animal until exhaustion super-venes. It will, for instance, go on to stimulate itself over 2,000 times an hour for 24 hours, then have a break for 20 hours' sleep, then start again. This is an extraordinary finding, which means that there is likely to be in our brains, too, though doubtless under more elaborate control, a centre or centres which mediate some acutely pleasurable response sensation. When one sets this along-side, for instance, Deneau's experiment on the monkey, or the clinical histories of heroin addicts, one finds it very hard to avoid the conclusion that cocaine, and morphine and amphetamine, are in some way activating the reward centres which Olds has activated by electrical means.

Suppose we now ask what the role of Olds' 'reward centres' can be; the answer must surely be that they serve, first to *promote* the completion of some effort, and second to *signal* its completion. For the rat, Olds suggests that the neurones are involved in food and sexual reward processes. For man, one should surely add those higher activities, aesthetic, mystical or intellectual, whose successful consummation brings pleasure or satisfaction. If one believes that neurophysiological activity accompanies mental activity, and recalls that feelings of pleasure and satisfaction are similar, even when the occasion or the course of events that led to them varies widely, from these considerations alone one would think it a sensible arrangement for the body to provide a neural centre 'in charge', so to speak, of this particular neurophysiological expression. But of course the existence of such a centre also means that in principle there could be procedures which activate it directly, and produce the response of satisfaction or pleasure, without the normally preceding activity or effort. This provides my psychic interpretation of the action of these orgasmic drugs: that they provide a chemical short cut to the feeling of reward which normally rounds off some successful physical or mental effort. One's attitude to such a conclusion may vary. One might say: 'How marvellous to be able to get this reward with so little effort.' Or again one might suggest that, for the human, there is something ultimately spurious, ultimately unsatisfactory, about a reward so obtained, Indeed addicts seem to move from the first position to the second as their addiction progresses. Be that as it may, my main argument is that the heart of the problem of hard-drug dependence is the nature of the reward it provides; and that the understanding, possibly even control, of that reward, is needed for any long-term solution.

But let us go on from these drugs, which, as well as providing some blunting of the realities of life, also have this orgasmic character, to those where it is a shift into a different psychic world which provides the attraction. This is the group containing cannabis, mescaline, LSD, and certain new tryptamines and amphetamine-derived substances. All these substances can produce disorders of sensation and change of mood which, largely according to the circumstances in which they are taken, may be pleasurable or unpleasurable. This derangement goes further still with drugs such as LSD (lysergic acid diethylamide), where quite profound psychic effects can be produced, going as far as hallucination and semi-permanent or relapsing psychosis. It is clear that with these drugs, continued administration can produce tolerance. Equally it is clear that when they are withdrawn there can be a feeling of let-down or loss. Further, despite what is said about their being non-addictive (and that scandalous example of suppression of truth and suggestion of falsehood which appeared as an advertisement in *The Times* made great play with this for cannabis), there is no doubt that they can produce a psychic dependence. It seems probable that some individuals can take cannabis a few times and never again (although 'never' is a long time); and yet others, more habitual takers, find that, in spite of all their protestations that they can stop at any time, it is difficult or perhaps impossible to do so without expert help.

I am sure it is true that the dependence is not normally strong, and some might think I make too much of it. But there is a little story about pethidine that is relevant. This is a substitute for morphine: it produces less euphoria, less tolerance and much milder withdrawal symptoms: so it was hoped, indeed expected, that it would be negligibly addictive. But because of this reputation, more people took risks: the end result (over the last seven years) has been between 100 and 130 pethidine addicts a year, as well as 150-200 morphine addicts. In considering risk, it is total risk that counts, i.e. the intrinsic risk multiplied by the number who take the risk: and, as my story shows, these two factors may interact.

Of this group cannabis is, for the present at least, far the most important. LSD has, justifiably, frightened people both because of its psychic effects and because of the evidence that it damages chromosomes; the other drugs have on the one hand proved less active than expected, and on the other are hardly available generally. I shall, therefore, restrict myself to cannabis, although the type of argument applies equally well to any drug. What, then, does one have to say as to the social and personal cost of cannabis dependence? It has, of course, been argued that it has none, or could even be advantageous. I think that there are some straightforward points: first, cannabis produces disorders of the sense of time, distance and spatial orientation. For an individual in his private house (if he has undrugged company) this could hardly matter. But one needs to remember that an individual receiving cannabis, if he happens to be in a position of some responsibility, is at least as dangerous as the car-driver who is drunk, or the lorry-driver who has been taking too much of some antihistamine, or the anaesthetist who has become addicted to sniffing the anaesthetic he gives to his patients. Whatever happens to cannabis, the restraints must be such that nobody in such positions of responsibility should take the drug while he is exerting that skill.

Second, these drugs have often been characterised as 'mind-enhancing'. There is in fact no evidence whatever that any of these drugs 'enhance' the mind, only that they distort the sensory mechanisms and perhaps modify the state of mental attention to outside events. Nevertheless, the claim has been made, and led to the further claim that as a result creative activity can be enhanced. This may prove to be one of the frauds of the age. It is true that detachment from reality by one means or another (by the drugs I've mentioned, or by anaesthetics, or even during the phase between sleeping and waking) can be associated with fascinating sensory distortions, even with feelings of 'insight', of being near to ultimate reality. The early experiments by Humphry Davy 150 years ago on nitrous oxide included vivid descriptions of this. But the actual insights brought back from these 'voyages' have always proved trivial. The brain, as well as having a mechanism which registers 'satisfaction', seems also to have a mechanism which, so to speak, registers 'insight'; a mechanism which, like the other, can be artificially but falsely triggered. Be that as it may, the claim to enhanced creative activity must be judged by its fruits; and I still wait for the Benjamin Britten, the Henry Moore, the Frost, Lowell or R. S. Thomas among the ranks of cannabis consumers. Indeed, the best evidence I have, gleaned from those close to students and schoolchildren, is that the habitual use of cannabis, so far from leading to improved performance, is more commonly a cause of their drop-out from academic life.

But these are perhaps minor effects, perhaps not. There are two other undoubtedly important, and neglected, aspects to cannabis. The first is that we simply do not know what the long-term effects of its administration are when given continuously on a large scale. Cannabis consumption of this sort is relatively new to this country and its impact on our culture is quite uncertain. Medically, of course, cannabis has been explored: it was removed from the British Pharmacopoeia after 1914, being demoted to the British Pharmaceutical Codex (which includes drugs of interest but of less therapeutic importance), and was removed from the Codex after 1949. (LSD has never been in either.) I would defend the case that there is no valid therapeutic use for cannabis whatever. People point to experience in the Near East, say Egypt, which has had cannabis perhaps for millennia without apparently being destroyed. Yet one may be cautious in evaluating such remarks. One would not expect, for instance, from some of the statements made, that the proposal that cannabis should be internationally outlawed came, not from paternalistic England or America, not even from the prudent Swiss or Scandinavians, but from Egypt and South Africa. Yet the evidence about the long-term effects of cannabis, discouraging though it is, is inadequate by modern standards. The only data we really have are from countries which have had, for many, a low expectation of life, a low standard of living, and much helminth infestation, particularly chronic anaemia from hookworm. Even in this background, the public health aspect of cannabis has aroused concern. Yet in such conditions any agent which made life more tolerable might be justified. But to apply this evidence to predict the effect of cannabis in countries such as ours or America, with quite different conditions of climate, diet, medicine, hygiene and general culture seems to me quite lunatic. I think the important thing to say about cannabis is that it produces disorders of sense and time and some euphoria, and that by modern medical standards, that is about all we really know—far less than about any of the 600 to 700 drugs in the Pharmacopoeia or about any drug submitted for consideration by the Dunlop Committee on the Safety of Drugs. Evidence of liver damage and of teratogenicity has now appeared.

The second aspect is this: that the interaction of cannabis (and indeed of the amphetamines) with drugs such as heroin deserves a much closer look than it has received. It is over the last two to three years that the idea that cannabis might 'escalate' to heroin has been canvassed really seriously in this country; and one can find some quite wise authorities who have said that they see no evidence for it. I have reached a different conclusion. But first one must be clear what one is saying: not that every person who takes cannabis is bound to go on to heroin; nor that I can identify *a priori* a process, started by cannabis, which must, physiologically or chemically, go on to heroin. It is simply a question of public health statistics: is there evidence or is there not, that taking cannabis gives an enhanced risk of addiction to opiates, and if so, by how much? If there *is* such enhancement, then the social cost of cannabis includes not only its own dangers, but that of the 'harder' drugs to which it may lead.

I would like to go into this in some detail, partly because it is important, partly because it illustrates a way in which I believe one can usefully think about drug addiction, that is, statistically, quantitatively, and socially.

The approach I would like to make is to set up, in contrast, a different hypothesis; that is that cannabis and heroin have nothing to do with each other, and then to test this hypothesis. It could be supported if one could for instance show that the age at which people come to take cannabis is in fact later than the age at which they take heroin. If this was the case, the suggestion that cannabis leads on to heroin would be nonsense. But the actual facts, as Dr Glatt has shown, are that in a group of heroin addicts, their history showed that on average they began to take cannabis or amphetamines at around 16 or 17, they began to take heroin at around 18 or 19, and in the experience of this particular group they were admitted to hospital psychiatric care around 21 or 22.

I think one has to say that the chronology is compatible with the escalation hypothesis.

A second approach would be to look at the growth, on the one hand of cannabis-taking, on the other hand, of heroin addiction. If one could show, for instance, that the one had developed historically much earlier or much later, or to quite a different degree quantitatively than the other, then the association between the two would become much less plausible. But again the only evidence one can obtain points in the other direction. Over the years from 1959 to 1967, after a relatively stable period up to 1958, there was, both in cannabis offences and in heroin addicts, a 20-fold growth. I find it rather remarkable that, despite the uncertainty of this sort of data (not all cannabis offences are recognised, and their annual incidence naturally fluctuates; nor are all heroin addicts known), the magnitude of the increases as well as their timing should be so close to each other. If there *is* a discrepancy in time, it is that the rise in cannabis offences preceded by one or two years the rise in heroin addiction. So again it is impossible to reject the idea that cannabis may lead on to heroin.

Finally, one can approach it statistically. Again let us suppose that cannabis and heroin-taking have nothing to do with each other. In that case the incidence of cannabis-taking among known heroin-addicts should be the same as that of the general population. The incidence in the general population is something of the order, according to rather rough estimates, of 1 in 2,000, that is, an incidence of about 0·05 per cent. But in fact it is a remarkable finding, quoted by many of those concerned, that almost all heroin addicts (80 to 100 per cent) have taken cannabis in the past. The incidence of taking it is therefore something like 2,000 times commoner than it would be if they had nothing to do with each other.

Now you could object that all addicts take tea or coffee, yet nobody suggests that these lead to heroin addiction. This ignores the crucial point in the statistics; that is that coffee or tea drinking is an extremely common activity, but cannabis-taking a much less common one in the general population. It is in the comparison between normal incidence and the incidence among addicts that the significance arises. This sort of argument is of the same kind as that which associates cancer of the lung with smoking, silicosis with certain dusts, industrial use of β-naphthylamine with bladder cancer, damage to blood-forming organs with chloramphenicol, consumption of alcohol with traffic accidents and the like.

One can, in fact, go a little further. Apart from knowing that cannabis is particularly associated with heroin, one would like to get an estimate of something for which an incidence is very difficult to get by direct enquiry, i.e. the incidence of heroin-taking among cannabis-takers. This one can do by using a method of inverse probability (a version of Bayes' theorem), used, *inter alia*, by astronomers, for whom comparable difficulties exist in making *direct* experiments on their objects of study. This calculation gives an incidence of 7 to 15 per cent, i.e. that of those who take cannabis, 7 to 15 in every 100 will be, or are, heroin-takers. The only other definite figure I have seen published is that by Dr Elisabeth Tylden, from a study of a group of 130 hashish smokers, of whom 10 per cent were known to be taking morphine and/or heroin.

I think one is bound to conclude that there is, at least for our culture, a far closer connection between cannabis and the opiates than is generally recognised. This connection may be shared to some extent by amphetamines, but it seems that alcohol (and barbiturates taken by themselves) do *not* share it. It is, of course, what one would expect if the escalation hypothesis is valid. But there are two other alternative explanations which I have heard advanced.

The first is to argue that opiate addicts are in any case psycho-pathic individuals who would have been addicts whatever happened, cannabis being an inessential but natural incident on the road. I would now unhesitatingly reject this 'predetermined addict' approach. Its only plausibility arises if you look at per-sonalities *after* they have become addicted; but if you ask those interested to define the personality which predisposes to addiction, you either get contradictory answers (whose average approximates to normality) or answers too general to be worth much. The fact is that no psychological characteristic has yet been shown to be of predictive value; many addicts frankly surprise everybody. One must suppose that if there is a psychological factor involved, it is a fairly common one. There is an undertone in this approach that I confess I dislike; that addicts are in some way intrinsically inferior people. *After* their addiction, possibly (and there are reasons for wondering if they can ever recover from damage done); but *before*, there is no hard evidence for this at all. It follows that, *if* they could be genuinely cured of their addiction, there is no reason to doubt that they could take their normal and rightful place in life (if they were allowed to).

Yet the question remains, why did these *particular* individuals become addicts? I think the truth may be rather different, and perhaps more illuminating: namely that it is largely fortuitous. Suppose that a young man, successful in his work, well spoken of by all, and happy with his girl friend, takes, or has taken cannabis for a bit of fun; who could say this was, in itself, dangerous? But let his friendships go awry, or let his experiments (if he is a scientist) or his job go badly, or let some other personal difficulty arise (and we all know how much luck there is in such things), then I think the chance of recalling his drug experience, of seeing an escape in it, becomes important. If he tries it, and it provides a temporary escape, the drug experience becomes very important. If the further chance of supply of other drugs occurs (and merely *knowing* an addict would be enough), then the sequence is nearly complete. Such a sequence is compatible with the lack of any identified psychological predisposition, with the seeming fortuitousness in the case-histories, and with the facts of infectiousness. It suggests that major factors in generating addiction are the chance of ordinary life, and the chance of availability of drugs.

But to return to the relation between cannabis and heroin: the second explanation is to agree that cannabis and heroin are indeed associated, and that this arises from the oppressive legal restraints on their use; release one or the other from their legal restraint, and the link would be broken. It is very difficult to test this contention, but some comments can be made. First, I think the intensity of legal restraint on cannabis is considerably exaggerated; true, it is there, but it is also clear that supplies are (if you are of the right age and appearance) easy to come by with an elastic market; and that the contentions by some pundits that there is nothing wrong with cannabis has produced for many of the young the feeling that cannabis-taking is little more than a technical misdemeanour. Heroin-taking has not shared in this development of attitude; and I think it is quite wrong to equate them. Second, this view would, of course, make all illicit drug-takings become associated with each other (and indeed all criminal activities to become linked to all). It is worth noting that for the teenager (and one must remember that heroin-dependence can begin at 14 years of age) the taking of barbiturates as well as amphetamines is in practice also illicit; yet neither of these drugs, nor alcohol, have so close a relation to heroin. Third, I am not convinced that, as a determinant of adolescent behaviour, it is legality that matters so much as adult approval or disapproval generally: and if this is the case, and if one admits a major increase in adult permissiveness generally over the last 10 years, then this change of attitude has been accompanied, not by a reduction in drug taking, but by an almost epidemic explosion. For my money, at any rate, therefore, what restrictions exist on cannabis-taking have saved us from an even worse heroin epidemic, bad as it is.

But whatever view one takes, one must notice that those who wish to legalise cannabis, and claim that this would reduce the amount of heroin-taking, have to assert that the *only* link between these two is their illegality. This is manifestly untrue. The mere taking of cannabis, that is, taking a drug *as such* to influence one's mind and emotions, carries one into a field for which everyone (regardless of the nature of their contacts) knows heroin as the (present) limit. It is obvious that the natural field of recruitment of heroin addiction is the population of those youngsters who have tried one drug for pleasure and might like to extend their experience. It is also true that while cannabis lacks the orgasmic offering of heroin, it shares with it the providing of euphoria, or of a day-dreamy detachment from everyday problems. As far as cannabis and heroin are linked, therefore, by illegality (if they are), one can argue about the effect of changing restraints on incidence; but in so far as cannabis consumption rose (presumably in time to a level comparable with that of tobacco or alcohol), the other links with heroin would produce a devastating incidence of heroin-consumption.

Finally, let us turn to the implications for individual or social action. First, and it is nearly a truism these days, research is needed. Exactly how to frame that research is not so easy to decide; but at least one can say that this is being seriously attempted on realistic lines, and that, in a way one could not say two years ago, there has been a considerable coming together of people in different disciplines in attempts to tackle the problem.

Second, I must deal with one obvious possible practical step: to attack the peddler. It is curious, when the peddler comes up in a discussion, how there is often a release of tension—here at least is an easy solution, and an easy common hate. True, the unaddicted person who makes money out of addicts is repulsive. But all the evidence points to his as a marginal role. Much of the supply is arranged by addicts themselves for each other. Disconcerting it may be, but strong opinion exists that even if one could get rid of all peddlers, it would hardly touch the problem.

Third, a severely practical point. Suppose a youngster does become a heroin addict; all is far from lost, if contact remains. But let him (or her) be disconnected from home, school, and university, without follow-up, then I think the writing often *is* on the wall. Further, one must regard any addict as infectious: so that the shorter the infection can be made, the better. A major responsibility, therefore, is somehow to keep in touch with addicts —intolerable though their behaviour can be. This means, too, a need to support social 'longstops' to the errors of our society, bodies like the Salvation Army, the Quakers, or the Association for the Prevention of Addiction.

But I think in all our minds is the much deeper question—what legislation or other social action is needed? Now although I know something of how a given dose of drug can produce some bodily effect, I know little about what dose of what legislation is required to produce a desired effect in the body politic: I hope somebody else has definite information (as opposed to opinions) on the subject. But I can only consider principles. One principle, however, I would advance very strongly. It can be argued that people should be free to go to the devil their own way. But we are dealing, essentially, with the question of the availability of chemical substances for large-scale human consumption or use. We know that there is a medical risk; and we know the risk is infectious. It seems to me that one should here follow the ordinary and *accepted* principles of public health and social legislation. We put guards on factory machinery, decompress the compressed air worker tediously, and so forth, often inconveniencing the experienced or the robust to protect the inexperienced or the weak. Equally I believe that no new drug (whether cannabis or something new in years to come) should become generally available unless it satisfies criteria at least as rigorous as those to be met by drugs used in medicine (under the Dunlop Committee), or by substances used as food additives; and that in assessing risk, one must take account both of intrinsic riskiness and of the numbers vulnerable, *and* of the interaction between these. Such an approach, I believe, could help to get away from the sterile arguments between the extremes of permissiveness and paternalism.

Of course, in theory at least, drugs may emerge (there is no evidence of them yet apart from tea and coffee and perhaps cigar smoking) which produce pleasure and can pass such tests. The question would then be one of individual moral decision. We can, in an interesting way, point to two scientific (or para-scientific) guides in such a choice. For one, Aldous Huxley, the guidance is familiar to us all, pointing to a rather highbrow, aesthetically sophisticated Lotus-land. The other, J. B. S. Haldane, may be less familiar: namely his remark that no drug he had ever tried produced an effect comparable to the thrill of a successful scientific investigation. Surely it is such a direction that the long-term answer to drug-dependence lies, not in repression and control, but in activities whose consummation brings a pleasure which can not only be expressed in emotion but also be endorsed by reason.

John Moat

THE ROAD TO INDIA

John Moat, author of the novel *Heorot*, describes here a young man who at first sight seemed to represent a 'problem', but who ended up by offering something more like reassurance.

A FEW HUNDRED YEARS ago, a man living where I live, that's in a backwood in North Devon, would have been right (as they say) 'out of the picture'. If he did ever get to hear of what was toward in the great metropolis or the outside world, it was probably from a misguided traveller or vagrant. Whereas today, thanks to Michael Barrett and Robin Day and company—even though reception in our valley is intermittent—I can confidently have a friend from London to stay in my backwood and know that the conversation, be it about the Incomes Policy or the length of skirts in the King's Road, isn't bound to be one-sided, since I stand every chance of being as well informed as my guest. And that's not all. A few months ago, an American friend flew in from Oregon on the eve of the Primary election being held in that State. He'd come non-stop, and still I was able to put him in the picture about a number of details, the candidates' campaigning methods, for instance, and to laugh to scorn his prediction of the result. In fact he proved correct, but that's beside the point. Or does it bring me *to* the point?

Occasionally I wonder whether my predecessors in the valley were necessarily so ill-informed; and whether (even today, for the man with his ear to the earth), there is not a strange hot line that carries to the most remote spot accurate and incontrovertible impressions; something akin to the Romany network that relays news like a whisper through the woods.

Take for example, students. Now, I, along with everyone else in the country, have become well-informed about the new student phenomenon: Danny le Rouge, the happenings in Berlin, Tokyo, Paris, Warsaw, Rome, Budapest, London, Manchester, Hornsey, and practically anywhere else you like to mention. Like almost everyone else I've had my own opinions, have got hot under the collar, and been prepared to throw punches. And then a couple of days ago, I, here in my backwood, met my misguided traveller or vagrant, one solitary student, and since then my whole opinion has been modified, and though still prepared to argue, I have grown not so hot under my collar. I'll tell you of our conversation, and you can judge for yourself.

This student was a hitch-hiker to whom I gave a lift. An art student, in fact, and he looked like it. A beret, long hair, tight, worn jeans, and travelling with a ruck-sack and a guitar. I confess that as I drew up, a number of prejudices were stirring, along with my hackles and my curiosity. But as he climbed into the car I received my first set-back. His blue eyes were soft and very clear, and his full clean features sensitive. For a second I had the feeling I'd met him before, until I saw that simply he was startlingly like the young Filippino Lippi in his self-portrait in the Uffizi. His expression was one of full composure; it was a beautiful day and he was enjoying it. When he was seated, I asked him where he was heading. He turned his head towards me slowly.

'I'm going home,' he said, 'to be with my parents for a bit before setting out to India.'

I felt there was something strange in the first part of this statement: 'going home to be with his parents'; but not the second. About that I was well-informed: pot in the garden of the guru.

'India,' I said. 'For enlightenment or employment?' And I was shocked by the sarcastic twist I put into those words. He may have noticed too, because he half-smiled.

'Oh, enlightenment I suppose, though if it came through employment, I shouldn't mind.'

My conversion was a simple as his smile. I was infected and wished I was going with him.

'Marvellous,' I said. 'When I was at University, Istanbul was about as far as we'd venture.'

'Today some get as far as Nepal, though it's difficult,' he said. 'Or Marrakesh. Some get to South America.'

'Do you run into a lot of opposition?' I asked, 'I mean people who suggest you're a layabout and a bum?'

'Er . . .' he hesitated, as if trying to remember. 'Yes, I suppose so. From time to time.'

'I did too,' I said. 'I had a piece of Saint Augustine which I learnt by heart and used to quote to them. "If you cannot by your own learning give the words a good sense, seek some learned and holy man that can instruct thee. Such a man cannot be found with ease? Seek him then with labour. He is not to be met with in thy own country? What better motive canst thou have to travel? No such man can be found on the continent? Then sail beyond the seas; if thou canst not find any one near the sea, pass further into the country, and even into the parts where the things happened of which these books speak." '

I chuckled, a little embarrassed—the quotation had seemed to me rather long.

He was silent for a minute, and looked about the sunlit country-side through which we were driving.

'I like that,' he said finally. 'It's funny, isn't it? the way a young bloke suddenly needs to get out and travel. It seems to be some-thing in his nature he just grows into, like suddenly having to shave.'

'Everyone grows a beard,' I said, hardly aware that my colours were now completely changed. 'Not everyone gets out on the road.'

Again he made nothing of my sneer. 'It's not that easy,' he said. 'That's one of the troubles. Nowadays, from the outset, right from infant school kids seem to be on a sort of conveyor belt. At first it's not so bad, but with every exam passed, with each place won in a new school or college, the pressure on you not to get off increases. Later you find you've invested so much that it seems senseless not to be true to all the previous effort, one's place in society is constantly at stake, and one's future and security. Nowadays people move from school to college to job without daring to question what they're doing, the pressure's so great from fear of being left behind or left out. These days you have to be lucky or daft to get on the road.' He didn't speak bitterly, but quietly and slowly, as he looked about him.

We stopped somewhere at a country pub, and I bought him the same as I had, bread, cheese and a glass of beer. He didn't thank me, and I saw that in the few years since I'd been on the road, even manners had changed. His gratitude was somehow demonstrated in the grace of his acceptance, in the unvoiced fact that we were men who got on well enough and that I had some money and he hadn't. Those seemed to me good enough manners.

We were alone in the bar, and sat comfortably silent in its still sunlight and pub's smell of scrubbed tables and morning beer. An old clock ticked on the wall, and outside above the square, the village clock sounded the quarters.

'I should like to live in a Devon village,' he said at length. 'Somewhere like this. One shouldn't have to leave it. So it must be later on when I'm prepared for my work.'

After lunch, we drove on, and when we had gone some way, he said: 'That was good, that piece from Saint Augustine. Practically no one goes out any more in search of understanding. I sometimes think I'd like to start a university. But I wouldn't get people to come to it. I'd wait till they came of their own accord, inquiring. Probably wouldn't work very well, though,' he added, smiling. 'But seriously,' he continued, 'I don't see how this standardised education is ever going to work out. Education seems to me to be one man talking to another. And finding the right man to talk to is all part of the hunt. It's the young man's job. A wise man shouldn't have to look for his disciples. Trouble is one sometimes wonders whether today there are any wise men around to look for.'

'Perhaps that's the cause of all the so-called student unrest,' I prompted him. I was suddenly interested to hear what he would say about that.

He thought for a while, and then he said: 'Well, maybe indirectly. But I think that the direct cause of the trouble is that nobody any longer wants to learn something just for its own sake. I see this at the Art College all the time. People learn to paint in order to get a diploma, not in order to learn to paint. They need the diploma. And because it is society that has subjected them to the need, they have a right—today everything's a matter of rights —they have a right to be taught, and to be taught nothing but that which will get them the diploma. That's what it seems to me student-power in this country is about. What frightens me is that this way we are about destroying our own freedom. The more power we have, the bigger grants we get, the more the state, as it were, invests in them, the more they will in fact have sold out to the state or society or whatever it is. As soon as we've got our diploma, we're dead ducks. Society as it were owns what we've learned, and society is going to make damn sure it gets a return on its investment. And that, as far as I can see, adds up to the finish of education.'

'Which is why,' I suggested, 'you choose the old high road to India.' He nodded. It was at this point that our ways divided, and I put him down on the side of the road.

Since then, here in the valley, I've felt relieved of the problem. The news of further disturbances has continued to come through by television and weekly paper, but I find I have been reassured not by what this student told me, but by the student himself. Or, in other words, by a backwoodsman's information.

III
TRAVELS

Reyner Banham

THE ART OF DOING YOUR THING

Reyner Banham is Reader in Architecture at University
College, London, and his most recent book is *The
Architecture of the Well-Tempered Environment*. Here he
reports on Los Angeles.

'GOOD GRIEF!' I said, steering narrowly round the crumpled
figure with the stripe across its chest. 'Was there a man in that?'
The family peered out the back window of the car down the
freeway. 'No, no,' they said, 'just an old wet-suit lying in the
middle of the road.'

The wet-suit is the surfer's cold weather gear, and it is therefore
something of a symbol of the continuing pride of Los Angeles in
what is still its most compulsive sport, and the fact that you really
can surf all the year round. The culture of Los Angeles—culture
in the anthropologist's sense—revolves around the physical
pleasures of the outdoors more than anything else. The range of
activities on offer is, by our standards, almost ridiculous: it is
literally possible to surf and to ski on the same day during the
winter months, without stirring out of the greater Los Angeles
area, because Mount Baldy isn't much farther from Downtown
than Disneyland is.

The visual culture of Los Angeles is soaked in, warped by,
subservient to, these pleasures. The range of involvement goes
from the so-called competition stripe across the chest of that wet-
suit to a concept of real-estate development called 'recreational
living' in which whole housing estates are grouped around a golf

137

course or, more and more frequently, an artificial body of water—Lake Havasu City, which has just acquired London Bridge, is a development of exactly this type. So, from the ornamentation of sports gear to the environmental planning of new suburbs, Los Angeles celebrates the culture of 'fun'.

The verbal insistence on 'fun' can get a bit wearing at times—even airliners flying into Los Angeles are called 'Funjets' or 'Funbirds'—but the visual elaborations of the concept are, to my eyes, the most potent demonstration that Los Angeles epitomises a civilisation. I use the word 'civilisation' in the old-fashioned sense that emphasised the existence of sufficient wealth and leisure to pursue activities that had nothing to do with the mere acquisition of physical necessities. In this sense the Angelenos are a privileged class—*the* privileged class of pop culture today. Their civilisation has invented and decorated artefacts that are the envy of the world and go so far beyond mere physical need as to be perfectly useless. This was what persuaded Tom Wolfe that the Kandy-Kolored Tangerine-Flake Streamlined creations of custom-car designers like Ed Roth and George Harris must be an art-form of some sort. The preoccupation of the designers with the fantastication of form and finish has left function nowhere; these baroque and peacock-hued vehicles of the imagination are usually undrivable. The brilliantly painted crash helmets produced by Von Dutch Holland are not seriously meant to be worn, except in a purely ceremonial sense. They turn up in art galleries, and writers on California pop-art who try to explain that Von Dutch 'is a professional painter of custom cars and not an artist' have got it wrong. Von Dutch is an artist *because* he is a customiser, and because he is accepted as an artist by many members of the Los Angeles art community like Billy Al Bengston. And Bengston bridges the gap from the other side. His paintings of motor-cycles done in the early Sixties celebrate the same culture, not only because he used to ride bikes competitively (and still follows the sport) but also because the finish and precision of his paint seems to accept the custom-car paint jobs as the standard at which to aim.

The technology and craftsmanship to contrive these extra-ordinary objects of art and automobilism and to give them their incredibly high finish are abundant in Los Angeles—don't let anybody kid you that great craftsmanship is only possible in a peasant economy. The reasons why these skills are so freely available must be complex; the vast reservoir of diverse and curious talent accumulated by Hollywood must have been a basic contribution, and aerospace has enriched it in more recent years. But there is something else there as well: a sense of dedication bordering on fanaticism. If you are a teenager, you must want it very badly to have your car given 11 or 12 coats of paint, each polished mirror-smooth before the next is sprayed on. To afford it you will have to work nights and weekends to raise the cash; or you may do it yourself, laboriously and meticulously, in months of spare time. The devotion to getting everything perfect and just-so is astonishing. Even if you are a professional and do these things for money—no, *because* you are a professional—you will be morally obliged to show the same dedicated fanaticism. It is not enough to be just the best pin-striper or surfboard-shaper, you must be the ultimate craftsman, perfect.

At its most rarified it is an abstract and private affair, epitomised in the mythology of the lonely surfer. However gross and beery the onshore antics of surfers can be, the cult revolves around supposed moments of truth out there on the board on the wave. Thus *International Surfing Magazine* said:

> There is no rhyme or reasoning with a wave. Once you are committed there is no way out except to make it or wipe out. Life is much the same to me, just one giant chance, and wave-riding simply reminds me daily of how infinitesimal I am in relation to the universe.

The apotheosis of this solitary communion with the universe will come when the perfect wave rolls in, and the dedicated surfer is ready for its challenge. To be perfectly ready, the archetypal surfer cultivates his muscles and his reflexes, avoids terrestrial work and lives on relief—which is easy enough, since his needs, beyond the surfboard, are as few as those of a medieval hermit: a pair of sunglasses, baggy shorts, the back of someone's car to sleep in, and an occasional hamburger. And when that perfect wave comes, and is perfectly ridden, the chances are that no one will see it happen, and no one will believe him when he tells them about it. Except—his face will shine like a man transfigured, for he will have done his thing.

The phrase 'doing your thing' has only gained international currency since the hippy episode in San Francisco, but it perfectly expresses what Los Angeles believes itself to be about. The promise of this affluent, permissive and free-swinging culture is that every man, in his own lifetime and to his own complete satisfaction, shall do exactly what he wants to. And for a large part of the population, especially the young, it appears genuinely possible to do your thing. Not for the whole population, even in Los Angeles: for most of the inhabitants of, say, the poor Mexican area east of Downtown, such self-fulfilment is not only an impossible ideal, but probably incomprehensible as well. But for the bulk of the population it is highly comprehensible, and if found impossible can lead to outburst of frustrated violence, as in Watts. It may be no more than an ideal, but it is the kind of ideal that colours all communications, infuses all expectations.

For instance, if you really expect to do your own thing yourself, there is less need to have someone do it for you in symbolic ritual. The kids watch the championship drag-racers less out of hero-worshipping admiration for figures with whom they impotently identify, than in order to discover the style and techniques they will have to use when they in their turn are champions. This lack of symbolic need, of course, erodes the arts of public symbolism; painters, sculptors, architects have even less to say in the public domain in Los Angeles than they have elsewhere.

In the eyes of the community at large, an artist is just another guy doing his thing, like the lonely surfer communicating privately with the universe. If he's the best, or perfect, then bully for him, but it's hardly a public matter. I feel that this must tie up somewhere with the absence of a public realm, of significant public spaces, in the fabric of Los Angeles. Other than the beach, the only public space that seems meaningful is Disneyland and that, above all, is a triumph of doing your thing—Walt Disney's two-dimensional celluloid fantasies realised in tangible, inhabitable three-dimensional form. Of take the case of Charles Eames, the city's most famous designer. Like many another Mid-Westerner, he found in Los Angeles the technical resources and the permissive atmosphere in which to flourish. He became so nearly perfect that he is now a world figure: his chairs and his toys and his movies have marked and characterised an epoch. And it has had hardly any public effect on Los Angeles at all. The city is not overrun with Eames-type houses, not illuminated with Eames-type graphics, not particularly furnished with Eames-type chairs. A world-wide achievement that could hardly pass in Europe without civic honours, one-man shows and royal medals, goes virtually unnoticed in this city where everyone is privately dedicated to his own thing.

At one time it did appear that an architecture related to the neat and unassuming steel and glass of the Eames house might emerge as an Angeleno domestic architecture. European readers of the Los Angeles magazine *Arts and Architecture* could see it in the ingenious Case-Study houses by Raphael Soriano, Craig Ellwood and Pierre Koenig, as well as Eames, all built in the Fifties and all in the same basic steel and glass idiom. But that style was an illusion, or at least a climate of opinion generated by a man whose 'thing' was to create climates of opinion. When John Entenza gave up editing *Arts and Architecture* and disposed of the magazine, the style seemed to wither away, and last year even the magazine died. Steel and glass architecture returned to its normal Los Angeles status of a private affair, almost a private joke.

A great deal of the fine art produced in Los Angeles has the air of being a private joke; or, rather, has a joke aspect which is public while its true art remains private. This is true of the custom cars, whose flamboyant shapes are public property while their mechanical niceties are reserved for the initiated, and it is also true of the cool paintings of Ed Ruscha. His coolness makes ineloquence and lack of comment into a weird virtue that shows in his books of photographs even more than his paintings. These books have titles like *Twenty-Six Gasoline Stations*, or *Thirty-Four Parking Lots*, which is the most recent. It contains photographs of 34 parking lots, captions explaining where they are, and nothing else whatso ever. The very obtuseness of the presentation compels attention. You are made to feel that the refusal to pass any of the customary town-planner's value-judgments implies some transcendental system in which parking lots are valued simply for being what they are, for doing their parking-lot thing.

This particular book was timed to appear on the opening night of Ruscha's last exhibition in Los Angeles, and the show consisted of a single picture, just one, about nine feet wide and four feet high. Meticulously drawn and coloured in a flat, monumental, simplifying style, it showed an aerial perspective of the Los Angeles County Museum of Art—*on fire*. An in-group joke, no doubt, but it sums up what most art people in Los Angeles seem to feel about the County Art museum, a pathetic and empty attempt at a public gesture in a context where public gestures are irrelevant. The only kind of architecture that makes any public sense there seems to stem from clear and present public need, like the engineering of the freeways or the great rock-cut amphitheatre of the Hollywood Bowl, or else it arises from doing a private thing to such a degree of liberated perfection that it finally transcends itself.

Los Angeles has, in fact, one such monument, the Watts Towers. Their feathery traceries and spires, faced with shards of coloured pottery and glass, photograph so well against the blue sky that they are always turning up in some magazine or other. They are quite beautiful, and they are not—as some European critics seem to maintain—in any way naïve or folksy. Their structure is immensely strong, the decoration of their surfaces resourceful and imaginative. And Simon Rodia—Sam of Watts— spent 33 solitary years making them, for private reasons that he once managed to rationalise with the words: 'I wanted to do something for the United States, because there are some nice people in this country.' The nice people of the country finally got together to preserve the Towers and declare them a national monument. But they remain splendidly and reassuringly personal. They are the most triumphant monument, ever, to the art of doing your thing.

Gwyn Williams

OUT OF ANATOLIA

Gwyn Williams is Professor of English Literature at
Istanbul University, and has written a book called *Turkey:
A Traveller's Guide and History*. He is also a poet and
novelist, and has translated Turkish poetry into English
and Welsh.

LAST SPRING WE spent five lovely days at a well-appointed
camping site at Korykos, east of Silifke on the south coast of
Turkey. It was mid-April and the sea was warm enough to swim
in after the first gasp of protest. The camp is set in an ancient
quarry which slopes gently down to the sea's edge and for miles
around the green foothills of the Taurus Mountains are strewn and
punctuated with evidence of the use of stone quarried here. This
is the city from which Cicero once governed this part of the
Roman Empire. Where we pitched our tent, the terrace formation
had almost disappeared under brown earth now rich with early
summer grass, clover and flowers, but where it reached the sea the
rectangular cuts of the last quarrying, 15 centuries ago, were swept
clean by the minimal tide and the occasional storm. I watched
Gwydion paddling in six inches of water, a giant moving over a
submerged city, and I wondered whether Hippodamus of Miletus
got the idea of rectangular towns from watching his 9-year old
son playing on a quarry floor. For it was along this coast that
modern towns started, conceived by Hippodamus in the 5th
century B.C. This chess-board or grid pattern of a town was re-

peated at Priene, at the Piraeus, in south Italy and south Russia and eventually in every corner of the world.

But the Hippodamian plan didn't just drop out of the blue. It wasn't the start of organised town-dwelling in Anatolia. Or of architectural experiment. One day at Fethiye we scrambled up a steep slope to a rock face into which had been cut the classical pedimented façades of Lycian tombs, in a style that can be traced to the upland Phrygian shrines of Midas Sehri. There, at the so-called City of Midas, occurred the first translation into stone of the two-pitched roof plan which had been made possible by the plentiful timber and the wood-working skill of the Phrygians. And on our way down to Korykos we'd passed near Catalhuyuk where 8,000 years ago there was a town which had much in common with the experimental houses of the recent Canadian Expo 67. In both these towns the other man's roof became your terrace and approach.

Nowhere in the world is there such an ancient and continuous tradition of urban experiment as in Antolia. Yet one doesn't think of it today as a region of town-dwellers but of proud, rugged, good-natured country people.

There were two castles near our camp, one a moated sea-fringed fortress with towering walls into which column drums had been set in a pattern and with a great ruined church which still has traces of fresco painting; the other an island castle across a mile of water. We got a boatman to take us across to that castle one blue afternoon and found it a fortified rock, a walled emptiness where a fine inscription in Armenian looks down on a tangle of barley and fennel and strange flowers. We went in under the elegant sensuous Armenian lettering, climbed up a spiral staircase until it broke off, open and unprotected over the rippled water, and looked out over this central sea which once carried the Anatolian notion of defensive building to Dover and Caernarfon. These twin castles were built by Armenians who came down from their upland kingdom in the 12th century to settle in Cilicia, snatched from declining Byzantium. This kind of defensive building is as old as the castellated, gated and posterned walls of the Hittite

capital at Bogazkoy, erected in the middle of the second millennium B.C. and it was caught up again in the land walls of Constantinople, raised 2,000 years later, which still, another 1,500
years on, astonish the traveller approaching Istanbul from the
west. This is a coast crenellated with castles: Korykos and
Camardesium with their projecting horse-shoe towers from
which to rake the enemy; Anamur, still perfectly castellated, its
extended outlines unhampered by any accretion of building,
absolute against the sea; Alanya step-laddering round a rising
promontory; Crusader Bodrum still holding the town at bay;
and little Marmaris crawled over with modest dwellings. It was a
coast worth protecting for its fertility, its unending timber and
the vast grainlands of its high hinterland.

Across the road from the camp we followed a track which
wound between fields of yard-high barley and past water channels
carrying clear cold water to tomato fields, through the fresh and
fragrant air to join an ancient way lined with immense sarcophagi,
past a domed bath and a roofless basilica up to two noble 5th- or
6th-century churches, roofless too. We stood and looked at their
columned windows, acanthus-topped pilasters and side-entrances
with barrel-roofed porches. Churches of cathedral size, with
immense courtyards. The first Christian churches were in fact
here in Turkey, St Peter's first congregation in the now pretty
grotto church outside Antioch, and the Galatian, Ephesian and
Colossian communities to whom St Paul wrote from his prison
in Ephesus. A bronze Demeter of the 4th century B.C. was fished up
along the coast. It's a bust, slightly more than life-sized, with a
head-dress draped down over her shoulders. She looks down, sad,
her nose long and slightly curved, a *mater dolorosa* who asserts the
chain between the Great Mother of ancient Anatolia, through
Kubaba, Cybele and Artemis to the Virgins of Renaissance Italy.
It is in fact the peak of the tradition, for this bronze has not been
surpassed in the west. We sat in the blessed shade of the walls of
the biggest church. Myrtles, bays, carobs and prickly oaks bushed
out from the tumbled masonry. Big horny lizards scuttled into
cracks. A huge acacia almost filled the half-dome of the apse. My

two daughters sketched a fine arch, and a few wide-eyed children left the cows they were tending to offer us chains they had made of golden wild chrysanthemum flowers. A farmer going by showed me a coin he had ploughed up, but it was only Turkish of the last century.

These five days at Korykos gave me leisure to think how near everything seemed to us, how comprehensible, how different from the cold inhumanity of ancient Egypt. Is it perhaps a matter of language and therefore a way of thinking? We don't know what language they spoke at Catalhuyuk but the Hittites, Urartians, Armenians and Lycians spoke Indo-European tongues. Or is it a matter of geography, climate and soil, or the happy blending of races? Lively, land-hungry Greeks came early in the first millennium B.C. from their barren peninsula to this more fertile coast. They saw the possibilities of its green valleys, pastures, cornlands, the varied forests, the indigenous olives and vines, the marvellous climate which swings from generous ripening heat to a brisk winter against a background of snow-covered mountains. They intermarried with Carians and Lydians, absorbed some of the discoveries of the long millennia of Anatolian experiment; they prospered and gradually achieved the luxury and leisure in which to inaugurate our western philosophy and science at Miletus, Ephesus and Cnidos. This was a country where men had clearly been living, building and inventing gods and goddesses for millennia before the Greeks arrived and the sense of history was born here in Herodotus of Halicarnassus, in this Ionian situation between Greece and Persia. Strabo, born between Ankara and Trabzon, was quite naturally an antiquarian as well as an historian.

Poetry too, for which you must have leisure, leisure to compose and leisure to listen. Homer walked out from the commercial hurly-burly of old Smyrna, some miles west of present-day Izmir, to put together the memories of the Fall of Troy and, since he was born and bred on the Asiatic side, to adumbrate our sympathy, confirmed by Shakespeare, for the Trojans rather than the Greeks. From Lydian Sardis, Alcman taught the Greeks and us to write love poetry, and, at Colophon, Mimnermos wrote the first love elegies and regretted the passing of life and love and pleasure in the sunshine. Anacreon lived at Teos and Sappho across the narrow water in rugged Mitylene. The movement of the Anatolian creative impulse has been westward towards us.

When the Turks came the direction was the same. The pointed Seljuk arch advanced from Erzurum, Sivas and Kayseri to the Gothic west and the Ottoman capture of Constantinople sent westwards ancient knowledge which was to restore our links with what had been thought and done at Cnidos, Miletus and Halicarnassus.

At lunch time at Korykos a bottle of cold Turkish beer refreshed us and each evening we walked up to the camp restaurant to watch the sun set into the sea behind the island castle and to enjoy grilled fish or kebab, with wine and fruit from not far away, white wine from Urgup in the moon landscape of the Goreme region, red wine from ancient Tenedos, and oranges from anywhere along this luscious coast. The strawberries were not quite in season but the artichokes and courgettes were in. There's nothing quite like Turkish lamb grilled on a skewer in gobbets with bits of onion, tomato and green pepper. And yes, even if you didn't know it you must by now have guessed. The wild sheep was first domesticated in south-east Anatolia and here too occurred one of the great revolutions in the story of mankind, the first Neolithic reaping of wild barley. From a hunter man here became a pastoralist and cultivator, meat became a luxury rather than a necessity and the pursuit of game a sport or a means of varying diet rather than a way of providing the next square meal. Not far to the north of Korykos a rock sculpture depicts a Hittite god presenting a grateful king with a bunch of grapes and a fistful of barley on its stalks. He obviously meant the Hittites and us to make good use of them. This is the original home of the grape-producing vine and surely of wine itself, and it is likely that beer was brewed here before ever bread was baked. The barley grains must first of all have been soaked in water to make a kind of cold porridge. Some of this, having been left uneaten, fermented. The blessing of beer was given to the world. The bread is good in

Anatolia too. Yes, it's a coast and a hinterland that seem to inten-
sify life. It's more than a museum of our origins. There's no
'abomination of desolation' here, no Pompeii, no Leptis Magna.
Handsome and friendly people live, cultivate, dance and wrestle
here. We found a little house and garden inside the land castle of
Korykos and a cow looked solemnly at us through a postern gate.
We left Korykos with regret and clung to the coast, great mountains to the right, a haze over Cyprus to the south, until the road
forced us inland at Antalya to cut through the mountains back to
Istanbul. We had motored 1,500 miles through wonderful country to find and appreciate our past and our present. How much of
our future shall we be lucky enough to save from it? It came home
to me on this trip that Anatolia offers us a continued insistence
on the goodness of some basic things; spring water, natural
well-baked bread, unsophisticated wine, grilled meat and fish,
fresh salad and fruit. And a dignified trustfulness between men.

René Cutforth

WAITING FOR THE DALAI LAMA

René Cutforth's broadcast reminiscences have won him a
wide public, and his autobiography is to be published
shortly. A previous book of his is *Korean Reporter*.

U P T O 1959 when the Chinese overran it, Tibet shared with the
headwaters of the Amazon a special place in the Western sub-
conscious. It seemed quite possible that something immensely old
and completely new could emerge from both to put mankind on
the right track. So in March 1959, when the news came through
that the Dalai Lama was riding hell for leather across the roof of
the world, through the blizzards and the Chinese, for the Himalayan passes and sanctuary in India, it was obvious that for
hundreds of millions of people who didn't care a damn about
world politics, this was a tremendous story. 'It's all very vague,'
my editor said. 'Nobody will say where the Dalai Lama is, in case
the Chinese get to know. The Indian government has some information, of course, and when they think he's safe, they'll let you
know where to go and meet him. I've booked you as far as Delhi,
and you can book yourself on. Wherever and whenever he comes
down the mountain, you'll be there to meet him.'

Unless the city of New Delhi is frying in the mid-day sun of the
hot weather, when every object in sight appears to be an incan-
descent white, with a short, dense black shadow at its foot in
which lies a dog or a cat, the best thing to do is to leave your
luggage at the air terminal and walk, for at least the first half-mile:
it's a marvellous way of dropping the English load. You can take

your pick of architecture, from the 'Ceremonial Imperial' done in red sandstone with the trailing curves of Art Nouveau (if architecture is frozen music, this is frozen Elgar) to the towering white office blocks and multi-storeyed, air-conditioned hotels of Middle Delhi; or you can take off sideways into an older tradition of colonial buildings with eroded cornices covered in weeds, and rows of wooden shutters with flaking paint where the monkeys dance along the edges of the balconies and bright rugs are hung out; and from there into the trading streets—packed rows of little open shop fronts and the full blare of Indian salesmanship. Whichever way you go, the pace is the same—an unchanging one mile an hour: the exactly proper pace to show off the languid splendour of a sari and how beautifully heads can be carried on necks, and hands on supple wrists; and to show how absolutely inessential it is to get from A to B at any particular time.

All along the edges of the pavements the neem trees were in flower—feathery trees rather like acacias, foaming with a sort of meadowsweet blossom and with a heavy scent of the same sort but darker in tone; and this, with a touch of curry, a whiff of burning cow dung and a tang of water-on-dust, is the smell of India. I breathed great draughts while the sun unbuttoned my spinal column and settled me down on my hips.

Delhi is dry, which means an embarrassing fiddle with the lift man who will put a bottle of Scotch in your room at a price. He was bringing it in when the telephone rang. It was a correspondent I knew well in London. 'I suppose you're on the Dalai Lama story. Well, so am I. We seem to be the only two in from London so far; the Indian government's in a tremendous flap about it, and Nehru has called in *The Times* correspondent for a conference which is going on now. I'm going to meet *The Times* man when it's over. I'll pick you up if you like and we'll all go along to Vice-Regal Lodge together.'

Nothing anywhere in England that I know looks half so English as Vice-Regal Lodge, New Delhi. The wonderfully kept lawns, the huge English trees throwing long shadows in the waning sun, looked as though they'd been there for 1,000 years in a wet climate, only instead of rooks, kites wheeled overhead in a flawless sky. *The Times* man joined us: 'The Prime Minister says he wants to see both of you since you're here.' Mr Nehru gave us whisky and told us: 'If I decide to allow the press to meet the Dalai Lama on his way down here, I want you to understand that it will be under the most strict regulations. The line you may not cross will be well south of Tibet. There will be armed sentries and they will shoot. Anybody found north of the line will spend several years in gaol. If anyone flies an aeroplane across, it will be shot down. I mean it.' And a day or two later the correspondent and I were flying in a very old Dakota into Tezpur in Assam, with strict instructions that the north road out of it, to the Himalayan foothills and Tibet, was strictly out of bounds except in government vehicles under escort.

Tezpur is an ancient city with traces of past grandeur and more than traces of present squalor. It has an antique fort and presents on one side a fine, dramatic skyline where the old fort and a group of great trees on top of a very steep hill are enfolded, together with half the city itself, in a great calm sweep of the River Brahmaputra, which, by the time it reaches Tezpur, has crossed the whole length of Tibet, turned a huge hairpin bend, and still has half its length to run before it reaches the sea. The first thing we did was to hire the only hireable car in Tezpur—about 15 years old—and make a survey of the place. It didn't take long. There was no hotel in the Western sense of the word. There was an Indian hotel, clean little rooms like monks' cells with a charpoy—a string bed—and a glass bowl and jug in each. But they didn't want us there. It wasn't until late afternoon that somebody told us about the Planters Club.

It was a mile or two out of the town, a large shambling structure of blackened wood, like a very solid Noah's Ark. It must have been built by the tea planters around Tezpur round about the early 1900s, to judge by the interior. There was a long bar of teak, and in one corner a mouldering billiards table, long abandoned to fungus and termites. There were some old-fashioned heavy teak Public Works Department armchairs, a clock with a Big Ben chime, a bathroom with a zinc bath on a cement floor, and a lavatory—which worked. The walls were covered with the pale yellow ghosts of photographs of King Edward VII leading in a Derby winner, the Tezpur Planters Association Cricket Team for 1909, and hundreds more, nearly all pre-1914, most of them just decipherable; there were cartoons and sporting prints by the dozen, badly mildewed. And there wasn't an Englishman left. Nearly all the planters were Indians, but there were a few Anglo-Indian heirs of the founders of the club and it must have been these who decreed that nothing should ever be changed.

Then came the negotiations. Could they put us up at the club for a day or two? Well, a member could hire a room but must provide his own bedding. Were we eligible for membership? Well, we were not of course Tezpur planters, but nothing could be discovered in the rule book which said we must be. If we would care to wait until about eight o'clock there'd probably be a quorum to vote on the matter; meanwhile we could be made honorary members simply by signing the book. At six o'clock they said that if we wanted anything to eat we could send the boy down to the bazaar for some curry, only we ought to send him now before the rain began. 'At half-past seven, it rains,' they said. So we paid the boy and we ate the good, black, devilish curry with chapatties and dal and bottles of beer. And at half-past seven, prompt—just like pulling the chain—the skies opened and for 11 hours, that night and every other night we were there, a deafening downpour thundered on the tin roof; conversation went on unevenly in shouts and the only sound which came through loud and clear against the storm was the chanting of the frogs outside. At half-past eight, there was a quorum; some of them had driven 100 miles. At nine o'clock, we were life members of the Tezpur and District Planters Club. At a quarter to ten we were buying drinks for the committee; at ten o'clock we had a room, and at half-past ten we'd found a very ancient horned gramophone and were settling down to the first evening of waiting for the Dalai Lama.

At half-past six in the morning the rain was promptly turned off, the sun shone, steam rose, birds sang, somebody started to play a flute outside. The old man who looked after the club made tea—very good tea, as you'd expect from a tea-planters' club. I noticed a telephone—a collector's piece—screwed to the wall; its earpiece—a fluted cylinder of ebonite weighing about three pounds—hung on its own wire separately from an ornate hook. I jiggled it. To my surprise it worked, and in less than half an hour I was through to our man in Delhi.

'Any news about the Dalai Lama?' I asked.

'Not a word. All they're saying is: "the nearest you can get to him is Tezpur." '

'But who are they saying it to?'

'Well, there are 16 Indian correspondents who think it's too early yet; the two big British popular dailies are due in this afternoon—whole teams of them; a big American group the day after tomorrow, two Frenchmen from *Paris Match*, and, I hear, some Germans and an Italian.'

'Shall I send a piece about Tezpur?'

'No good. Everything is embargoed by the government.'

So I rang off. 'Now then,' I said, 'the whole place is going to be bung full of correspondents with money to burn. First thing to do is hire this old car for a month, paying in advance and getting a receipt. Then we want blankets, tins of biscuits and fruit, and go and have a look at the telegraph office.'

At the telegraph office we aroused with great difficulty an elderly man with a large grey soup-strainer moustache, who was sleeping on his back on a bare wooden bench. When he opened his eyes, they were bright crimson. We showed him our cable cards, and it was clear he'd never seen their like before.

'Telegram,' we said, 'to London.'

'London,' he said, 'London . . .' as if he recognised the word. He held out a form. With luck you could have got 12 words on it. 'No, no, 400, 500 words.'

'Four hundred words impossible.' He groped in his mind and found the formula. 'No cable facilities.' We didn't waste his time.

That afternoon five more correspondents turned up, three

British and two American agency men. By half-past eight they
were life members of the Tezpur and District Planters Club. By
a quarter to nine they were buying drinks for the committee. By
nine o'clock they were in despair.

'Well, where's the nearest cable station?'

'Shillong, there's one in Shillong.'

'How far's that?'

'About 90 miles.'

'How long by car?'

'You can't get to Shillong this time of year: all the rivers are
flooded, man.'

'Can a plane get there?'

'It could, I suppose: there are airstrips. There is no service.'

The next night the club was full, and the night after that it was
bursting. In the Indian hotel, Indian correspondents were sleeping
six to a cell. Anybody in Tezpur who owned a verandah had a
dozen correspondents sleeping on it. One correspondent, James
Cameron, came in so late that there wasn't a place for him at all—
but in the yard at the back of the Planters Club there was a sordid
little structure of four poles and a low straw roof, under which a
goat normally spent the night. Cameron appropriated this
shelter: whether he turned the goat out or shared with it I don't
know, but in the morning an Indian, who went to wake him with
a cup of tea, came back in great agitation and signalled us all to
come outside. Round and round Cameron's shelter, pressed deep
into the mud, were rings of monstrous paw marks. An old,
white-whiskered bright-eyed shikari was borne into the com-
pound from the town by a great crowd of people eager to see the
sight. It took him about two seconds to make his diagnosis.
'Tiger, sahib,' he said.

So Cameron spent the next night on a verandah.

That day, no doubt in response to all the frantic telegrams and
telephone calls which every correspondent had been sending day
and night since his arrival, the Indian government announced that
we would be permitted to go up in government transport with
a military escort to the line south of the Tibetan border where we

should, on the appointed day, meet, we hoped, the Dalai Lama. It was about 15 miles north of Tezpur at a place called Foothills. The road to Foothills turned out to be a country track between banks of bright green jungle with a stifling green smell. Every leaf glittered as if varnished, and the vegetation was piled up on steep hillsides on either side of us. The road, too, led steeply uphill and had a surface of broken rock which reflected a kaleidoscope of glare from the sun. It was a surprise, after about an hour in which our old buses made about 12 miles, to come out in an open space where the jungle had retreated a quarter of a mile on each side of the road. Here there was grass and flowers and long, low huts of bamboo and thatch, and we could see in front of us the foothills—considerable mountains, thinly clad with jungle, and behind them an even more considerable range, rather more thinly clad. Wisps of steam-like cloud moved along their flanks. The air began to smell damp and cool and still our red-hot old bus engines ploughed on uphill in bottom gear until suddenly we made a right-angled turn and there they were, the Himalayas. They rose from the foothills like trees from grass and they were utterly alone and remote. They might have been ten miles from us or 100. They made scale seem ridiculous. The sun shone placidly on the calm snow of their upper halves and we could see dangling like a thin, twisted fly-paper from a ceiling the track down which it was hoped the Dalai Lama would eventually arrive. And now the road turned another abrupt angle and right across our way was a barrier, one of those poles with a weight at the end, and at that end was a Gurkha sentry, with a great grin, standing at ease with his rifle.

It was a company of Sikhs who'd been given the job of super-intending us and now, jovial, bearded, immensely obliging, they began to explain the lie of the land. They had a bamboo barracks and their discipline was obviously ferocious. There was a mon-astery, they explained, some six miles up the track from us and hidden from our view by a spur of the hillside, and there they expected the Dalai Lama would stop the night. They would bring us up in the early morning to meet him. They were terribly pleasant; they soothed us as if we were children. 'But not past the barrier, oh no, sir, oh no. Ha-ha, ha-ha.' They laughed the whole time. I wouldn't have tried to pass them for anything on earth. So we all stood around looking pretty squalid with the Himalayas behind us and smoked in silence. We said very little, and after about half an hour we got in the buses again and went back to the club.

If you included the stringers and the stooges and the pilots and the drivers and the interpreters, there were now about a hundred newsmen in Tezpur and it was possible to take a look at the runners and assess the form. First, the heavy stuff: the two great British dailies with enormous circulation had each brought its own circus headed by a correspondent whose name everybody had heard of. Each of these had an aeroplane, a pilot, a car, a driver, an immense stock of hard cash, a couple of interpreters, and a secretary or two and a few angle-men and assistants. If sheer weight of money and supplies could do it, they were most likely to get the story.

By now all the correspondents knew where the real story lay. Anybody with eyes in his head could make some sort of piece about the actual physical descent of the Dalai Lama to the foothills. That didn't matter. The real question was who was going to get from either the Dalai Lama or his escort the first-hand story of their escape from the Chinese in Lhasa. On form, it looked as if the lesser of the two big dailies had the best chance. They were equipped with the cars and aircraft and interpreters that the other had, but in addition they had brought off a very smart stroke: they'd hired Heinrich Harrer, a mythical man, who'd escaped from a British prisoner-of-war camp during the war and walked across the Himalayas to Lhasa, where he'd become a personal friend of the Dalai Lama, learned Tibetan and become a sort of adviser to the Tibetan government. He's written a very good book about it. And here he was, amongst us—a haunted figure, in fact, followed about everywhere he went by a formidable female journalist on the staff of the paper which had hired him. She was there to see that his special knowledge of Tibetan affairs should not be used to swell the colour stories the correspondents were all busy writing, against the day when the embargo would be lifted. The only place you could talk to Harrer was in the gents, and even there not for long. 'You writing anything?' I asked him, in there one day. He turned a hunted look on me. 'I write long pieces every day, good solid information about the foundations of the Tibetan way of life, and every day they are taken from me and I see them again in the evening with my name on and I do not recognise a word.'

'Oh, well,' I said, 'it's not your fault and you must be making masses of money.'

'Not all that money,' said Harrer.

'Look, I wonder if you could tell me,' I said, 'the present Dalai Lama was discovered when he was five. Isn't that unusually old?'

'Certainly,' Harrer began, 'in old times it was usual . . .'

'Mr Harrer,' came an imperious female voice from just outside the can, 'can you spare a moment, please, most important?' And he bustled out, rolling his eyes.

On form, I thought Harrer will probably pull it off, but there were plenty of dark horses. The agency men were keen, deadly operators; the Indian papers had a pull, most of their correspondents spoke half a dozen Indian languages; *The Times of India* correspondent, an Englishman, was playing it very cool—something up his sleeve, watch him. The Frenchmen from *Paris Match* I thought had little chance. They were a sharply contrasted pair: the cameraman was a bright, very modern Frenchman with a crew-cut and a cool look; his companion, who was about 50 and did the words, was a long-haired literary romantic. The prolonged absence of the Dalai Lama hadn't worried him at all, and he'd practically given up the story in favour of one about the British in India. He roamed about the club, noting down the captions under the sporting prints. He stood for hours in a reverent attitude before the photograph of King Edward.

'What a race,' he would say to me, 'what a race. Here on the confines of the habitable earth, the billiards champion and King Edward's horse.' 'Not a hope,' was my assessment.

The only other one who had a hope was a Canadian girl correspondent: she was pretty enough to get herself anything she wanted.

It was round about this time, when we'd been waiting for the Dalai Lama for ten days or so, that the correspondents began to go a bit mad. It began with the malicious spreading of rumours.

'Well, we got the story, then.'

'What story?'

'We know where they are.'

'Who?'

'The Dalai Lama and his party.'

'Well, where are they?'

'Mean to say you haven't heard? They're up at the monastery. Been there a week.'

'How d'you know?'

'I have my sources, old boy, which you wouldn't know a thing about.'

'Well, it just could be true.'

'I'm flying over it tomorrow.'

'You'll be shot down if you do.'

'Who told you that?'

'Well, if you want to know, Mr Nehru.'

'You can't believe that, old boy.'

'What?'

'The Indian government shooting down a British civilian plane.'

'It's an Indian civilian plane.'

And so on. But in the end everybody believed the monastery story. Everybody made plans which they chewed over in corners by themselves. I had my plan: I hired an elephant.

It's extremely easy to hire an elephant in Tezpur. There were elephants all over the town carrying great bales of firewood or loads of hay, and I simply stopped a driver, who was ambling along by the side of his elephant, and said: 'I should like to hire an elephant.' He looked all round him several times and then put his finger to his lips, rolled up his eyes and moved on. Later that might he turned up at the Planters Club with a friend who spoke English and we did the deal.

My plan was to take off through the jungle, north-east of Tezpur, and join the Dalai Lama's track four miles or so beyond the Gurkha sentry, take a good look at the monastery for an hour or two through field-glasses and—I might have a story. 'All right,' the elephant driver said, 'that'll be 100 rupees a day for the elephant and me and 15 rupees for the elephant's food which we'll have to take with us. I'm not taking you in European clothes, but I will provide you with Indian garments for ten rupees and some dye to rub on the bits of your skin which will show. Meet you by the fort at six o'clock in the morning.'

I cannot think now why I ever assented to such a mad plan, but at the time, after nearly a fortnight mewed up in the Planters Club with a trip to Foothills by bus once a day like a school outing, it seemed not only enterprising but sensible. I did have a qualm as I climbed on the elephant; I was dressed in a very voluminous dhoti with a long shirt and a lot of cloth to cover my hair, which was the wrong colour, and the elephant driver had anointed my hands and face and legs with a brown preparation which stank. The elephant was carrying about a ton of hay, and in front of that, me, and in front of me, its driver. It had only just stopped raining and everything on the elephant's back was sopping wet. I hitched up my dhoti and tried to find something to catch hold of and the elephant climbed off the track and lolloped into the jungle with a crashing noise.

I think we'd made about a quarter of a mile, when somebody ahead of us blew a shrill whistle and went on blowing it in a hysterical sort of way for about two minutes. And then all of a sudden a Sikh major with a revolver in his hand came bounding out of the dense shrubbery and stood in front of us. When he saw me he began to laugh. He laughed till I thought he would injure himself, and then he had to sit down against a tree and laugh all over again. Finally he said: 'I see you, sahib. Come on down.' I came down, clutching my finery about me, and the major led me through the undergrowth for about a hundred yards to a bamboo hut. Five Sikh soldiers inside it were laughing their heads off. The major sank into a chair, and when he got his breath back, he said: 'Taking into consideration the entertainment you have provided, I fine you 100 rupees to be paid on the spot. I shall then provide you with an escort to the road.' And so he did, but to a very special piece of the road—the one that runs the whole length of Tezpur market before it reaches the taxi rank and the road to the Planters Club. The brown stuff was still brown, but not so stinking, when I landed in London weeks later.

It was at this juncture in the correspondents' bitter lives that the Indian government sent down a representative to talk to them. I have never admired a man more than I admired Mr Chowdri—I think that was his name—that morning. The correspondents were like mad bulls; there were actually placards hung out saying 'To Hell with the India Press Office' and 'Nehru, Wake Up the World wants a Story.' The Americans were making most of the noise.

Mr Chowdri arrived in a splendid car. He was a slim, elegant, very good-looking man in his thirties. As he got out of his car, he was surrounded by a dense mob of correspondents who bore him along to the big table of the bar and sat around him shouting and screaming and shoving their great red faces under his chin, while they banged on the table with their eyes bulging out.

'If India don't get me to see the Dalai Lama then India's going to have the worst American press that India's ever had,' roared the loudest voice.

'Oh, I don't think we should care about that,' Mr Chowdri said. The noise redoubled. During the tumult, Mr Chowdri glanced appreciatively around the Planters Club, waved at me—I can't think why, but I waved back because I liked his style—and when they were all exhausted he said: 'I came down here to say, but it's been a little difficult, that the embargo is lifted from three o'clock today. You will have cable facilities here in Tezpur tomorrow morning and we believe you should meet the Dalai Lama inside three days.' He then rose. 'Nice to have met you. Don't drink too much—it's dangerous in this climate. Goodbye.' He climbed into his car.

We all spent the rest of the day rewriting the sheafs of irrelevant colour stories which we'd all been working on for weeks. We all telephoned in voices full of emotion and alcohol and then we spent most of the night on whisky.

It was about half-past five that morning, I suppose, when I was awakened by a rough shaking and a voice which said: 'Sahib, sahib, Dalai Lama come.' Out into the pelting rain with my recorder and then stuffed into the bus with 30 or so competitors, I jolted for the last time up the track to Foothills. There it all was, the glorious sun, the glittering leaves, the mountains from another, grander planet, the giddy track like a narrow, twisted flypaper hanging from the ceiling. And now I could see on the flypaper a group of minute dots.

From where we first caught sight of them until they passed through the Gurkha's barrier it took the Dalai Lama and his party nearly five hours. And then the big, sturdy Tibetans, in their fur hats and fur coats, their faces crimson, dismounted from their little tough horses at the barrier surrounded by a ring of Sikh soldiers, and in the middle was the Dalai Lama. A great surprise: like a large handsome specimen of American college youth straight off the campus, with his round intelligent face, his round intelligent glasses, his large size and his expensive Western suit. As he emerged smiling from among his followers, the press leapt on him like an animal. He was borne very slowly along in the middle of an almost silent mob, except that one of the interpreters, in a low whining voice like a beggar, besought him in Tibetan all the way to the Sikh major's house to say something— anything. In the scrum I somehow managed to keep my microphone close under his mouth the whole time, but during the 150-yard journey, while moving his hands like a bishop blessing his flock, the Dalai Lama said absolutely nothing, and kept up a sort of wordless murmuring, too low to be recorded on my tape. 'Ulla, ulla, ulla, ulla,' that's what it sounded like. Then the Sikhs snatched him and his attendants inside and the door shut. That was all we got. Later in the day, when he left on a special train from the railway junction, we got even less. He remained locked impenetrably in the train and this time the journalists meant nothing to anybody. The station was crammed. It was almost collapsing with all the Buddhists in North India who'd been able to get there. Four hours the train puffed away in the station unable to move for the throngs of worshippers prostrate on the railway line. Tibetan horns mooed in concert on the platform, women held up children, and men, weeping on their knees, turned prayer wheels, chanted, prayed and beat gongs. It was marvellous, but it was all we got.

It was all we got, all except one of us. The *Times of India* correspondent had had a cool look. He had also concealed in Tezpur a Tibetan youth. At Foothills, indistinguishable among the drivers and interpreters and secretaries, this youth had slipped into the jungle and changed into his native mountain clothes. Then he had mingled with the horsemen from Tibet and spent two hours in the Sikh major's house, chatting the story out of them. So the *Times of India* scooped the world on a story which must have cost the press round about, well a million pounds. It printed it two days later—three paragraphs, nearly at the bottom of an unimportant page.

Eric Maple

RETURN TO THE WITCH COUNTRY

Eric Maple has for a number of years been inquiring into
survivals of witchcraft, and similar practices and beliefs, in
the English countryside. Amongst his books is *The Dark
World of Witches*. Here he tells of a return visit to Canewdon, in Essex, where he had first discovered a continuing
belief in witches in 1958. The dialogues that are included
are transcribed from tape-recordings that he made.

THE CANEWDON STORY had begun, for me, just ten years
before when I had decided to investigate the last surviving legends
of the Essex witches, white and black. A black witch was one who
placed you under an evil spell—so they said—but there were
undoubtedly white witches—men and women who removed
spells, and went into trances. They discovered things that were
lost, and occasionally cured illnesses by herbs and charms. They
could be troublesome too—if you upset them they'd curse you.
And the curse of an angry white witch was, if anything, even
more devastating than the curse of a black one. Canewdon, a tiny
village just ten miles north of Southend-on-Sea, had a most
sinister reputation in the past. It was supposed to possess a permanent establishment of six witches under a master of witches.
There are two traditions about this—one is that their identity was
unknown, though three wore silk and three wore cotton; the
other that two of them at least were always the butcher's wife
and the baker's wife, but that the Master of Witches was always
a man; the last, a Mr Fred Pickengale, died many years ago.

It was generally believed that every time a stone fell from the church tower one witch died and another took her place—and that only when the tower finally fell down would witchcraft in Canewdon become extinct.

When I first inquired into the Canewdon story all those years ago only a few of the old people remembered the legends, or would talk about them, but I noticed that the village had avoided having either a butcher or baker. Outside the village there were always a few people with a lurking terror of Canewdon witchcraft. Some laughed it off but others were certain that misfortune threatened all who ventured there. One woman told me: 'My mother would *never* let me go to Canewdon. Why? Because if you did *they'd* get yer.'

It was not so much the witches they feared—after all, at least they were human—but their imps, 'the little old white mice'. The hallmark of a Canewdon witch was the possession of these diabolical animals, and some very odd tales were told about them.

Once, after an old Canewdon woman had died, hordes of screaming white mice were found in her house. Even the cat fled in terror when it saw them. And there had been only one way of getting rid of them—by burying them in the coffin with the witch.

The cottage of the last Master of Witches, old Mr Pickengale, had been regarded with awe during his lifetime, but after his death it was shunned like the plague. Those who peeped through the narrow windows swore that they could see the shining red eyes of the 'little old white mice' inside—waiting.

All the Masters of Witches were men of great power. They could go into trances and find lost and stolen property, but it was dangerous to cross their paths for they had the uncanny knack of bewitching all forms of wheeled transport. Horses and carts a well as human beings, came to a sticky end.

Now in 1968 I was in Canewdon once again—expecting to find the witch legends completely forgotten. Standing in the long narrow street I saw the church tower looming up before me.

Well, I thought, there *ought* to be witches in Canewdon since the church tower still stands, but I wonder if anybody will remember the story now. What was my surprise when I discovered that far from dying out, Canewdon's witches were on everybody's lips. It was not so much the country people who were prepared to talk about them, but rather the newcomers, scores of whom are now accommodated in contemporary houses surrounding the village street. What was more, Canewdon apparently possessed a new Master of Witches, a country labourer called Bibby Kemp, who is reputed to bring disaster upon those who offend him—particularly men in motor cars. The village still talks about the car-load of reporters who arrived in the village one day and inundated Bibby with their questions. Within two weeks their newspaper had closed down for good.

It was with considerable trepidation that I asked Bibby what happened to those who crossed his path.

BIBBY: When I say it happens, it happens.

MAPLE: What happens?

BIBBY: Never you mind, matey.

MAPLE: Is this because they've upset you?

BIBBY: Yes. Definite.

MAPLE: So it doesn't pay to upset Bibby . . .

BIBBY: No. Never does.

MAPLE: What was this queer story they told about you and the man in the motor-car?

BIBBY: Well, he upset me.

MAPLE: What happened next?

BIBBY: He run out the barn and jumped into his van. It started up. When I twigged him coming I stopped it. Twice I done it.

MAPLE: Stopped his motor-car.

BIBBY: I stopped the engine. He come back in, he said 'I ain't going to have no more to do with that.' I said 'Right-o'.

MAPLE: Were you watching it happen?

BIBBY: No. I was a mile away . . .

MAPLE: Mm.

BIBBY: See. And that's true.

MAPLE: You know, Bibby, that all the old witches are supposed to have this power of bewitching things with wheels.

BIBBY: Mm. I don't believe in that. Don't believe in it.

MAPLE: But you have the power.

BIBBY: Mm. Don't believe in wheels. No, don't believe in wheels. No. I don't believe in it.

MAPLE: Do you think some people feel a little cautious about upsetting you, a little wary?

BIBBY: Yes. Very wary. Very wary. Yes, they do.

MAPLE: What else can you do, Bibby?

BIBBY: Well I can do a lot of funny things. Yes. If I say a thing is going to happen, it happens. And that's flat.

MAPLE: What, do you see it in your mind?

BIBBY: Yes. If I want to find a thing here I go to bed and sleep on it.

MAPLE: If you want to find something that is lost?

BIBBY: Yes.

MAPLE: Do you mean that if I lost something and I came to you . . .

BIBBY: Yes.

MAPLE: . . . you could find it for me?

BIBBY: I could find it.

Witchcraft and magic are in the blood. According to witch-lore, the power is always passed down from father to daughter, and mother to son. From whom had Bibby Kemp inherited his own magical powers?

BIBBY: My mother.

MAPLE: You know these powers that you say you have, that if you upset people they come to grief, do any others of your family have this power?

BIBBY: None. Only mother.

MAPLE: You take these from your mother, then.

BIBBY: My mother did that. She put it on anybody. And she'd pick a match-stick up, put it in my hands. I'd watch that grow.

MAPLE: A match-stick would grow.

BIBBY: Anything would grow. What she put in. Anything.

MAPLE: She had a kind of magic in her.

BIBBY: Mm.

MAPLE: You know these stories they used to say—I think I've got it right—there would always be witches in Canewdon.

BIBBY: So long as the church stands.

MAPLE: So long as the church stands.

BIBBY: Yes.

MAPLE: Tell me what they said.

BIBBY: That's what they said. The last one dies and the church is supposed to fall down.

MAPLE: So when the last witch dies the church tower falls down.

BIBBY: Falls down.

MAPLE: So if that's true, there must be a last witch here still.

BIBBY: Definitely so. You've hit a point.

MAPLE: So there is still a witch somewhere in Canewdon.

BIBBY: Canewdon . . . Well there is.

MAPLE: Can she do harm?

BIBBY: Yes. Great harm to people.

MAPLE: What kind of harm?

BIBBY: Any harm you like.

MAPLE: How can you stop her doing harm?

BIBBY: You can't stop her. She's got a willpower over you, so you can't stop her.

MAPLE: Are some people frightened of her?

BIBBY: Yes. They are.

MAPLE: Not children?

BIBBY: Children, no. No. No.

It is difficult to discover exactly how Bibby's neighbours feel about him. It is obvious that any worker of magic in a community is bound to be regarded with mixed feelings, to say the least. There is not the slightest doubt, however, that he is respected and liked. Mrs Felstead, who owns the Chequers public house and is

RETURN TO THE WITCH COUNTRY

permanent hostess to Bibby and his fans, probably sums up the feelings of the village fairly accurately.

MRS FELSTEAD: Whether they're afraid to upset him or not, I wouldn't like to say. But he's looked up to in the village, by the customers at the Chequers anyway.

MAPLE: So in spite of his power he is, as you say, an extremely important person in this community.

MRS FELSTEAD: Yes. Because he's the man that will help anyone else out in any way he can. He's always willing to give a kind word to the children, and he is generally liked, I should say; very much so.

MAPLE: What do people think about the witches of Canewdon, your customers, people who come from outside?

MRS FELSTEAD: I think you'll find that the local people are very cagey. They won't say whether they believe in them or not. But I think they all feel that there is something there.

MAPLE: Do you think yourself that there are any of the old witches still left in Canewdon?

MRS FELSTEAD: Oh, I'm sure of it. I'm sure of it.

Bibby can cure as well as curse. He tells how he once restored the use of a man's bad leg by rubbing it with salt and water, only the limb had to be rubbed upwards. Why upwards? Was this magic? White magic!

Now in the old days people in the Essex countryside had always linked magic powers with the possession of little imps. I persuaded Bibby to tell me more about it—and whether his powers were shared by other members of his family.

BIBBY: Yes. Oh yes. All through my family. All through my whole family.

MAPLE: Has anybody else in your family got these powers now?

BIBBY: They've been handed down to one.

MAPLE: To one.

BIBBY: Yes.

MAPLE: From you?

BIBBY: Yes. But I'm not going to say who.

MAPLE: No, that's fair.

BIBBY: I'm not saying.

MAPLE: Is this one of the secrets you mustn't say?

BIBBY: Yes. It is.

MAPLE: One of the secrets.

BIBBY: Yes.

MAPLE: You know years ago they used to talk about the witches...

BIBBY: Mm.

MAPLE: ... and the little old white mice?

BIBBY: Mm.

MAPLE: Am I right in saying that people thought the witches had white mice?

BIBBY: Yes. Of course they'd put a white mouse on you.

MAPLE: This was your way of saying you'd do harm to them?

BIBBY: Yes. Yes.

MAPLE: They must have thought, you know, that you were a kind of witch when you said that.

BIBBY: Oh well, that comes . . . See what I mean.

MAPLE: So have you really put the white mice on people?

BIBBY: Yes. You've got to. You have it on your mind. On your mind.

MAPLE: How many are there?

BIBBY: There's only three.

MAPLE: And they are not ordinary mice.

BIBBY: Ordinary mice—bless you, no. Of course they ain't. Definitely not.

MAPLE: So you think of these?

BIBBY: Mm.

MAPLE: And these make things happen.

BIBBY: Yes. If you want to think anything you put it on your mind. It'll come to you.

MAPLE: Did you . . .

BIBBY: They make you shudder. You give a shudder. Wakes you up.

Bibby's wife is one of his most loyal supporters. I asked her what she thought about it all, and whether in her opinion Bibby's spells really worked.

BIBBY'S WIFE: Oh, they do.

MAPLE: Have you known that to happen recently?

BIBBY'S WIFE: No, not recently. Some time ago.

MAPLE: Can you tell me about it?

BIBBY'S WIFE: If he tell you anyone was going to have bad luck they'd have it. If they upset me.

MAPLE: I see. He looked after you.

BIBBY'S WIFE: Yes, definitely.

MAPLE: Did you want him to do this, or would he do it off his own?

BIBBY'S WIFE: He'd do it off his own accord.

MAPLE: Were you pleased if somebody who upset you had this happen to them?

BIBBY'S WIFE: Yes, because I didn't want them to upset me.

MAPLE: Seems to have this power of, say, putting the mockers on people who . . .

BIBBY'S WIFE: Oh yes, he will.

MAPLE: He will.

BIBBY'S WIFE: Mm.

MAPLE: Your husband was telling us about the mysterious white mice. He says he sees them in his mind at night. Well, is he restless to sleep with?

BIBBY'S WIFE: No. Sometimes . . . well, sometimes he'll jump and I'll say 'What's the matter with . . . what's the matter with you, then?' because, you know, really he jumps. He says, 'Oh, it's something I'm sleeping on.'

MAPLE: And do you think it's the white mice again?

BIBBY'S WIFE: Oh, he doesn't say. But he says he's gone to bed with something on his mind; he's going to sleep on it. But he doesn't say what it is. But I find out . . . he jumps and I say to him, 'Well, what's the matter with you then? Anything the matter?' 'No, I've just got something on my mind . . .' 'What is it?' He says 'I'm not going to say'.

How had Bibby acquired his remarkable reputation for magic and witchcraft in the first place? Had some of the mystique of the old Witch Master, Mr Fred Pickengale, rubbed off on to Bibby's own shoulders? Perhaps it was only a coincidence, but when, all those years ago, the old wizard's cottage had become vacant, through death, it had been Bibby of all people who moved in.

BIBBY: In his cottage where he died, went out.
MAPLE: Were people afraid of that cottage at all?
BIBBY: They were afraid of old Fred, because he put it on . . .
MAPLE: Not everybody would have gone to have lived in his cottage.
BIBBY: Certainly not. Certainly not. So it was left there for me . . .
MAPLE: So you stepped . . .
BIBBY: Some of it.
MAPLE: So you stepped into his shoes.
BIBBY: That's it. He never had any shoelaces to lace them up with, matey.

So the ancient thread of Canewdon witchcraft continues to be spun—in the imaginations as well as in the lives of the villagers new and old—the tradition that as one witch dies, another takes their place. What keeps the old beliefs alive is something of a mystery. At first I thought that the publicity I had given to Canewdon's story in books and on radio was responsible for this latter-day revival of witchcraft in its most ancient form—but now I am not so sure.

To find similar stories of witches and their imps one would have to go back to the witch trials of the 17th century. Why, I wonder, has the fear of witches, or at least respect for them, still survived in this one village, only two hours' journey from

London? Perhaps the answer to this mystery lies hidden in the most tenaciously held tradition of all—that just so long as the church tower stands there must be witches in Canewdon, and that only when it finally crumbles to the ground will the last witch die—only then perhaps will those strange white mice cease to trouble the dreams of those who live in this haunted countryside.

Ray Gosling

BLACKPOOL

Ray Gosling is a journalist and a regular broadcaster, with a programme on Granada Television in the North called 'On Site'.

Before I talk about Blackpool I want to tell you of a dream I had the other night. It was a very pleasant dream, but it was not about Blackpool. I dreamt I'd been given the job of changing the image of the Co-op. I threw away all the plate-glass packaging and I brought back mosaic tiles and proud gilt lettering, 'Industrial and Provident, Equitable Co-operative Society Limited—Grocery Branch No 7', and I advertised Nutritious Food and Strong Working Clothes. I put giant photos of Keir Hardie and Engels, and Bevan and Frank Cousins, and all the Rochdale Pioneers, all over the store, and on the outside we hung embroidered banners: 'Workers of the World, Unite,' 'At the Co-op shop the Toiling Masses,' 'Solidarity with the Co-operative Bakers of Wholemeal Bread,' 'People Like You Make the Goods, People Like You Serve People Like You at your Co-operative,' 'You needn't be afraid at the Co-op,' 'Walk inside. No snooty assistants. No trendy gimmicks. No one puffs you up at The Society.' I even had Chairman Mao in 365,000 coloured light-bulbs outside the Royal Arsenal, until I remembered that Mao Tse-tung smokes State Express 555. And then I awoke.

Blackpool is a town half-way between London and Glasgow, beside the Irish Sea facing west towards the Isle of Man. It grew,

like the Co-op, in the latter part of the 19th century as a playground for the workers in Lancashire cotton towns, and expanded
to become where people arrived for their week's annual holiday
from all over the North of England, from Glasgow, the Midlands,
and to some extent London.

In front of the old Euston Station was an enormous sign
advertising 'Blackpool, playground of the world, only five train
hours from here'—and although the Lancashire resort is *the* town
of tall stories, that boast of being playground of the world was
not untrue.

Coney Island just outside New York has roller-coasters and
honky-tonk like Blackpool, but not a summer season where 14
live theatres take over £2 million in the box-office. There isn't
a British variety star worth his name who hasn't played Blackpool. Fifty years ago it was Florrie Forde, and G. H. Elliot, the
chocolate-coloured coon. Everybody's played Blackpool—Sid
Field, Harry Lauder, Tommy Handley, Can-You-Hear-Me-
Mother? Sandy Powell, the Cheeky Chappie Max Miller, diddy
man Ken Dodd, Tony Hancock, Arthur Haynes, Frankie 'oo'
Howerd, and Al Read, who has played the central pier so many
times, he vies with Reginald Dixon as Mr Blackpool.

In America, although the big stars all play Las Vegas, no one
lives there, and I can't imagine the political machines holding
their convention at Vegas. In Blackpool they do. 1968 saw the
Trades Union Congress, the Labour Party and the Conservative
Party all holding their annual conferences there. They stayed at
the big hotels, all of them built before the war, and walked in the
morning along the Golden Mile to the Opera House, the largest
theatre outside London. They walked past the fruit machines and
the penny falls; beneath your tickling stick and candy-floss came
Heath and Wilson and Woodcock; and following them the
foreign correspondents who dutifully report the proceedings—
and some of them reported on Blackpool.

They were amazed, as foreign correspondents are every year.
They go out and walk the Golden Mile late at night, slip on the
hot-dog papers—appalled at the vehement colours, the tatty

barkers, the bingo halls; the shellfish in vinegar. It is not at all the King's Road, nor even the Earls Court Road.

The first political figure to use Blackpool in my lifetime was George Woodcock, who, when he came for the TUC this year, combined his visit with doing the first BBC television commentary on the Crown Green Bowls Championship. Blackpool is a people's town. Above every showman's head is the phrase: '240 pennies equals one pound.' Unlike in Brighton or Bournemouth, you can usually find a room in one of the big hotels even at the height of the season. Where you have a problem is finding room in the 5,000 guest houses which between them find bed-space for half a million people at prices you can afford.

In the old days Blackpool's season was built on the Wakes Week, a unique system of staggered holidays where each town in the North of England closed down for two weeks by rota. Often whole streets would move *en bloc* in Wakes Week to Blackpool and the whole street stay in the same boarding house, all together. You could bring your own food and the landlady would cook it. You marked your own eggs with your initials and kept them on the shelf in the dining-room. Meals would be steak-pudding and chips, rissoles and chips, fish and chips. There were and still are donkeys to ride on the sands. In one splendid year, 1905, they actually had camels on the sands. Tea on a tray on the sands, and league cricket and Rugby League, Blackpool Borough and crown green bowls and snooker, and the fun-fair to take you back to your brief teenage dream. A town where there was always an answer—where there is always an answer—to the question: 'What can I do now, Mum?' Tommy Trinder has called Blackpool 'the Woolworth's of show business'. It is.

Blackpool is not so grand if you have to live there and are poor —and some are. Blackpool Corporation spend a fourpenny rate subsidising the Illuminations—the greatest show on earth, and it must be that. The Strip in Las Vegas is only three miles long; Blackpool Front is seven miles. Blackpool spends a fourpenny rate subsidising the lights, and yet no matter how you interpret statistics the town shows up very, very badly in the way it looks after its old and its homeless and its handicapped. Every town is a little crooked. All of us have failings, but no town is ever as crooked as a seaside town.

This year, in the middle of the conference time, I was investigating the welfare services in Blackpool for a local television programme. Everywhere I went people were saying: 'I can't say anything,' 'I don't want to talk.' It was two in the morning and very wet and I'd spent hours trying to find a town councillor I wanted badly to interview. I said to the taxi-driver, 'Give up,' and I told him what I was doing. He said to me, 'I knew all that and I knew who you were,' and he smiled, and I smiled. And then he said: 'Do you know what the motto of Blackpool is?' I said: 'Yes, sure, it's "Progress"—a good simple English word.' He said: 'I'll tell you what it really is. It goes like this:

If you're bent, pitch your tent.
If you're straight, you can wait.

That's the real motto of Blackpool.'

Natives of Blackpool are called sand-grown men—the football team, old Stanley Matthews's team, used to be First Division; it's now in the second and doing well this season. At the beginning of the match they brought on a mascot, a character wearing a flowing tangerine-coloured robe, and he holds, like an orb and sceptre, in one hand a duck and in the other a huge stick of rock. Blackpool is a show-business town, it's a fairground town, a gypsy town, and there is a tradition among show people that if there's a punch-up on the stall next to yours, do *not* intervene. Each stall-holder must fight for himself. This is a town of enterprise where the cut and thrust of competition is enjoyed, and so it is remarkable that over the last few years Blackpool has, through its Corporation, its Council and most of the local people, made some decisions about the future.

People will get richer in Britain, and the old Blackpool pattern of holidays can't go on for ever. More and more people go abroad every year and while Blackpool is in no way declining it isn't expanding as fast as it should. Not only is there a drift to abroad. On the Lincolnshire coast there are already more shacks and caravans than bed-spaces in Blackpool, and so Blackpool town is turning more and more of its boarding houses into do-it-yourself flatlets. And it has begun a long-term campaign to attract German and American tourists into the town for week-long stays. If it can tempt visitors from the Continent, the theory runs, then British holidaymakers will look at Blackpool in a new light. But I think the sand-grown men, for all their guile, have missed one vital statistic. We go abroad not only for the sun but for the haphazard chance encounter. It's a problem of sex. How do you keep the burp, the belly laugh of noise, the Incredible Giant of the Andes, the gastric joke, the honestly vulgar and quite inoffensive family Blackpool? How do you keep that and attract young people who are out for a rather different good time?

Brighton does it because she's so close to London, and Bournemouth by bringing in foreign students, but neither of the big South Coast resorts have this sheer weight of lucky numbers— eight million a year into Blackpool who want family entertainment and slapstick fun. What I am sure of is that the change can't be done by the big companies alone, who have recently acquired so much of traditional Blackpool. EMI now control the Blackpool Tower Company, and Rank and Forte's are large owners of what was once the pitch of local men.

Maybe the lobby groups who come into Blackpool with every party conference will one year tire of the politics, and tire of mocking the Woolworth's of show business, honest Blackpool and they'll set up—I don't know what, but the postcard industry needs new life. McGill's bloomers and double-meanings are now period pieces. You can't buy a photo of Stanley Matthews on a postcard in Blackpool—it's his town; nor tea towels of the Peterloo massacre. How about Tariq Ali shaving-mugs? Or face flannels with Enoch Powell's picture? Or how about piggy banks in the shape of Cohn-Bendit? You can't get James Dean, nor Marilyn Monroe, nor the Jarrow Hunger March, nor Sydney Street, nor Lowry, nor D. H. Lawrence. Nor Albert and his stick

with its horse's-head handle—you can't even get that in Blackpool, and I'd like to buy one of those. Some people say that what
must be done with Blackpool is to change its common image. I
mean, every seaside town, even Rhyl and Minehead, has its rep
theatre, except Blackpool, nor I believe should it. Many towns
hold an arts festival. How about a fun competition in Blackpool
—directors of fun, Cedric Price, Joan Littlewood, Albert Hunt?
A vulgar *International Times*; a populist *Private Eye*; camels on the
beach again, and revive Max Miller.

In the bars and along the crowded sands in the hot season walk
pedlars of *smile, dammit smile* two or four-page broadsheets. They
have mock small ads and a blank space for those who cannot read;
definitions—'Pram: last year's fun on four wheels.' Or this one—a
big ad for Hugh Rhine Ale: 'looks bad, tastes bad, and is bad, the
beer with a bash in every burp.' Come on, we can do better than
that—or can we?—all those student-rag magazines. But come up
to Blackpool and have a look. Don't underestimate this town.
Two flies were playing football in a saucer. One said to the other:
'You'll have to play better than that; don't forget we're in the
cup next week.'

Norman MacCaig

BY LOCH ASSYNT AND LOCH CROCACH

Norman MacCaig is a poet, whose last book was *Rings on a Tree*. He has recently held a Fellowship in creative writing at Edinburgh University.

PATRIOTISM IS A word whose meaning just about escapes me, at any rate as it's used notably by penny-in-the-slot politicians and boozers in pubs. When I hear someone say 'I'm a Scot and proud of it,' I can't help wondering 'Why? Why should you be *proud* of a country just because, as a result of a million accidents, you were born in it?'

Of course, it's possible to love one's native land, or at least to get used to it. And if you resist the seduction of emigrating to the greener grass on the other side of the fence, you have, of course, the duty of any member of a society to try to improve its lot. But if you don't like the place, what's wrong with clearing out? What's wrong with *denouncing* it? If you're being a traitor, you're only being a traitor to a geographical accident.

Well, I'm one of those who didn't clear out and I've no intention of doing so, though my feelings about Scotland are very complex indeed. I love its landscapes and detest its philistinism. I like its weather and loathe its parochialism. Historically, I admire the battle it fought for freedom while strongly suspecting the motives of most of the self-seeking thugs who led that battle. I respect the Scot's independence of mind and can't stand his submissiveness to the wrong authorities. And so on. But the fact remains I stayed there, and chose to. And I find this matter of choice applies more locally, within the narrow boundaries of Scotland itself.

My father came from Dumfries, in the very south of Scotland; my mother came from the Outer Hebrides, from Harris; and I was born in Edinburgh—three beautiful places, three places that mean a great deal to me. But in the end, my closest allegiance is to none of these, but to a part of Scotland with which I have no such connections. It's that wild and deserted area in the far North-West, in the county of Sutherland, the coastal strip which stretches from Ullapool to Kylesku and, in particular, the central part of that strip that forms the parish—but what a parish—of Assynt.

Well, there are reasons for everything, though they're often hard to come by, and I do know very clearly some of the reasons why this place so engages my mind and my affections. The look of the place, for a start. Now, however beautiful a woman is, she has a skeleton inside her. And it's the geology of this landscape that is the bones of its beauty and that differentiates it from any other landscape in Scotland. In a way it's simple enough—at least, if it isn't, I'll simplify it. The basis is a bamboozling complex of low hills, up to 700 or 800 feet high, formed of Lewisian gneiss, a rock that's mostly greyish-pink, but comes in many colours—and changes them too in the innumerable shifts of the light. This base is admirably called by geologists the 'ruffled foreland', and in an extraordinary number of the ruffles water lies—small lochs with reeds and waterlilies, that wink and blink and entice you to walk farther than you meant to.

Millions of years ago—the phrase shows I'm no expert—that ruffled foreland was overlaid with a deep sediment of sandstone. Then the glaciers came, travelling west, pausing, and melting backwards towards the east, all the time gouging and scraping the soft sandstone, forcing passages to the sea. What they left was a line of mountains perched on the harder gneiss, separated from each other by these passages and rasped and chiselled and worn into the most individual and sometimes fantastic shapes. The mountains are not high—round about 2,400 feet. And that's important.

For I'm a man who generally prefers small scale things to large. For instance, I'd rather listen to Bach's Chaconne in D for a single fiddle than to his Mass in B minor. Also, since the details of this landscape are small, you've to walk only a very short distance—and there's a new view. The elements that make up the landscape are few in number. But the fantastic inventiveness of wind and weather and time has composed from them an unending series of brilliant variations that echo, but never mirror each other. Also, the lumps and bumps of the ruffled foreland demonstrate what distance is by a recession of horizons, one behind the other like waves on the sea but not so tidy, not nearly so tidy.

Clearly this is a marvellous landscape for walking through. And if you're a fisherman—well, the lochs are, most of them, so small and so close together you can wander about all one long day without seeing a soul, and come home with trout taken from six, eight, ten lochs.

In most of them a trout weighing a pound would be a good fish, but there are some, which I refrain from naming, where they run much larger than that. My own personal best was $6\frac{3}{4}$ lb. It came out of a loch set in a landscape of crags and corries that you could walk round in a quarter of an hour, and a number of deer, minute on the skyline above me, watched me with interest as I played it.

Trout, salmon, sea-trout in the rivers; red deer, roe deer, otters, foxes, wild cats in the hills and woods; ravens, eagles, buzzards, hawks in the air: these are only the beginning of a long list of the creatures that add their enlivening interest to the landscape, and it has made no mention of the teeming life in the sea, and above it. And wherever one goes one is never very far from the sea—clean and pure, exploding on cliffs, poking inland as sea lochs or creeping up over sandy beaches almost as white as salt.

It was, naturally, the physical beauty of the place that first attracted me. But as I returned more and more often, it began to go deeper than that. I knew something, of course, of the past

history of the Highlands. I knew about what is called the Clear-
ances, when crofters were ruthlessly evicted to make room for
sheep and a long and sad emigration began which hasn't stopped
yet. And I knew that this corner of Scotland suffered most of all,
so that Sutherland now is far and away the most thinly populated
county in Britain.

But I knew all this in my head, I had only a tiny historical
imagination and it was half asleep. By going there so many times
and getting to know the people, and by seeing the sad ruins of
crofting communities deserted for generations, that imagination
began to yawn and stretch and wake up; and even to grow. I take
this to be a good thing.

That was a gift I didn't expect. And I got another one. I used
to say I was apolitical. I couldn't understand politics. They bored
me. I realise this meant I was living slightly adjacent to reality.
By going back so often to this tinily populated place, I began to
get to know it in depth, in a way that's impossible in a place on the
scale even of Edinburgh. I began to learn of the relationship of
the landowner (an Englishman) and the locals, a relationship in
many respects uneasy, to put it mildly, and to notice the divisions
and conjunctions amongst the local people themselves. I got
interested in the economics of crofting, fishing and tourism. I
even noticed the prices of food in the local shop—and, believe me,
they made my eyes blink—and to find out about freight rates—
that curse of outlying places.

It's a matter of scale again. Because this was a small community
I, even though I was, and am, an outsider, began to see, demonstrated in petto, how economics and politics work (or don't) and
to feel involved in them. I don't say I see very clearly or very far,
but it was an eye-opener—an unexpected bonus for a man who
thought he went there only for the beauty of this most beautiful
corner of Scotland.

IV

IMAGININGS

Mary Douglas

NOMMO AND THE FOX

Mary Douglas, who is Reader in Social Anthropology at
University College, London, here considers how we might
learn to release our imaginations by taking a hint from a
Sudanese tribe and their oracle.

A GREAT DEAL IS said these days about creative thinking.
Everyone agrees we should learn how to harness the muse. We
need more inventiveness in every direction: how to feed the
world, for instance; and how to communicate with one another;
how to renew enthusiasm; how to avoid wars. Professor Hoyle
has said that in science the pace of invention has been slackening
off since the splitting of the atom. In his John Danz lectures, three
years ago, he said that there were in physics alone about 20 major
discoveries lying around for someone to pick up. It seems that the
next great invention will have to be one about how to switch on
inventiveness. But I notice a kind of helplessness in the attitude to
creativity. It is a mystery. Its behaviour is wild and free. Inspiration is treated like a horse which gallops off when you try too
hard to catch it, but may come and nuzzle your face when you
decide to give up in despair.

It's true that every creative worker knows the sudden feeling
of receiving a new idea, out of the blue. Fred Hoyle's best setting
for revolutionary ideas is a fishing trip, away from it all—and
especially away from the laboratory. Every scientist who has had
a great idea knows the feeling of being passive, subject to a
sovereign thought. Francis Bacon says he feels that he is not in

control when he is hard at work on a painting. Other people have solved theoretical problems after finding the answer in a dream. It seems to be no accident that Archimedes shouted *Eureka!* in his bath. Evidently the thinker has to switch off his own rational control of the problem-solving act and give it up to his free imagination.

If only that were enough! We could say to our great brains: 'Hey! Take it easy. Play some healthy games. Go fishing.' If they still seemed tense, we could try threatening them: perhaps cut off research money, until they relax. The trouble is that nothing like that would work. The muse refuses to be switched on. So we return to the helpless feeling that the imagination is untameable.

But actually there are some clues we could follow. Other peoples in other parts of the globe have a different way of treating the problem. They have some special techniques for turning off rational control and freeing the imagination. One of them is a trick for standing back from a question and looking at it in the most general possible terms. This allows the whole range of a person's commitments to be seen afresh at long range. I am convinced that a scientist solves his theoretical puzzles when he suddenly sees them relating to his own inner life. I believe that he gets blocked because (for whatever reason) the technical problem has become separated from his deepest concerns. Therefore I believe that a technique for standing back and presenting all one's problems as part of the total pattern of one's life may be the way to release the imagination.

People who use oracles for solving personal problems assume there are two ways of existing. One is at the level of appearances of formal behaviour; the other at a deeper level. To get through appearances to the other reality is the diviner's task. The contrast corresponds closely to our ideas about two kinds of understanding. We distinguish systematic reasoning from imagination. The idea of intuitive reasoning fascinates us. It even seems to be a truer kind of knowing, since we tend to suspect that the more cumbersome machinery of logic distorts our understanding as well as slowing it down. So with this bias in favour of intuition we should be able to understand the tribal cultures which hold that knowledge gained in trances, dreams and oracles belongs with the night, or the moon, or the left hand, or femininity, while formal knowledge belongs to the day, the sun, the right hand and manhood. When they consult an oracle they mean to make that very dive into the depths of the free imagination that Fred Hoyle makes on a fishing trip, or Archimedes made in his bath.

A particular oracle I'm interested in is laid out in straight parallel lines and marked-off squares, into which symbolic objects of different kinds are put. It is used by the Dogon, a tribe in what used to be the French Sudan, and seems to be a most practical oracle. They consult it daily, as matter-of-factly as a stockbroker consults the *Financial Times*. Outside the village there are sand-covered flat rocks. In the evening they draw up on the rocks a blank questionnaire form, put in it certain data they want more information about, scatter food around and go to bed. In the morning, when they get up, they go straight to the oracle. In the night the white foxes that live in the Sudan will have come, taken the food and left their little tracks over the questionnaire. This is how it is filled in, and the diviner starts to interpret the answers to his questions.

The Dogon universe is governed, on the one hand, by a deity, Nommo. He represents order and reason. But his power is balanced to some degree by his brother, who has the form of a white fox. The Fox is depicted as the obverse of order—not a sinister obverse but a richly creative one. He stands for nonsense, contradiction and confusion, but it is the kind of nonsense which the Surrealists have hailed as the work of imagination, un-trammelled by the sense of realism. The Fox is represented as being always in a complex kind of opposition to the reality of appearances and of social order. Realism and society are limited by time and space, and have their own kind of truth. But the Fox can operate without these limitations. So he can pierce through appearances and reveal hidden truths. He's on the side of humans and helps them to make decisions by filling in their oracle questionnaire. So the Dogon who consult the oracle explicitly reach into the confused energies of their imaginations and fish up precise answers to their daily problems. They have a technique for taming the imagination without destroying it: for don't let us forget, the oracle has to be interpreted.

Now look at the shape and lay-out of their questionnaire. They draw three long rectangles in the sand. One represents God, one Man, and one the Fox; or say that they represent heaven, earth and death. Each is divided into an upper and lower rectangle. The upper rectangle always deals with more general matters, and the lower one in each case refers more personally to the consulter himself. For example: the first rectangle, God or Heaven. Its upper portion concerns the whole spectrum of powers that formally govern the world. Are they well-disposed to me or not? If the tracks of the fox go upwards towards that rectangle, the sign is good; if down and away, it is bad. The lower portion concerns my religious duties: should I make sacrifice, and if so on which altar? In the Man's section, the upper part refers to all outsiders, foreigners, strangers, other villages, sorcerers. The lower part refers to myself, my own home and my own family and personal concerns. In the two squares of the Fox, the upper part deals with death in general and the lower part, called the cemetery, is my grave.

So here we have a blank form representing the universe. But the questioner soon fills in the framework with little symbols: a stone, a stick, a wisp of straw. A whole set of conventional objects represents tools, houses and people. He places these in the appropriate squares, taking care not to symbolise his private problem so obviously that any passer-by can read it. I can just imagine the sense of peaceful expectation with which he must go to bed and sleep soundly, having clarified his mind about what his real problem is and given up responsibility for solving it.

Then in the morning he runs to the oracle. Here he may find that the fox has settled the matter quite clearly. If it was a question of whether to undertake a journey, he may find the pebble representing himself in foreign parts has been kicked back home —or the fox may have walked straight to the cemetery. So the answer is no and the matter is settled. But sometimes the fox has scuffed up the different squares and produced a baffling confusion of signs. When this happens they say the fox is stuttering. So after a rite of sacrifice, the problem is posed again. Wouldn't this give the man a great chance to rethink his whole problem? I bet he doesn't set it out a second time in exactly the same form. Sometimes one fox runs one way and another one runs another way—this they decipher as contradiction. Again, here is the questioner being given another chance to reconceive his problem from the start; and always in the widest possible frame of reference.

Ever since Jung himself wrote about oracles psychotherapy has realised their potential for mental health. But alas, few studies of oracles in working order have been made with enough understanding of the social structure in which the consultant is gripped. It is this social context which has created his problems in the first place. So of course we can't assess the kind of peace of mind the oracle produces—or its effectiveness as a decision-making system. But we can still try to draw some guidance from it for the question of channelling inspiration.

The Surrealists brought out into the open for us the difference between two kinds of experience: the real, which was good enough for most people, and the surreal, infinitely better and the only kind for them. But they denied the possibility of the surreal being brought under control and would have been scandalised at the idea of putting the glorious, free imagination into harness to serve realism—which is what I am interested in. There is an older writer, though, whom they greatly admired, and whose work is close to my theme—Raymond Roussel. He found a technique of writing which he thought revolutionary. He would choose two words, almost alike but with a small difference in spelling; then he would choose two others exactly alike in spelling but with a different meaning. Then he would combine them in two sentences, in one sentence drawing on one set of meanings and in another sentence on the other. He would spend as long as two weeks on choosing the words that gave him two usable sentences on this basis. Once they were chosen, he set himself to construct a story that would begin with one of the sentences and end with the other. Usually he sandwiched little folk-tales between these fixed openings and endings. They were very trivial and his means of arriving at the pre-ordained last sentence was laboured in the extreme: it wasn't so much literature as a parlour trick.

When he was 19 he had had a psychological crisis, the opposite of a depression—he was filled with a vivid sense of glory. He fully expected this experience to come true and waited for fame and glory to follow the publication of his stories. But nothing happened, no one noticed. He went on writing and developed his technique. It became more complicated but more flexible. He began to choose the names of his characters by the same technique of playing with the meanings of words. Whole episodes were suggested by the breakdown of familiar phrases. He used the technique to stimulate and free his imagination and eventually produced the most extraordinary results. Who else, writing a story about a young Frenchman from Marseilles, would give him the unlikely name of Carmichael? Roussel did because his secret technique had produced that name and he stuck faithfully to whatever it found. A story that began with a comment on the greenish tinge on the skin of an over-ripe prune develops into a melodrama of poisoning in which the victim is an over-ripe brunette with a complexion of a greenish tinge—no wonder after she had eaten the fruit? He took the phrase *Napoléon Empereur*, and considered it in its separate parts. *Nappe*, table cloth; *olé*—this suggested Spanish, so he developed a scene in which a Spanish dancer is dancing on a table with a cloth.

He had a technique which maximised improbability. So it was that André Breton declared him to be the writer with the most richly fertile imaginative power of his day. But the important point to note is that his imagination, as it floated up between the crevices of the words he maltreated, drew up his own personal problem. This was how to be creative effectively and get world-wide recognition for it. As he concentrated on his word-splitting technique, his stories were free to develop as they would. One after another they told of brilliant scientists, inventors, artists, whose fantastic inventions brought world renown and wealth. Usually the invention was of a work of art which was able to produce other works of art freely so long as it was switched on. Often the central episode consists of an admiring crowd looking into a frame in which they see an admiring crowd gazing at a work of art in which is depicted an admiring crowd gazing—and so on. Roussel himself finally solved his own problem: he achieved his ambition of seeing an admiring crowd gazing at his work of art in which an admiring crowd was gazing at a work of art—and so on.

The moral for Roussel was that in the first stage he had his technique, but he played it cold. The trite little stories he used between his acrostics were just page-fillers. He himself was not involved. Gradually he mastered his technique and gave himself to it freely. He let the absorbing passion of his life bubble up through the words. He also let the technique express the many different levels on which his self had to achieve success if it was to achieve it at all. But only when his own personal concerns were fully engaged in the technique did the writing have power to stir other people.

To me, his rigid techniques recall the oracle of the Fox. I imagine that the Dogon who consults the oracle uses its fixed structure as a device for letting his passions express themselves. The oracle's three compartments allow him to think of the problem of organising himself at three different levels. The compartment of Heaven shows him facing his conscience as represented by moral pressures all around; the compartment for Man shows him interacting with his fellows in the hurly-burly of everyday life. The compartment of the Fox is his unconscious self from which all the answers come in the end. The lay-out lets him see himself looking at the problem in a perspective which *shows* him looking at the problem. The solution should help to organise him at all these levels.

I suggest we should abandon the random theory of inspiration. On this view, the great solutions only come by chance, in dreams, in baths, when the mind is switched off. It is about as reasonable as the stork theory of how babies arrive. Think of all the anglers who sit fishing day by day, and no flash of inspiration breaks through. The kind of oracles I have described do much more than just switch the mind off. They also switch it on to the problem at different levels of personal involvement. I believe that there is nothing random about the inspired idea's choice of a moment to arrive, that it comes when the thinker's other experiences in some abstract way dramatise the problem at issue. In a new arrangement of his social relations there may suddenly appear an abstract patterning of his theoretical problem.

Any formal pattern may trigger off recognition. The Dogon think in terms of heaven, earth and the Fox, or home, abroad and my grave. But a game of football or roulette could carry the same load of meaning: a theatre or ballet, or the struggle to outwit a fish. The analogy leaps to the receptive mind. It sees the narrow problem under a new guise. Then the thinker can go and have his dream or bath. This, it seems to me, is how inspiration finds its way in. In some vivid experience the thinker has recognised a simplified abstract patterning of the theoretical problem. The imagination has not had to make any very wild, capricious leap. It has passed smoothly from the pattern in an unsolved form, to the same set of elements in a new pattern, and back from there with the answer. Some people have this habit of being receptive to these free-floating analogies. But if the imagination is hitched to a knotty problem it won't come up with a brand-new solution unless its own depths have been stirred. They can't be reached by an academic presentation of the question: it has to be posed in a way that evokes strong passions.

Linear programmers devise computer games to simulate complex decision-making. Here is something they could think about. They should try to write in some equivalent of the Dogon oracle's sections for heaven, earth and death. Then the technical question can be formally linked with profound questions of personal identity and meaning. They might end by producing a formula for inventing inventions.

Peter Burke

THE CUNNING OF UNREASON

Peter Burke lectures in the School of European Studies at Sussex University, and is writing a book about Italian culture and society in the 15th century.

I—*The Dreams of Archbishops*

A FEW MONTHS AGO, I was sitting on a train when the man opposite asked what I did for a living. I said: 'History.' And he said: 'It's a funny subject. I mean historians always assume that human beings act rationally, don't they?' Well, there's a great deal of truth in that remark. Yet if it's completely and necessarily true that historians neglect the irrational, I think they might just as well give up altogether. So I shall try to escape from this dilemma.

There seems to be a historical connection between the rise of history and the rise of rationalism. Ancient Greece; the Renaissance; the Enlightenment: they were all great periods of historical thought. And they were also periods when great value was set on reason. The great historians of these periods—like Thucydides or Gibbon—don't exactly ignore the irrational. I mean, they don't impute rational motives to everyone all the time. Gibbon would be much less amusing if he did. But the historians of the Enlightenment, for example, do tend to label the irrational and then dismiss it: they tend to impute irrationality to 'them' (the masses, the clergy, the Middle Ages) and never to 'us'. The great 18th-century labels are 'superstition' and 'enthusiasm'. When these men come up against the irrational, they don't analyse; they moralise.

GOOD TALK

This idea—that history is only about the rational—becomes conscious in Hegel. He was fascinated by what he called 'the cunning of reason', working itself out in history. But he rejected the cunning of unreason. He attacked those historians who make their heroes, as he said, 'appear to have done every-thing under the impulse of some morbid craving, suggesting, for example, that Alexander the Great was possessed by a morbid craving for conquest'. All this he dismisses as 'Thersitism', prompted by envy. I think that this view of Hegel's has been the dominant one among historians in the 19th and 20th centuries whether they all realise this or not. To give just one example, an explicit one: R. G. Collingwood declared that the irrational was not part of history. He says: 'Irrational elements, the blind forces and activities in us, are not parts of the historical process.'

But of course, not everyone agrees with this; the attitude has been challenged. Dramatically so in 1912, when the French psychologist Gustave Lebon was very scathing about the his-torians of his own day, when they were confronted with the problem of explaining the French Revolution. He claimed they simply didn't know what to make of it and this 'was simply the result of the habit of having recourse to rational interpretations to explain events dictated by influences which were not rational'.

This criticism is splendid; but where do you go from here? You need concepts and you need methods. Well, you can, of course, turn to Freud. Freud was very interested in history; his famous study of Leonardo goes back to 1910. Some historians read Freud from the start; in 1913 the American historian Preserved Smith applied Freudian concepts in a brief study of the early development of Martin Luther.

Luther is a marvellous subject for a psychological approach. Marvellous because of the problems he raises for more traditional historians. There's the story of his fit in the choir at Erfurt when he was a young monk; he shouted out: 'I am not!' He went through severe depressions. One of his revelations came to him on the lavatory. He is fascinated by anal language; the devil's dirt, the Pope's stinking trousers keep on recurring in his pamphlets.

196

He has visions of the devil, who is filthy and smelly and shows Luther his backside. For traditional historians, things like this are an embarrassment and an irrelevance. For historians who want to take the irrational seriously, they're valuable clues. For one student of Luther, the psychiatrist Erik Erkison (whose interpretation lies behind Osborne's play) Luther had been 'a highly restrained and retentive individual'. This was true both psychologically (he kept quiet) and physically (he suffered from constipation) and perhaps ideologically (he kept his unorthodox ideas to himself). Then came his sudden revelation, on the lavatory. It was at once a physical, a psychological, an ideological breakthrough all in one. He turned into what Erikson calls 'an explosive person' with an explosive message.

The importance of these interpretations, it seems to me, is that they've reclaimed an area of Luther for history. What was thought of as inexplicable, irrelevant, meaningless, and was therefore ignored, is now seen to be part of a pattern. In the same way, the psychological approach to Gandhi, to Lenin, to Trotsky, to Woodrow Wilson have all integrated into the pattern incidents of their lives which had always been left outside it. And historians are always looking for patterns, in the behaviour of individuals and of societies.

Of course, seeing patterns isn't everything; the question is, is it the right pattern? Did Luther behave in this way? In fact, I deliberately didn't discuss the significance of Luther's fit in the choir because there isn't enough evidence that he had such a fit; it is a story told by biographers who believed—and here is an example of 16th-century psycho-history—that Luther was possessed by a devil. Again, it is obviously tempting to do as Erich Fromm does and relate Luther's attitude to God and to the State (that is, to authority) to his attitude to his parents, especially his father; tempting because other people's attitudes to authority and their parents seem to be related in this way. But then we know so little about Luther's parents.

What I want to argue is not that a particular interpretation of Luther is true; but that a certain type of interpretation is worth attempting. To take an example in rather more detail. The one I've chosen is Archbishop Laud. Let's start from Laud's conscious, adult behaviour, especially during his period of power during the reign of Charles I. Laud was authoritarian. He was deeply concerned with the problems of order and unity. He was a supporter of tradition and of ritual. He tried to make the clergy wear surplices, and the congregation bow at the name of Jesus. He stressed uniformity of observance in the Church because he thought 'those men who are sacrilegious against God and his Church' (as he called them) were likely to be rebellious in matters of state too. He had what friends called 'a hasty, sharp way of expressing himself' and what enemies called 'arrogant pride'; he made enemies easily.

Laud's political views aren't surprising in a mid-17th century Englishman. But they're not universal either. They might be related to his character. It is interesting that Freud's famous description of the 'anal character'—the man characterised particularly by his orderliness, his parsimony, and his obstinacy—fits Laud well. It is tempting too, to press into service the famous concept of 'authoritarian personality', with its suggestion that a particular style of upbringing, a particular relation to one's father, encourages a particular attitude to religious and political authority. Unfortunately, we know even less about Laud's parents than about Luther's; we simply know that he was his father's only child, but his mother's tenth. What we do have, to make up for this, are some of his dreams. He recorded about 30 of them in his diary over a 20-year period, 1623-43, which includes his period of power.

The very first dream he recorded was this: 'I did dream that the Lord Keeper was dead; that I passed by one of his men, that was about a monument for him; that I heard him say, his lower lip was infinitely swelled and fallen, and he rotten already.' The Lord Keeper was John Williams, bishop of Lincoln, a great enemy of Laud's. So here's a wish-fulfilment of his enemy's death. It was in this year that they seem to have become enemies. They were rivals for the favour of a common patron, James I's favourite the

THE CUNNING OF UNREASON

Duke of Buckingham. Then the Bishop of Lincoln quarrelled with Buckingham; but in 1625, Laud noted in his diary that Lincoln wished to be reconciled with Buckingham. The next night, Laud's feelings on this reconciliation took dramatic form:

'I dreamed that the bishop of Lincoln came, I know not whither, in iron chains. But returning loosed from them, leapt on horseback went away; neither could I overtake him.' Eighteen months later, 'I dreamed that my lord of Lincoln came and offered to sit above me at the council table, and that L.H. came in and placed him there.' A typical 17th-century quarrel over precedence; and at the same time a dramatic expression of Laud's fears of being pushed out by Williams.

These three dreams show Laud as aggressive and insecure. Other dreams suggest that his jealousy of a rival was all the greater because his feelings for Buckingham were not simply those of a client towards his patron. Laud, who was now in his fifties, seems to have been attracted towards Buckingham, a man 20 years younger. At all events: 'in my sleep it seemed to me that the duke of Buckingham got into my bed, where he showed me much love.'

James I was also attracted towards Buckingham; he used to write letters to him beginning 'sweet child and wife': indeed, Buckingham's whole career depended on this fact. Prince Charles shared the attraction. But Charles and Laud never seem to have been on friendly terms, despite their common aims. Perhaps their common devotion to Buckingham came between them. At all events, although from outside it may have seemed that the King and the Archbishop were very close, they were not; Charles did not trust Laud and Laud knew this. His dreams show that he knew it: 'I dreamed that the King went out to hunt; and that when he was hungry, I brought him on a sudden into the house of my friend Francis Windebank. While he prepared to eat, I, in the absence of others, presented the cup to him after the usual manner. I brought him drink, but it pleased him not. I brought him more, but in a silver cup. Thereupon his majesty said: you know that I always drink out of a glass.'

199

Another dream makes the point less dramatically and more directly: 'I dreamed marvellously, that the King was offended with me, and would cast me off, and tell me no cause why.'

These are not the only anxiety dreams of Laud's. He once dreamed that he was in Oxford: 'I went to St John's, and there I found the roof off from some parts of the college, and walls cleft, and ready to fall down.'

Here I think that the college may be a symbol for Laud himself. It was his old college; he had rebuilt part of it; and a house often symbolises the dreamer himself. The St John's dream came in 1642, when Laud had good reason to feel insecure, or 'ready to fall down'. But he had insecurity-dreams well before this; for example, in 1627 he twice dreamed that he lost his teeth, a common dream which is sometimes interpreted nowadays as a sign of insecurity.

Another important theme in Laud's dream is the Church, as one might have expected. For example: 'I dreamed that I put off my rochet, all save one sleeve; and when I would have put it on again, I could not find it.' The rochet was the bishop's surplice; here it's perhaps a symbol of the Church of England. Puritans at this time were attacking both bishops and surplices; and Laud was attacking Puritans. Yet in this dream we seem to catch him uncertain about what he is defending. Perhaps he was closer to the Puritans than he liked to admit; he wore his hair short like them, he believed in austerity and discipline like them, he came from a merchant background like many of them. Perhaps he had to persecute the Puritans to convince himself that he wasn't one of them.

Laud was also pulled in the opposite direction. He was often accused (by the Puritans) of being a 'papist' in disguise. The Catholic Church believed it too; Laud was twice, secretly, offered a cardinal's hat. More surprising still, Laud's unconscious seems to have held the same opinion; for he once dreamed that he was reconciled to the Church of Rome. In waking life, Laud maintained that he was a moderate, avoiding the twin extremes of Catholicism and Puritanism. Yet his methods weren't moderate;

it's as if only his methods could express his unconscious yearning for extremes.

Laud said at his trial in the House of Lords, 'by my diary your lordships have seen the passion of my life: and by my prayer book the greatest secrets between God and my soul; so that you may be sure you have me at the very bottom.'

I am not sure what is the significance of all this material. I don't want to exaggerate it. And yet a basic pattern does seem to emerge. That of an aggressive and insecure man, aggressive partly because insecure; a man who stresses unity because he is internally divided; who uses ritual as a defence against his anxieties. One might have guessed that Laud felt insecure without his dreams; for he was of low birth and low stature. But it's one thing to expect a man to feel insecure; you're on firmer ground when you see this insecurity expressing itself through the dreams. It's easier to understand why Laud wouldn't compromise, after seeing what his policy meant to him in psychological terms. He couldn't compromise, because he made success a test of his personal worth, as insecure men often do.

At this point you may well ask how much Laud's insecurity has to do with the English Revolution (or, for that matter, how much Luther's anality has to do with the Reformation). No more (and no less) than great men have to do with great events. There's an irony here; psychoanalysis (seen as a tool for historians) was a tool which arrived at the wrong time. In 1900, historians were just beginning to abandon the view that the private lives of great men were the key to history; they were beginning to emphasise structural factors. To use the new psychological approach seems to commit one to an old way of writing history; to give the new answers you have to ask old questions.

But it may be possible to use psychological approaches to study groups as well as individuals. Let's go back for a moment to the French psychologist Gustave Lebon, and his criticism of the historians of his day for their rational interpretations of the French Revolution. He suggested that the behaviour of men in crowds and assemblies (then as always) was different from their normal behaviour; they went to extremes of violence and cowardice, they were insolent to the weak and servile to the strong. Certain emotions were encouraged by the revolution, among them hate, fear, ambition, jealousy, vanity, enthusiasm.

These ideas were taken up by the great French historian George Lefebvre. He was much more cautious, much more precise. He distinguished different kinds of crowds and groups. He put rather more emphasis on the importance of individuals and of conscious decisions. But like Lebon, he was very much concerned with what he called 'collective mind'—*mentalité collective*. In another book Lefebvre studies the famous phenomenon of the *Grand Peur*; the rumour spread through France in the summer of 1789—the brigands are coming, the brigands are coming. But the brigands weren't coming; the rumour was a collective hallucination. Lefebvre carefully draws maps of the spread of the 'great fear', and relates it to the progressive distortion of news from Paris about an aristocratic plot; but he also sees the fear as the crystallisation of unconscious collective anxieties, about hunger and vagabonds and so on.

Lefebvre's book is some 35 years old. In the last few years, there's been much more interest in the psychology of social movements: in millenarianism, for example, or antisemitism. Professor Norman Cohn, for example, looks at the ideas expressed in social movements as shared fantasies which can be analysed in the way that the dreams of individuals can be analysed. These fantasies often seem to be paranoid; the Brethren of the Free Spirit in the 15th century, Nazism in the 20th century. This isn't to say that all the individual members of the group were paranoiacs, mentally ill; but that as a group they behaved like paranoiacs. It's difficult to know quite what to make of these metaphors; dreams which aren't dreams, paranoiacs who aren't paranoiacs. But what's the alternative? Historians did not discuss these questions before; the content of collective fantasies had been dismissed as being of little interest—like the dreams of emperors and archbishops. So this approach, like the psycho-historical approach to Luther, is reclaiming something human for history; suggesting that there may be a pattern where no pattern had previously been seen. I don't doubt that in 50 years time, all our present psycho-historical explanations will seem old, superficial, confused; and at the same time, I'm convinced that all historians have to move in this direction if they want to understand their own subject, human behaviour.

II—Chairs, Mirrors and Autobiographies

I have suggested that psycho-history—the history of the unconscious and irrational—is necessary, and that it is possible. Necessary—historians need to be concerned with the irrational if they're going to understand their own subject. Possible—historians really can find something out about the unconscious lives of individuals and groups, still using conventional historical sources, but asking new questions, questions like the questions asked by psychoanalysts and social psychologists.

But there's a big difference between historians and psychologists. Historians are not studying contemporary society, so they can't take the social context for granted. Freud's essay on Leonardo, the famous one, shows what goes wrong if you do. Freud noticed that Leonardo's painting of the Madonna and St Anne showed Anne and Mary, the mother and the daughter, as women of equal age. It seemed odd. Freud's explanation was that there had been two young women in Leonardo's infant life; his mother and his father's wife (Leonardo, of course, was illegitimate). But it's been pointed out that showing Anne and Mary as women of more or less the same age, was in fact, a 15th-century convention. If you give a psychological explanation of that convention, you've got to give it in terms of social psychology.

So Freud's mistake leads to an important conclusion. Not just the point that people who write biographies need to do their homework on the historical background; but also that the irrational has its own history, that there is such a thing as psychological anachronism. It's just as big a mistake to attribute to an Elizabethan motives exactly like ours, as it is to imagine him dressed in modern clothes instead of a doublet and hose. I think that's an exciting conclusion but a rather daunting one. It opens up a field of research, fascinating and difficult. For example it looks as if we should be able to have a history of madness; as if people suffer from different mental illnesses, or different forms of them, in different periods. A Dutch doctor-historian said recently that we shouldn't take of neuroses but of 'socioses', since what causes them is not 'the nerves' but social tensions. And social tensions have a history.

I don't think many historians share this view at the moment. But it's rather like the view of some modern anthropologists. In recent years a whole new subject—psychological anthropology— has developed. And it's concerned with the extent to which men in different cultures dream different sorts of dream, and rear their children in different ways, and suffer from different mental illnesses.

This view runs counter to the classic historians' view, put forward by Thucydides, by Montesquieu, by Gibbon, that human nature is always the same. David Hume made the point as explicitly as you could wish. He says: 'Would you know the sentiments, inclinations, course of life of the Greeks and Romans? Study well the temper and actions of the French and English; you cannot be much mistaken in transferring to the former most of the observations you have made in regard to the latter. Mankind are so much the same, in all times and places, that history informs us of nothing new or strange in this particular.' In the 19th century, this classic view began to be questioned, to be rejected. The Danish historian, Niebuhr, criticised Montesquieu for exactly this 'transferring' of sentiments and inclinations; for presenting the ancient Romans as if they were 18th-century Frenchmen. At much the same time as Niebuhr came the historical novels of Scott and Manzoni, and they show an awareness of psychological anachronism and try not to modernise the psychology of their characters. Yet in general, in the last 150 years or so, historians have been a bit slow to follow the example of the historical novelists. Nietzsche lamented in 1882: 'So far, everything that has given colour to existence still lacks a history. Where could one find a history of love, of avarice, of envy, of conscience, of piety, of cruelty?' Nearly 60 years later, the French historian Lucien Febvre echoed him almost exactly: 'We have no history of love. We have no history of death. We have neither the history of compassion nor of cruelty. We have no history of joy.'

In fact, these criticisms are a bit unfair. As Nietzsche must have known, his friend Jacob Burckhardt had published, in 1860, a book on the civilisation of the Renaissance in Italy, which discussed topics like self-conciousness, the sense of fame, the sense of ridicule (related to envy, surely?), morality and immorality (which included conscience and cruelty). Again, as Febvre knew (because he reviewed it) in 1919 the Dutch historian Johan Huizinga published the book we know in English as *The Waning of the Middle Ages*. In this book, Huizinga studied the collective psychology of the 14th and 15th centuries as it revealed itself through literature and art. He remarked, for example, on the irritability, the 'facility of emotions' of the men of his period in France and the Netherlands, of what he called the 'perpetual oscillation between despair and distracted joy, between cruelty and pious tenderness which characterises life'. More recently, Lucien Febvre was working on a study of the 16th-century Frenchman, which was completed by his disciple Robert Mandrou. One of the leading points Febvre and Mandrou make is that the Frenchman of the 16th century was much less of a visualist than the Frenchman of the 20th century, that hearing and smell were much more important for the 16th-century man.

Well then, there really are some general studies of historical psychology; studies of Europe in the 15th and 16th centuries. Serious criticisms have been and can be made of all of them. One of the most serious is the objection that these writers all seem to suggest that only in their area and their period did men behave in these particular ways, whereas this is not the case. Huizinga criticised Burckhardt because he exaggerated the distance separating Italy from the Netherlands and from France, and the Renaissance from the Middle Ages. Febvre in his turn criticised Huizinga for suggesting that violent emotional contrasts were specially late medieval, and argued that the 16th century was also a time of emotional oscillations. Mandrou has also been criticised because in his book it is difficult to see what is specially French or what is specially 16th-century. He emphasises contrasts between France then and France now—but similar contrasts can be between modern urban industrial societies on the one hand, and traditional rural agricultural societies on the other.

What these criticisms suggest is that the defects of the books I've mentioned are the defects of pioneers. What we need is more history of this kind; a psycho-history of Western man from Homeric times to the present. I wonder how much of this we will have by the end of the century. Such a general history would have to discuss questions like these. Was the 3rd century A.D. an 'age of anxiety'? Was romantic love invented in 12th-century France? Did Victorian Englishmen have a mother-fixation? Contributions to all these historical problems have, in fact, been made in the last few years, although I think it's fair to say that many historians are somewhat suspicious of the whole subject.

Of course, there's some reason for suspicion. If historians, unlike novelists, have so far taken relatively little account of psychological anachronism, this is to some extent because they didn't want to write historical novels under another name; they wanted evidence. The problem is that all evidence is evidence of something; that is, you have to formulate a question before some relic of the past becomes evidence, becomes relevant to the answer. But then you can't ask new questions without new concepts. There's a sort of conceptual bottleneck in this field. To break out we need to borrow concepts, as historians have often done; in this case, from social psychology. For example, the concept of 'social character', meaning by this that part of character which a man shares with other members of his society, or of some social group within it; a refinement of the old concept of national character. Historians have often used the concept of national character, but usually as a sort of joker in their explanatory pack, brought in to explain something when other attempts have failed. If they follow the social psychologists, historians will see national character not as a solution but as a problem, some-thing to be defined by comparative study, to be related to the social environment, to be seen changing over time.

In the study of social character, there are a number of concepts being used which may be useful to historians. For example, there's the distinction between 'shame culture' and 'guilt culture'; that is, between societies which rely on public shaming as a means of ensuring conformity and societies which rely on a private sense of guilt. Professor E. R. Dodds has applied this distinction to Greek history and suggested that a transition from shame culture to guilt culture did take place in archaic Greece. Again, David Riesman has brilliantly discussed the changing American social character in terms of a transition from what he calls the 'tradition-directed' personality-type (which corresponds to the shame culture) to the 'inner-directed' type (which cor-responds to the guilt culture); and then he has added a third concept and spoken of the rise of the 'other-directed' type, the contemporary American, whose guide is neither tradition nor inner light but the people around him, who conforms neither out of a sense of shame nor a sense of guilt but out of a diffused sense of anxiety: the typical member of the 'lonely crowd'. Other concepts which have become established in the field of social psychology and might profitably be put to work by the historian include 'anomie' and the 'authoritarian personality'. Anomie is a state of 'normlessness' in individuals and groups. Behaviour as if there are no rules, no constraints, no limits on what one may or may not do. It may well be that Huizinga's 'waning' Middle Ages should be characterised as an age of anomie, and that modern discussions of the social background of anomie would suggest useful lines of research into why it should be in the 15th century that men were like this. Again, the authoritarian personality, rigid and repressed, conventional and compulsive, a man like William Laud, is a social type, created or encouraged by a certain strict style of bringing up children.

Of course, it's difficult to guess which concepts are going to be the fruitful ones before the research is undertaken. So I should like to end by looking at some examples, at particular changes in the social psychology of Europeans in the 15th, 16th and 17th centuries. I shall try to put concepts next to examples, in the hope that some trends may emerge. Let's look at three possible changes or shifts; from group to individual, from spontaneity to control, and from the ear to the eye.

The first shift might be called 'Burckhardt's shift': the rise of individualism, which, according to Burckhardt, occurred in Italy at the Renaissance. The trouble with the idea of individualism is that it is so vague. It can mean self-consciousness; competitiveness; freedom; isolation; uniqueness. I think that it was the self-consciousness and the competitiveness of Renaissance men that Burckhardt wanted to stress most. He may well be making the same points in different words as David Riesman was making with his concept of 'inner-direction'. The Renaissance would mark a shift from tradition-direction to inner-direction. What is the evidence? On the self-consciousness side, there's plenty; the rise of the autobiography and the biography, the portrait and the self-portrait; the habit of signing works of art more often; perhaps even the increased use of chairs, as opposed to communal benches, and mirrors. Competitive individualism is a more difficult subject. I don't doubt that one can find a great deal of competitive behaviour in Renaissance Italy; the difficulty is that of being sure that there was not as much in the Middle Ages. Yet it is interesting to see how competitiveness in schools was encouraged during the 16th century, especially by the Jesuits: the modern system of points and houses and school plays and prize-givings starts with them. In the same 16th century, economic competitiveness seems to have become respectable; a virtue, not a vice. Further than this it is difficult to go; although a team of American social psychologists have recently tried to measure the desire for achievement (surely related to competitive individualism) by counting what they call the 'achievement images' in literature. They have looked at ancient Greece, medieval Spain, Renaissance England, and concluded that a rise in the 'achievement imagery' in a national literature is followed (at a 50-year interval) by a rise

in economic growth. I have some doubts about their approach—
it's difficult, for example, to decide just what counts as an achievement image. But the study of changing patterns of imagery as
evidence of changing social character looks as if it may be a
promising field for historians in future.

The second shift might be called 'Weber's shift'. This is
spontaneity to control. I can't say 'self-control' because I mean
control over the self, but not necessarily control by the self. From
spontaneity to discipline might be a better phrase. I call it 'Weber's
shift' because a considerable part of his famous book on the
Protestant ethic and the spirit of capitalism is about this change;
Weber was concerned with the effect of feelings, as well as the
effect of ideas, on economic behaviour. He suggested that the
Benedictine and Cistercian monks developed a systematic method
of rational conduct, of control over irrational impulses. In the
16th century, this 'rationalisation of life' (as Karl Mannheim
called it) spread more widely and became secularised. Perhaps it
was a necessary condition of the rise of capitalism.

Weber's thesis is one of the most famous historical theses of the
century. It is usually criticised for being too wide; but so far as its
psycho-historical side is concerned, it may be useful to widen it
still further. For example, to bring in the 14th century. Historians
of the later 14th century, working on England or on Italy, have
found themselves talking of a rise of 'puritanism'. There is a
shift, expressed in sermons and paintings alike, from the love of
God to the fear of God. There is a distrust of the body; a stress on
repression, on discipline. Why the late 14th century? It seems
plausible to relate this change to the Black Death, that sudden
disaster in which a third of the people of Europe died. The
disaster made people feel guilty. At the time, men said that the
plague was God's punishment for their sins. A modern psychologist might say (as one, Robert Lipton, has said about the survivors of another disaster, Hiroshima) that what people really
feel guilty about is surviving when others die. At all events, 14th-
century puritanism may be a reaction to a sense of guilt induced
by the plague. Not the only reaction. The unstable, 'anomic'

behaviour described by Huizinga may well have been another one.

In the 16th century, Catholics and Protestants developed control further and spread it further. The aim of Ignatius Loyola's Spiritual Exercises was, he said, self-control. Calvin described discipline as the nerves of religion. Calvinist discipline was all the more significant because it was family discipline, and so affected the way in which childern were reared.

In the 16th and 17th centuries, there was a rise of self-control expressed in secular ways too. In courtly circles, noble behaviour was associated a little less with fighting, and a little more with good manners. There is a rise of courtesy-literature, which includes advice to the reader not to scratch or yawn in public, not to relieve himself while others are looking on, not to smell someone else's food or wine, not to offer him an apple out of which one has already taken a bite, not to make pellets of bread and throw them at other courtiers at table; in a word, self-control. The fork and the handkerchief, which began to be regularly used by the upper classes in the 16th and 17th centuries, may be seen as mechanical agents for spreading the self-control recommended in the courtesy books. Another kind of self-control is that practised by the merchant; deferred gratification, thrift. This too seems to spread. So does school discipline. I wonder: has there been a steady rise of control in Western Europe from 1350 to the present, or have there been what one might call 'tender' or 'laxist' reversals?

The third problem might be called that of 'Febvre's shift' from the oral to the visual. In a famous book on Rabelais, Febvre discussed the relative unimportance of the sense of sight in the 16th century. He suggested for example that Ronsard's images are frequently images of sound and smell, or again, that it's significant that geometry had not developed in the 16th century. Mandrou has added other examples: the importance of having the king's 'ear' in the 16th century (rather than catching his eye); the fact that Luther called the ears the only organs of a Christian man, because: 'The bread we see with our eyes, but we hear with our ears that Christ's body is present.' The thesis is a fascinating one, which can be extended in time so that the 15th, 16th and 17th centuries are seen as the period of shift from oral to visual, first in Italy, then elsewhere in Europe. The invention of printing and the consequent extension of literacy were important in the shift (as Marshall McLuhan keeps saying); but before printing was invented, there was already a new awareness of space in 15th-century Florence, and a spread of enthusiasm for landscape in 15th-century Italy.

The evidence seems overwhelming—until one stops to think of counter-examples. One catches oneself saying that the Middle Ages were visual ages. The frescoes in the Church were the poor man's Bible; so was the stained glass; so was the sculpture on the west fronts of cathedrals. The 15th-century Franciscan Luca Pacioli and his friend Leonardo argued that the eye was nobler and more important for knowledge than the ear. It looks almost as if the 16th century was a period of the decline of the visual, not its rise, with Luther stressing the ear as the only organ of the Christian man and Calvinists smashing images.

In fact, I think that the 'rise of the visual' is one of those dangerous half-truths like 'the rise of the middle class'. The simple formula needs to be translated into a number of more precise statements; about changes in picture space, or about the shift from concrete imagery to abstractions (which covers the trend from shop signs to numbered houses in the 17th century; the rise of geometry; and the trend from stained-glass windows to a printed Bible).

But my real point is not to support Febvre or attack him; simply to suggest that the rise of the visual has joined the rise of the middle class or the rise of democracy as a proper subject for historical research and controversy. We have moved a long way from the irrational in Martin Luther or the French Revolution. An approach which grew out of dissatisfaction with existing answers to old questions has now developed questions—and even fields—of its own.

John Donat

LIVING IN GLASS HOUSES

John Donat is an architect who now specialises in photo-
graphing, writing about and broadcasting about architecture. He edited the annual review *World Architecture*
for four years.

WINDOW CLEANING MUST surely be one of the most secure
jobs in the 20th century. I suppose most of think of windows as
fairly simple devices to let light in, to let us look out and to
protect us from the elements. But the French architect Le Cor-
busier went so far as to say that 'the history of modern architecture is the history of the struggle for the window', and the
American architect, Frank Lloyd Wright, said: 'The greatest
eventual difference between ancient and modern buildings will
be due to modern machine-made glass.'

In 1914, Paul Scheerbart, an expressionist poet and science-
fiction novelist, predicted an architectural paradise of glass in
his book *Glasarchitektur*: 'Glass brings us the new age.' He imagined buildings with walls, floors, ceilings and stairs all made of
glass. Arthur Korn in his book about glass in building, published
in the Twenties, also talks about a new world of glass: 'The
window is the wall, the wall is the window'. He endows glass
with almost metaphysical qualities: 'It is there and it is not there.
It is the great mystery membrane, delicate and strong at the same
time.'

The glass dream was a dream of infinite space dissolving the
traditional boundaries between inside and outside; a dream of

sheer glass towers insubstantially composed of ambiguous transparencies and reflections, of sheer walls invisibly suspended in the thin air, brilliant by day, glowing like a jewel by night.

Another architect—Saarinen—said: 'Windows are like fireplaces, they're nice to have around, but rarely used for their original purpose.' As if to prove his point, he built a research centre which has a continuous wall of glass three storeys high and a thousand feet long—all it does is light a corridor, the laboratories behind haven't got any windows at all, they're artificially lit by fluorescent light, artificially heated, cooled and ventilated by air-conditioning.

Of course in many ways the glass dream has come true. Practically every city in the world has its complement of glass architecture. But the trouble was that as soon as the glass dream started to get built it transpired that extensive areas of glass created far more problems than they ever solved. Too much glass meant too much light, too much glare, too much heat, too much cold, too much noise, too much condensation and not nearly enough privacy. In fact, some rather extraordinary things began to happen. We can usually rely on the rain to come down vertically, but at the United Nations building in New York, that great tall slab of glass, they found that the wind striking the vertical faces of the building was blowing the water up, and of course all the windows were designed to throw off the rain as it came down. Rain coming up blew into the building, soaked everybody, and the whole thing had to be redesigned and all the detailing had to be altered. That building was a prototype for the classic matchbox of modern architecture. The classic matchbox building has one characteristic which is that it is the same all the way round. It bears no relation at all to the way the sun faces, so that you get colossal heating loads on the north and east faces (in the Northern hemisphere) and terrific cooling loads on the south and west. This problem reached an amusing extreme in an office building in Denver, Colorado. Because the country around is flat desert, one tends to assume that it's at sea level, but of course it is nothing of the kind—it's actually over 5,000 feet up. Some architects built a high office block. What happens at that altitude is that in the winter you get very high sun temperatures and very low air temperatures, so in the same building at the same time there was one side sub-tropical while the other side was sub-arctic. The air-conditioning had to cope with this simultaneous predicament.

Having created the problems, we then go on to create all kinds of inventions with which to solve them: air-conditioning, heat-absorbing tinted glass, the *brise-soleil* (an elaborate external sun-shade), Venetian blinds, double glazing and so on. The trouble is that too often we build glass buildings without benefit of the elaborate mechanical services they need to really work properly. These are what I call photographic buildings because they are built in imitation of photographs. They look exactly like their American counterparts in the magazines, but because they're not air-conditioned they can be sheer hell to work in.

Glass admits short-wave rays—the heating rays from the sun. These get absorbed by the furniture, wall surfaces and so on in the buildings and are then re-radiated as long waves which can't get out through the glass. This gives rise to what is neatly des-scribed as 'the greenhouse effect'. This particular effect on one building in England, a new town hall, was that the temperatures inside exceeded the permitted maximum in Her Majesty's ships of the Royal Navy in the Red Sea.

Of course it's often hard to distinguish between real problems and imaginary ones. When I was an architect in the LCC Schools Division, we used to receive lists of complaints from headmasters and teachers (my favourite one, which I suppose as architects we should have anticipated, was of gym-shoe marks on the ceilings). The most regular complaint was the charge that they fried in summer and froze in winter as a result of large areas of glass. In Nottinghamshire—justly famed for its new schools—they suffered similar complaints, but it became evident when they measured the room temperatures that they were exactly as calculated and exactly correct. What the teachers didn't like was that it was all done automatically and they had no control. So the architects suggested that if they fitted individual thermostats in each of the rooms, so that the teacher could control his own conditions, perhaps everything would be all right. The thermostats were fitted and the teachers found it a very satisfactory solution. I don't suppose anyone has ever pointed out that the thermostats were never wired up and had no effect on the system whatsoever—the problem was entirely an imaginary one.

Another example, from the UNESCO building in Paris. This has heat-absorbing glass screens which are suspended outside the windows at a special angle to absorb the heat from the high summer sun, but allow the low winter sun in—so you get a warming effect in winter, a cooling effect in summer. It only took one fantastically hot day in May—and everyone in the building nearly died. Heat gained from the sun is one problem with glass architecture, heat loss is another. Glass isn't much of an insulator in a single sheet, and most of the heat goes outside, as one lecturer used to tell us as students, 'to warm the birds'.

One of the beauties of glass is its transparency—then you have to stick horrid bits of tape all over it so that people realise it's there. I know of one chap who had seventeen stitches in his head after walking through his own glass front door. Then there was a hapless teenager who went flying through the window of our local supermarket—it cost him a bruised behind and cost the shopkeeper 135 quid just to replace one large window pane.

Then there's the problem of maintenance. Just imagine the cost of cleaning an all-glass building. At New Zealand House, the green glass tower next door to *The Fiddler on the Roof* in London, the architects came across another problem—vertigo—the problem of people feeling pretty dizzy standing next to big sheets of glass and looking vertically down. They solved it by projecting each floor-slab outside the building so that you can't look directly down, but one can't help thinking they'd have been better off by simply not creating the problem in the first place.

Glass also creates the problem of security—no problem to a burglar that a well-aimed brick won't solve—and of privacy. Philip Johnson's ineffably elegant all-glass house in New Caanan,

Connecticut, is marvellous if you own an acre or two of the Garden of Eden, not quite so appealing on a housing estate in Slough. Timothy Birdsall, who used to do marvellous freehand drawings with his own commentaries on television, did a beautiful little piece once called 'Picture Window House'; he started by just drawing a simple rectangle and said 'This is a picture window,' and he filled out the lines of perspective and you saw a lovely living room with the picture window at one end, and he put in some furniture, curtains, a few people, and then started drawing other little rectangles in the big rectangle and the commentary went something like this: 'And here's another picture window house, and here's another picture window house, and here's another picture window house, and here's another picture window house'—until the whole picture window was full. Someone once said: 'People really want houses with huge windows inside and tiny windows outside.' It's a pity Lewis Carroll wasn't an architect.

The need for privacy gives rise to the much-despised net curtain which diffuses light, reduces glare and improves privacy—but why create the problem in the first place? I remember one very beautiful new building at Cambridge University, a hall of residence for students which had lovely big glass windows opening out on to communal terraces. One of the students had put a sign up on his window saying, 'Do not feed this animal.'

As each problem arises, the glass manufacturers produce some ingenious new product with which to solve it. They have produced toughened glass that is extremely strong called armourplate. At a glass manufacturer's showroom (it may still be there) there was a staircase made of this glass. I don't know if you can imagine the horror of stepping on to treads of thin glass which actually bend under your weight as you go up, but it's that strong. Then they use tinted glass to absorb heat—the Corning Glass Building in Manhattan is covered with four and a half acres of it. Then they make darkened glass for ambulances so that you can't see in. There's the Bell Telephone building in America, 700 feet long, of one way mirror glass. Glass shatters in fire, so they've invented wired glass to hold it together. Double glazing was invented to conserve heat and reduce condensation. With a wide enough gap it's even quite good for sound insulation—but acoustically murderous, imagine an all glass music room. (I wonder what hi fi sounds like in Philip Johnson's house?) There's a special tinted glass, a vile yellow colour, developed for jam factories, abattoirs and dairies which is apparently loathed by flies— unfortunately it has much the same effect on people: it wrecks their eyes and is generally injurious to health.

The choice about when to use glass is obviously crucial. If you take a typical Middle Eastern town, made of mud bricks, with shady bazaars, narrow streets and tiny windows (if there are any windows at all), the whole thing is really a micro-climate control —the shade, narrow streets and high walls create equable climate conditions when the temperature outside is very high. Then some oil Sheikh flattens this micro-climate control, builds wide avenues, big glass office blocks fully air-conditioned, and he goes from his air-conditioned office in his air-conditioned American car over to his air-conditioned palace—while his wretched subjects are frying to death in the unprotected streets.

Air-conditioning is one of the clues, of course. Glass needs tremendous support from mechanical services really to function properly. In America now, half the cost of a new house goes to mechanical services and equipment. Every suburban house in America has its bulky air-conditioning units that stick out of the windows as though someone had tried to shove a chest of drawers through and got stuck half way.

There's no reason why the glass dream shouldn't become more and more fantastic, more and more true—providing we're prepared to spend a good deal of hard cash making sure the dream does come true and doesn't turn into a nightmare.

Richard Cobb

MAIGRET'S PARIS

Richard Cobb is a Fellow of Balliol College. His books include *Problems of French Popular History* and *A Second Identity*, and he is a Chevalier des Palmes Académiques.

THE BEST HISTORIAN of Paris, had he ever set his mind to it, would be the *afficheur*, the man who climbs his ladder to stick up, with the indifference of the technician, bill-posters, advertisements for patent medicines, announcements of public sales by auction, decrees of general mobilisation, electoral declarations and political denunciations, on the considerable amount of space still left available after the passing of a much repeated law of July 1889. The damp, leprous sides of Paris houses have, for at least two centuries, screamed with the strident history of the capital: red on black, black on yellow, black on white, blue on white, in butterfly variations of anger, denunciation, self-justification, promise, threat, command, information or cajolery. The pursuit of the Parisian cannot be confined only to the Archives and to the works of reference; he is to be followed, in two centuries of novels from Restif and Mercier, through Maupassant and Darien, to Charles-Louis Philippe, Dabit, Fallet, Guimard, Aragon, Sarrazin, Queneau and Simenon. And the Parisienne is to be followed further into the intimacy of her artifice in the popular weeklies: *Confidences, Pour Lire à Deux, Marie-France*, and to pin down the legendary Marie-Chantal, the rather inane middle-class girl from the XVIme, in *Elle* and the other fashion magazines. Literary sources, advertisements, parish magazines, the announcements of marriages displayed outside *mairies*, the popular press, are often far more informative than the official records; or, rather, they inform at a different level, and about different things.

Le 6 octobre, the first volume of the immense *Les hommes de bonne volonté*, opens with an evocation of the approach to the capital, as an express train runs screamingly through the leprous suburbs: the chaotic mass of villas of Villiers-le-Sec, the damp, black tenements of Aubervilliers and Pantin, capitals of tuberculosis, a green bus seen on a small square, a 30-foot face a greenishgrey, in high collar, staring out of the murk, the huge posters painted on the cut-off sides of steep houses: *Suze, le jambon Olida, Porto Antonat*, the approach to the Gare de l'Est. And, later, Romains describes the flux and reflux of the working population in the course of the day, from North-East, East, North-West, to the VIIIme, the Ier, the IXme, the Xme, more rarely to the VIme, the IIIme and the IVme. This was in 1906. But, even in 1969, the currents of movement have followed similar axes; the greatest mass comes from the eastern suburbs, the most frequented point of entry is the bus station at Vincennes, the line most in demand is Vincennes–Neuilly (East–West), though, thanks to the *autoroute du Sud* and the displacement of *les Halles* to Ris-Orangis, new channels of communication are beginning to emerge that break out of the contours fixed by Romains, by Dabit and by Simenon. The shop-girls and typists pour in from Saint-Denis, Aubervilliers and Pantin, to work on the Right Bank (VIIIme, IXme, Ier), bringing back in the evenings, with eyes awash with mascara, to the barrack-like wastes of their suburban communities, the civility, a little of the taste and a lot of the impudence of Paris: it is they who 'clean up' the young men who work in the factories on the spot. Nor does this moving population take the shortest possible route, whether by *Métro* or by bus, in order to conform to the iron laws of sociology or to the unimaginative dictates of the town-planner. Even the humblest of travellers under Paris or on the surface of Paris must be allowed an element of fantasy—some will change three times, in order to travel part of the way with a girl, some will make bizarre zigzags by bus, because they like a certain line or appreciate the wit of the *conducteur*, some will go out of their way in order to follow the quays of the Seine, others to fly through the air *Nation-Etoile*. The *Transports en Commun* mean what they say, they are not the tubes that used to be employed in drapers' shops to bring back one's change in three farthings, they are an exercise in sociability, meandering through an underground Tunnel of Love and surrealim (*Les Filles du Calvaire, Bolivar, Barbès-Rochechouart, Marcadet-Poissonnière, Reuilly-Diderot, Sèvres-Babylone, Corentin-Celton*—is there an underground system in the world that can boast such bizarre and evocative combinations?).

Between 5.30 and 7.30, the papers seen most frequently underground are *l'Humanité* and *le Parisien*. These are the hours too of caps, berets, leather jackets, breath strong with garlic, bouffant hair styles, flower ear-rings, *Pris-unic* scent; the handbags are not of real leather. At 7.45, *le Figaro* begins to make a timid appearance, by 8.30, it has swamped even the 2nd Class, and from 9 to 10 it holds the field, as clothes improve and the volume of traffic from the West to the Centre increases and that from the East to the Centre decreases. *L'Huma, le Parisien* travel in from the north and east; *le Figaro*, like Maoism, comes in from the west. Unlike any other paper, *le Figaro* is printed on the Champs-Elysées. *L'Aurore* tends rather to stay at home; it is the paper of the concierge and the small shop-keeper; it is much read too by publicans and by policemen (whom it flatters). It also has the best crime coverage and would, one suspects, be the favourite reading of Maigret, for the *commissaire* is out of harmony with the technocratic age and has little sympathy for high police officials or *juges d'instruction* in their forties or less and who have got up on written work. *Poujadisme* does not travel, it lurks in the dark recesses of small shops.

In Simenon too, people are always just leaving or just arriving, his reader right behind them, keyed up by the same excitement, curiosity and uneasiness with which these battered travellers get off or arrive at destinations most of which they have not previously known. It is good stuff to read, especially on departure, as the train, this time, gathers speed and Villeneuve-Saint-Georges careers by in a racing jumble of white and pylon, lending to each journey the satisfaction of ambience so well observed, of intimacies gradually, but completely, penetrated (each feminine character in this *littérature de l'arrivée* does not have to wait long before being subjected to a sort of moral strip-tease—in one case she does a physical one too, before ending up naked on the beach —carried out with clinical precision—the contents of the handbag, the *carte d'identité* stained with lip-stick, the battered suit-case containing a black bra and no nightdress—but not devoid of compassion, for most indeed have so little to carry, and that so pitiable, so soiled). His endless attraction, then, is his sensitive rendering of atmosphere, of the feeling of a locality, and the acuity of his social observation. He has both the eye of a detective and of a popular historian, and the concern for individual eccentricity that distinguishes him from the sociologist. He is so constantly, and so attractively, reminding one that history, too, should be walked, seen, smelt, eavesdropped, as well as read: the historian too, he seems to say, must go into the street, into the crowded restaurant to the central criminal courts, to the *correctionelles*, to the market, to the café beside the canal Saint-Martin, a favourite hunting-ground, to the jumble of marshalling yards beyond the Batignolles, to the backyards of semi-derelict workshops off the rue Saint-Charles, to the river ports of Bercy and Charenton, as well as to the library. He has a particular affection for the rue des Francs-Bourgeois, but it is not because the Archives Nationales are there—an archivist, not Simenon, is the author, under a pseudonym, of a detective story entitled *Crime aux Archives*—he may not even know they are there, but he does know that this part of the Marais used to be, still is to some extent, the centre for wholesale haberdashery, as well as the likeliest *point de chute* of the recently arrived orthodox Askhanazim, Polish- or Yiddish-speaking. The Marais, as it was before M. Malraux took over, washed its face, pulled down the clusters of hutments that encumbered the secret courtyards of semi-submerged *hôtels particuliers*, is very much part of the Maigret quadrilateral: rue des

Archives, rue de Turenne, place des Vosges, rue du Roi-de-Sicile, quartier Saint-Paul, rue Vieille-du-Temple; this is where he likes to place his lonely, secret, little people, because he knows that it is, or was, a *quartier de petites gens*. He is as fond of it as of Maubert-Mouffetard, the XIIme, or the café by the lock at Conflans or Joinville. His geography is completely unpredictable—and that is its attraction, both to Maigret, who dislikes desk work and is endlessly excited by the prospect of smelling out the ambience of a quarter never previously visited, or neglected for many years, and to the reader, who is thus taken well off the routes of any guide (even that of the *Paris mystérieux*) and to places well away from the centres of learning. For Maigret, although he can see the Pont-Saint-Michel from his office, seldom crosses it, keeps well away from the VIme, skirts the Vme at a safe distance from the Boul-Mich—one suspects that he rather dislikes students and *lycéens* and one admires his aesthetic judgment in thus always giving a wide berth to the place Saint-André-des-Arts and the rue de Rennes (even if he does live boulevard Richard-Lenoir) and is only briefly, and grumblingly, seen in the precincts of Saint-Germain. (If it is to be *boîtes*, he prefers Pigalle and the place Blanche.) Aware, very much aware, of Saint-Médard, he is not of most of the XIVme—he is not missing very much—but he has spotted the old carters' inns and the *restaurants des chauffeurs* (*boeuf gros-sel*, etc.) rue des Favorites, in the XVme. He has, on occasions, to penetrate the hostile steppes of the XVIme and the XVIIme, go up in voluminous but slow-moving lifts, climb up heavily carpeted stairs, even show his card to discreet, shocked *concierges*, boulevard Malesherbes, boulevard de Courcelles, but he is not happy there, not at least, until he can get away from the wide avenues into some side street, to find a small café, opposite a *boulangerie*. The Ternes is much more his style of things, and one can appreciate why the rue des Acacias, with its individual houses, might be in provincial France. Maigret is admirably selective in his omissions. Pigalle, the rue de Berri, the rue de Ponthieu, les Halles had to be in, but he manages very well without the Latin Quarter. And so can we.

The historian, at least, may well have been obliged to follow him to a place of work that he shares with the *commissaire*. And, if some of the regular customers of the historian are stowed away, in green boxes, at the top of the *Police Judiciaire*, 36, quai des Orfèvres, he should have an eye too for those who are there, in the flesh, hand-cuffed between two rugger-built inspectors, or sitting nervously on the green plush benches (there has been an improvement since Maigret's time) in the corridor, on the first four floors, as he climbs the steep, curving, rather dusty, staircase, in the wake of the puffing, short-breathed *commissaire*, for whom this climb is a daily exercise and represents, especially after an *enquête* involving an unusually heavy consumption of *ricard* or *calvados* (the drink will be appropriate to the milieu in which Maigret is temporarily involved, it is all part of 'putting oneself in the picture', of 'getting the feelings of things'), the rather alarming barometer of ageing ('Better say something to Pardon'; no wonder Maigret has already had one *cure* in Vichy!). For history is not only at the top, on the fifth floor, among the bombs and pistols and guillotine blades, alongside the fingerprint people, it is vertical too, so that the historian climbs through a sort of inverted order of crime and delinquency, mounting from murder and homicide, through embezzlement, to blackmail and counter-feiting. Perhaps, in fact, the order is purely the accident of a building bursting at the seams. But it is as much the job of the historian, as that of Maigret, to observe, and to explain, at least the changing pattern of clientèle in the *PJ*'s week, as seen from the corridors: Monday, *ces demoiselles*, a noisy, chattering, impudent, loud-mouthed, humorous chain-smoking, garish throng; Monday too is reception day for the hangers-on of that ancient trade: *souteneurs*, hotel-keepers, and so on. On Wednesday, it is the turn of the counterfeiters, *Section Financière*, while the summer season, that rarefies the usual presences in the hazy corridors, multiplies that of small, well-dressed lithe, professional-looking men, their dark hats on their knees: cat-burglars and house-breakers for whom the holidays of most represent the working season of the few. Murderers, male and female, in *crimes passionels*, may be seen emerging from the inspectors' rooms, hiding their eyes against the flash bulbs of the Press, very early in the morning or very late at night: they are not day birds. Elderly couples in black, dressed like provincial employees or in the ancient suits of peasants, in their Sunday best, are the parents of the assassins or the assassinated, they have come up by the night train. Saturday's haul will include young men in leather jackets, the uniform of the suburbs, who have invaded the city, on their strident, two-cylinder red motor bikes, and who, plying hilariously in gangs drawn from the same factory and the same barrack-like block of *HBM*, have been involved in punch-ups with middle-class students, in an effort to make pay night seem more memorable. Sunday is a quiet day in the *PJ*, but it is not for the *morgue*, the hours between 1 and 4 on Sunday morning being favoured by participants in *crimes passionnels*—infidelity is likeliest to be a weekend luxury, at least when found out, for there can be little check on the 2 to 4 p.m. variety—even murder takes time and has to be fitted into leisure—and, for exactly opposite reasons, suicide will favour the same night hours of the beginning of the weekend, for that is the time when lonely people will feel loneliest.

Maigret's *enquêtes* have brought him, too, an intimate, and perhaps, dangerous, because too intimate, awareness, of another calendar, one that marks the hours, rather than the days, like that of the *transports en commun*. For he at once has an eye—and we with him—for the *gros Auvergnat*, standing, in his blouse, washing out glasses, as well as for his customers, as they succeed one another during the day and, near les Halles, porte de la Villette, rue Brançion, during the night: the 7.45 employees, *pousse-café*, the nine o'clock painters, building workers, *vitriers*, in their white smocks and paper hats—*un petit blanc sec*—the eleven o'clock *commis voyageurs*, *représentants*—*un petit blanc sec*—the midday to one rush of *ricard*, *pernod*, *chablis*, *beaujolais*, the afternoon solitary *marc* or *calvados*, the furtive *martini sec* offered by the customer, *après consommation* in a neighbouring hotel room, to the prostitute, who has time on her hands, 4 p.m.; the six o'clock rush, the

apéritif regiment, the evening card players, the solitary 3 a.m. on
repeated *marcs*, the Sunday morning queues at the *PMU*, the *gros
rouge* of the all-night horse slaughterers. It is a drinker's day, as
complete as that described, nearly 200 years earlier, by Mercier.

To savour the sharp, irreverent humour of the Parisian, the
popular historian should take up position on the open platform
of a bus, between a policeman and a man leaning heavily on the
rail, with a cigarette stuck to his lower lip. The most irrepressible
humorist of all is the conductor, but he is only to be found on
certain routes, most commonly those that take in a maximum
number of hospitals, cemeteries and prisons (the 75 is especially to
be recommended). Conductors who ply on lines between stations,
shopping centres, the quarters of entertainment and vice, the
Ecole Militaire, the Invalides and the boulevard Malesherbes are
tight-lipped, surly and melancholy; but the sight of the Palais de
Justice, which is a bus stop, will nearly always inspire an outburst
of ironical humour. When he had the time, this was Maigret's
favourite method of travel, especially after a good lunch.

Simenon is a teacher as well as an entertainer and an observer.
Maigret is a historian of habit, of the *déjà vu*; like any good
policeman, he is a historian of the predictable, and, even in the
1940s and 1950s, one still feels that he is an observer of the 1930s,
whether in Paris or the provinces. He is a historian too because he
has a sense of ambience and of period, can in fact convey the *taste*
of a period, by describing a building or by listening to a street
band or to the eloquence of a street salesman, can convey a season
by the colour of the sky.

He is also a historian of class. He is at once at home with the concierge (as befits a policeman) with whom he is so much in accor-
dance, as his own father was a gamekeeper and thus likewise a
faithful retainer of the well-to-do and the high-born. He is
basically loyal; he has much in common with the bank clerk, the
shop-keeper, with the young provincial semi-failure in the Paris
setting (so many of his books are about frustrated ambition, or
about disillusionment with ambition too easily satisfied, so many
of his characters are *demi-ratés*, in the economic, social or sexual

stakes). He is also at home with the middle ranges of regular crime, though some of his criminals are so petit-bourgeois as to be scarcely credible. He himself has petit-bourgeois values that have been grafted on to a peasant sagacity and prudence: like so many Parisians, he still has mud on his boots, dreams of retiring to the country and wishes to be buried in the village churchyard of his birthplace. He is not wholly a townsman, still something of a peasant, he can smell the impending shower, he is like the Breton greengrocer next to the Maine-Montparnasse conurbation, an elderly lady who states that it will be wet tomorrow, because the martins are flying high. Maigret is in fact so very much the archetypal Parisian of the 18th, 19th, and 20th centuries, still half a countryman, with rural values, still carrying the native province with him in the Paris streets, still making collective judgments on people in virtue of their provincial origin: Auvergnats are dour, careful, tribal, ambitious, rather mean, Bretons are tribal too, they intermarry, they drink too much, are violent, and think constantly of their province, Picards are strong, brave and straightforward, Ardennais make good soldiers, Lorrains are pig-headed, Marseillais boastful and unreliable, and so on. It is, of course, a brilliant stroke to have Maigret live on boulevard Richard-Lenoir, in the XIIme.

It is all an entirely predictable world. Weekends are spent eternally fishing on the Marne, newspaper tycoons have mistresses called Nadine, doctors sleep with their nurses, the *Théâtre du Palais-Royal* prospers—the old plot: lover, caught without trousers, hides under the bed or in the wardrobe, those who meet regularly *chez Véfour* become *Académiciens* (Simenon is very impressed by the *Académie*), all the successful have mill-houses, *manoirs*, tastefully converted, in the Yonne, the Brie or the Beauce, and the scope of the Paris weekend can still be circumscribed within the limits of mid-1930 transport, that of mid-week Paris infidelity to the odd night in the *auberge* within a thirty kilometre radius: Houdan, la Ferté-Allais, Saint Nom, or, more modestly, Joinville-le-Pont. Maigret is pre-Sagan, pre-Godard; if he were to tackle England, he would locate the dirty weekend at

Maidenhead. It all forms a whole with the *contrôleur des wagon-lits*, Paul Morand, Deauville-Trouville, the Hispano, scandal in high places, a worried, badgered police. Simenon's favourite actor is, predictably, Jean Gabin. We are stuck eternally in the Third Republic. This is why Simenon is so reassuring to people of a certain generation. It is a cosy, slippered world. The *patron*, in his blue overalls, standing behind his aluminium bar, breathes heavily over the glasses as he wipes them with the corner of his apron, something funny is always going on in the little café by the canal lock, *truands* head for discreet *guingettes* on the Marne, to plan operations or to lie low, boxers past their prime take to running bars in the neighbourhood of the Champs-Elysées, their wives, one-time strippers, have gone to fat, go in for blue rinses and are excellent cooks. Simenon, like Eugène Sue, has the secret of eternal youth; both are profoundly counter-revolutionary writers. Sue canalised popular violence into myth, Maigret explains away youthful revolt in pipe-puffing, paternalistic terms, an invisible tear in his eye, for he *knows*, while he waits for the inevitable eventual blubbering breakdown of the young man who, for hours, has been fighting so hard to keep it all back; it has to come out in the end.

Maigret is then perhaps a bad social historian in so far as social history is the awareness of change as well as of continuity. But he is a very good popular historian in so far as popular history is the observation of habit, routine, assumption, banality, everydayness, seasonability, popular conservatism, especially in leisure, eating habits and in clothing, the pattern of the week, that of the weekend, that of the *grandes vacances* (how he loves the empty Paris of mid-August, but how he curses, like any *aôutien*, the fact that virtually every *crêmerie*, every *boulangerie* is shut!); he thinks nostalgically of a quiet, shady green spot down by the Loire, but he never goes; he is always about to retire, but he never retires. He knows about the importance of weekends in terms of human relationships, particularly at the lower middle class level; he knows that holiday or weekend connections can be as important, as close, and as permanent as those of trade, profession or quarter. He knows that shopkeepers take their weekly day-off on Monday, and Museum attendants on Tuesday. He knows that people from the North of France—Lille–Roubaix–Tourcoing—tend to live near la Trinité, huddling together, that Bretons, and more generally those from the West, seldom move far beyond the vicinity of Maine-Montparnasse, the rue du Départ, the rue de l'Arrivée and the rue de l'Ouest, the old stamping ground of Bubu and of poor Bécasine, once she has fallen and been recruited into the trade; he knows that young men from Nantes crowd together in hotels off the rue Tournefort, that the poorer sort of White Russians live in the XVme and the richer ones near the rue Daru, that cafés frequented by Belgians are to be found round the Gare du Nord and on the quays, the Walloons going to the former, Flemish bargees to the latter (there used to be one quai des Grands Augustines, opposite Maigret's window), He has noticed that cafés are particularly numerous opposite the entrance to cemeteries and prisons, that these are most commonly called *On est mieux qu'en face*, that undertakers' assistants have red faces, are noisily joyous and drink a lot, that waiters are the best authorities on horses and that they habitually suffer from fallen arches. He ought to know that bus conductresses on the *RATP* are frequently married to the drivers of the buses on which they serve, and that, when this is not the case, it is very likely to be in the near future; any bus dépôt will see the driver climbing down on to the mud-guard from his high seat and walking off arm in arm with the conductress, once she has handed in her harness; and, *en cours de route*, there are frequent conversations through the little partition behind the driver's seat, mostly about the behaviour of difficult female passengers. If he wants schoolboy humour and rumbustious horseplay, he has only to head for the restaurant frequented by the Professors of Medicine, a noisy, back-slapping lot, with the stupendous appetite of the fatstock farmers, wholesalers butchers and slaughterers of la Villette. If he wants to be publicly insulted by the *patron*, made a fool of, there are plenty of rather expensive restaurants that provide this additional service; such places are much appreciated by the young married technocrat and the provincial businessman, both of whom feel that being insulted by a *traiteur* qualifies one for recognition as a full-blown Parisien.

Immediately after the Liberation, the *Puces* at Saint-Ouen were still a source of social history, literally on the ground, the wretched soiled intimacies of three or four generations of Parisians, mostly petit-bourgeois, mostly too of provincial origin, an enormous, chaotic, fascinating rubbish-heap of bad taste and bizarre designs, broken telephones with swivel devices, plates representing the Allies in the Crimea or the newer alignments of 1914, chamber pots with an eye in the bottom, busts of Poincaré and the King of the Belgians, faded wedding photographs, the *poilu* of 1914, still in blue tunic and red trousers, seated against a photographic backcloth—a well, a trellis of roses, or his torso poking out of a grotesque aeroplane—seamstresses' models, the heads, legs, arms and dismembered torsos of shop window dummies, the *bicornes* of Polytechniens, the pointed helmets of the Kaiser's army, kilometres of bric-à-brac, a maze of steak and chip cafés in hut-like structures, accordion orchestras, the confused encampments of an Asiatic besieging army, fences, junk merchants, rag and bone men, the poor *secrets d'alcôve* of the 1900 shop-keeper, of the 1913 petit bourgeois, derisory obscenities of the Belle Epoque (A Night in Paris, La Dame des Wagon-Lits), a shattering, scattered litter of raped intimacies, like the wallpaper of bombed houses, like the mass of heterogeneous objects thrown up as by an insane hand by the impact of a V-1 around the remains of an Anderson shelter, in a back-garden in Wapping: hair clips, love letters on lilac paper, picture postcards (Having a Lovely Time in Brighton), an artificial silk stocking—it was still rationing—with a leg inside it, cut off at the thigh, a Dali-like rubble. Then, in the 1940s the *Puces* were still the physical archives of social history, the music was still that of the *bal-musette*, of the *java* of the Twenties and Thirties. Later, 'tourism' came that way too, spontaneity withered overnight, and the Porte Saint-Ouen went the same way as Montmartre with its pseudo-artists or the place de l'Estrapade with its American intellectuals, come to Paris to write the novels they never will, and huddling together, as in Hemingway's time, to keep out the French.

From Maigret we can learn thus of habit, of predictability, as well as of insecurity. The Parisian, both in Simenon and in real life, is an elusive being, hard to define in terms of place of birth. Paris might, after the Second Empire, make fun of the southern accent, mock the gawky Auvergnat or the unlicked Lyonnais who put on black sleeves to protect his jacket, generalise about the alleged greed of Normans, laugh at the way Belgians spoke French, and refer to the simplicity of Breton girls. Such attitudes would often conceal the fact that the mockers themselves were of southern descent, had Auvergnat parents, had only recently arrived from Lyon, or, like *Bel-Ami*, from Rouen, had, on arrival, gone to the Hôtel des Nantais, reassured as they were meant to be.

Even today there is no one more energetically Parisian than the young man who is making his way in the city, ensconced in those little tribal corners of *pays* that, time and again, in the course of his investigations, Maigret succeeds in revealing, tiny ant-heaps hidden from the passing eye, the family relationships of which, a whole network between Paris and the native village, the attentive *commissaire* has managed to unravel. When Gaby, or Marcelle, or Dédée or Micheline is found murdered, in a maid's bedroom in the XVIme, she is likely to have come from Narbonne, or Pézenas, la Rochelle, Roubaix, Quimper, Douai or Moulins, rather than from Pantin or Vanves-Malakoff.

Simenon is right to have made so much of the girl with the fibre suitcase as she nervously feels her way through a Paris terminal. He is a novelist of loneliness and alienation, of the process of urbanisation in individual terms. If he has no deep understanding of individual conduct, like any good provincial observer he can perceive the hidden network of groups, by quarter, by trade, by common provincial origin, by shared weekend habits, by the yearly exodus of the *grandes vacances*, by the national origins of certain skills, by the chance encounter of a baptism or a funeral, by the complicated genealogies of in-lawry.

Few writers could be more aware of the family; he is a 20th-century Physiocrate who implies that the country boy should have stayed at home and that the *petite Moulinoise*, if only she had listened to her mother instead of doing a bolt up to Paris, would have come to no harm. His books are full of matriarchal figures, and most of those who come to a violent end, are disgraced, abused, mocked or ruined, have stepped out of the family unit. The ties of family are so persistent that, after an absence of nearly 30 years, *la Tante* suddenly re-emerges, to take over what is left of a sinking ship. Perhaps what is most depressing, most petit-bourgeois about Simenon is this insistent presence of aunts, cousins, sisters-in-law and grandparents. It is much the same with Dabit's *banlieuesards*, with Chevalier's *métallos*, as well as with Simenon's admirable illustration of the family basis of the restaurant trade and of all those concerned with les Halles.

Much of what he sees and writes is already an evocation of the past, but so long as Maigret is with us—and we cannot let him retire, much less die—there is still hope for the *pêcheur à la ligne*, for the Sunday painter, for those who like to drink standing up at the counter, for those who seek simple, modest, harmless enjoyments, for those who like to sit on park benches, for those who can smell spring in the air, for those who, like Maigret, are descendants of the proverbial Parisian *badaud* and who are inquisitive about small things. So ultimately our debt to Simenon is not only as an unconscious historian, but as a poet of a world of fraternity and simplicity already almost submerged, and remembered with nostalgic affection, the uncomplicated world of *le Grand Bob* and of so many other weekenders on the Marne.

Patricia de Berker

OEDIPUS AND THE FORSYTES

Patricia de Berker was until recently the honorary organising secretary of the Association of Psychotherapists.
Here she casts a psychoanalytic eye on those surprising
new folk-heroes, the Forsyte family, and on their creator
John Galsworthy.

'THE FORSYTE SAGA' offers a set of variations on the theme of
how to cope with an unresolved Oedipus complex. Galsworthy
is wrestling with his own confusion between the sexual and the
maternal woman. All this takes place without his being in the
least aware of it, and all the more tellingly for that. Let us take a
closer look at Irene Forsyte, her loves and her hates. To me she
is the only woman who really comes alive in the Saga. Perhaps
she was the only one who came alive for Galsworthy, and when
she virtually withdraws from the scene, the story loses most of its
zest. But when Irene is in her heyday, she carries the whole tale
along, with a mysterious, crazy plausibility. Would it be too far-
fetched to suggest that in the three principal men in her life we
see Galsworthy working out the struggle between the divided
aspects of his own masculinity? Might it not be Soames Forsyte-
Galsworthy who is tormented and shamed by her, Jolyon
Forsyte-Galsworthy who worships her chivalrously, Jon Forsyte-
Galsworthy whose young lovelife is blighted by her? If we
suppose this, may we not go further and see Irene essentially as a
symbol of the untouchable, seductive mother-goddess who has

inhabited the heart of every male infant on this earth, and who perhaps is never quite deposed?

Irene certainly has many of the characteristics of a goddess. She is the remote egocentric that the Victorian or Edwardian mother-on-a-pedestal could afford to be. There is a nimbus of mystery, of unattainability, about her which Galsworthy represents as the peak of feminine attraction. The true lover must venerate, not consummate. In the Soames affair, Galsworthy has revealed the low status he accorded physical sex, and the man who persists in his demands for it from a woman of refined tastes deserves trouble. Soames got it.

Second husband Jolyon achieves marital harmony because he is content to adore and make no sexual demands. You may point out that Irene and Jolyon produce a son, and so they do. I only question how. For Jolyon seems anxious to disclaim any share in Jon's conception, and Soames perceives Irene at Queen Victoria's funeral walking with a statuesque grace that seems incompatible with advanced pregnancy. It would be consistent with Galsworthy's fantasy for his ideal woman to be physically inviolate, despite the birth of a child.

Jon, the youngest and most vulnerable version of the Galsworthian psyche, remains united with the seductive mother at the cost of his own maturity. There's no marriage for him until Irene ceases to occupy her obsessive place in Galsworthy's inner life. And even then it is a poor, shallow substitute for the pleasures and pains of life with Mother.

What is she like, this dream-woman of the not-so-distant middle classes? When Galsworthy traps himself in details, he can be banal, as when he compares Irene's eyes variously with bits of brown velvet or the eyes of an Alderney cow. He is at his most effective when he evokes the dream-like atmosphere with which senti-mentalists tend to clothe their earliest memories. Irene sways through most of the Saga clad in violet-grey gowns. She always contrives to smell of flowers: and all things male, from ancient grandsire to little child, tremble when they catch a whiff of violets. No naughty French perfume for Irene. Old Jolyon in his

87th year says of her: 'Seductive, yes, but nothing of Delilah in her.' Certainly no one could strive more strenuously than Galsworthy to cover his own tracks. For instance, on Irene's return from what the story inescapably implies to have been an afternoon of fornication, her hair and body are said to have breathed perfume, like an opening flower. With this heavily overlaid symbolism he reveals that even at this climax of his tale he cannot admit straight out that his mother-goddess has indulged in real sex, that down-to-earth, odoriferous activity of ordinary mortals.

For students of the Oedipus complex, it is a nice touch that before she becomes involved with Jolyon, Irene has a platonic affair with Old Jolyon, his father. Jolyon is thus able to pull off what many men have desired: he marries his father's woman, the nearest thing he can get to Mother.

The last but most important of Irene's seductions is of her own son Jon, and seduction it unmistakably is, in all but the most literal sense of the word. Irene moves into position when Jon is eight years old. We learn that up till now his heart has been monopolised by his nurse. His mother has remained a shadowy figure who has appeared sometimes at bedtime to stroke his forehead just before he falls asleep—a precious but remote person. The foundations of a cripplingly sentimental attitude towards Mother have already been laid, and without much effort on her part. But now, in the brief interval between the nurse's departure and Jon's dismissal to boarding-school, she must strike indelibly and mark him for her own. And so the nuptial night arrives for little Jon. He experiences for the first time the full impact of his mother's omnivorous claim on him. He is an easy conquest. 'I—I want to stay with you and be your lover, Mum,' he stammers. That night he says his prayers: 'Our Father which art in Heaven, hallowed be Thy Mum.' It is a confused intuition that his own father shares a mother with him. He goes on to ask her: 'Is Daddy in your room?' And she replies, expectantly: 'Not tonight!'

And so, years after his infantile love affair with his mother should have been allowed to develop and then die naturally away, she reactivates it, and to put the seal on the situation, invites him into her bed. His subsequent ineffectualness when we next meet him at the age of 19 shows that she timed her coup well. But Galsworthy seems quite satisfied with his impoverished young man. The problem is too near home.

Finally, Irene forces Jon to choose between herself and his fiancée Fleur. This is ostensibly because Fleur is the daughter of Soames. Not that Fleur as a young girl in love carries much conviction. She is one of Galsworthy's other breed of female—sexless, sisterly, pert. Jon needs her simply because she *is* so different from the terrifying mistress of his subconscious. She does not stand a chance against the mother from whom he has never yet kept anything. He slips his arm about Mother's girlish waist and appeals to her to explain the family feud, but she only quivers and suggests a voyage abroad, *à deux*, for two months. What a splendid recipe for an adolescent nervous breakdown! Even Father Jolyon feebly wonders if frankness might not now be preferable, but the voice of common sense is seldom heard in the Saga and certainly never listened to. Jolyon decides that it is not for him, a mere father, to go against a mother's instinct.

In Spain Irene reinforces her position. We see her communicating with her son in those ultra-simple sentences of hers which can mean so much—or so little. He re-experiences his mother's dangerous intensity directed blatantly at him. He has too much time, poor fellow, to ponder the confusion of his feelings.

He could not frame what he felt about her. Her life was like the past of this old Moorish city, full, deep, remote, his own life as yet such a *baby* of a thing. His mother's life was as unknown to him, as secret as that Phoenician past was to the town down there. He felt aggrieved that she should know all about him and he nothing about her, except that she loved him and his father and was beautiful.

So in a few words Galsworthy has pin-pointed the Oedipal conflict as it welled out of him: the passion for Mother, with her secret life that is closed to him, the baby; the incipient jealousy of Father. No wonder Jon falls quite ill.

On their return, Fleur persuades Jon one afternoon to take her to Robin Hill. Here she meets Irene, who gazes at Jon with an expression which makes him feel like a worm. Father joins them and contributes a few innuendoes about the selfishness of the young. And so this elderly couple, who are supposed to have defied convention for love, who have nursed a grievance for half a lifetime about the possessiveness of others, feel justified in depriving their son of *his* love, even stooping to the old lie: 'We don't care for anything but your happiness.' All this evidently presented no problem for Galsworthy or his readers.

And now once again Galsworthy is in the position of having to get rid of Father so that he can follow the urgings of his fantasy and allow the younger man sole possession of Mother. Jolyon supports Irene's plan to seduce her own son with a sort of orgiastic denial of his own claims upon her which may be seen as the ultimate triumph of true devotion, or of the death wish, according to your standpoint. He sees her playing the piano in the lamplight and thinks: 'It's Jon with her, all Jon. I'm dying out of her—it's natural.' 'Unnatural' might seem the better choice of word.

At last he puts Irene's boy in the picture in an eloquent letter. Irene is still, he asserts, suffering after nearly 30 years from feelings of horror and aversion. It would be almost as humiliating to her to share grandchildren with Soames as it would have been to share children. 'She will soon have only you,' he pleads. 'Don't break her heart.' Irene approves the letter. 'It's wonderfully put. Thank you, dear.' Jolyon hands it over with a final appeal to his son: 'Think what your mother's been to you, Jon! If you don't give up this love affair you will make Mother wretched to the end of her days.'

It is all too much for Jon. It will be too much for many modern readers. Yet it is interesting, for it is a climax which brings Galsworthy as near to passion as we ever see him. Illogicalities tumble over each other in his determination to make Irene's attitude plausible. The reader is not spared the ultimate in ham drama. Jon roams house and garden distracetdly, picturing his mother being owned like a slave by Fleur's father. Then he comes upon her posturing in his bedroom—a favourite haunt of hers— murmuring his name and gazing at a little photo of himself as a tiny boy. She can now safely risk a phoney renunciation: 'My darling boy, my most darling boy, don't think of me—think of yourself.' Actually it is Father they both ought to be thinking about, since that worn-out individual has just suffered a fatal heart attack in the dining-room.

After his capitulation that evening, Jon dreams he sees his mother's name, crawling on his bed. The disguises of the sub-conscious have worn precariously thin.

The orgy of incestuous solitude continues for some weeks. In due course Jon smothers the last traces of resentment at his defeat, and slips his arm again about his mother's waist. She rewards him, we are told, with a swift kiss, 'given with a sort of passion'. Soon, to seal their complete reunion, they will leave together for life in the United States. Almost our last view of them is in his bedroom. In a strange sentence Galsworthy summons up a strange predica-ment: 'The beauty and grace of her figure, the delicate line of the brow, the nose, the neck; the strange, and as it were remote refinement of her, moved him.'

It is the language, not of filial devotion, but of filial infatuation.

Philip Collins

THE DECLINE OF PATHOS

Philip Collins, besides being Professor of English Literature at Leicester University, is also well known for his public dramatic readings from Shakespeare. He is the author of *Dickens and Crime* and *Dickens and Education*.

'It may reasonably be doubted,' wrote a journalist in 1867, 'whether there has ever been a more thoroughly sentimental time than the present. The 19th century is flooded with a perfect inundation of sentimentality far above anything known or seen before. People grow up from childhood drenched through and through with it, and the character of women in particular is sodden with it before they arrive at maturity.' Twentieth-century commentators on Victorian life and literature have noted 'the general dampness of the age', often with derision or disgust ('Blast their weeping whiskers', as Wyndham Lewis put it), or at best with puzzlement: but there is surprisingly little discussion of the when and the wherefore, or indeed of the precise character of Victorian pathos and its sentimental excess.

'Victorian', however, is here—as often—a dangerous term, not only because similar forms of sentiment occur before Victoria's reign but also (and this is my subject today) because taste changed notably inside the reign. It would be a curious study, remarked another literary journalist in 1897, to trace the changing form of pathos in English fiction of the past half-century. Back in the Forties, he said, literary tradition encouraged writers to be luxuriously expansive over grief, but something had happened since then to make their pathos seem absurd. He suggested that readers now expected novels to be more realistic: Anglo-Saxons had never thought it good form to display powerful emotion, but earlier novelists had preferred emotionalism to verisimilitude.

This won't do as an explanation, however. Lachrymosity was not merely a literary phenomenon. Anyone familiar with Victorian life can remember many anecdotes of the manly tear being shed, and not only in literature or over literature: people bursting into tears at the magnificence of the Crystal Palace; headmasters weeping with their staffs after a disagreement, or with boys whom they had reproved; families, and even boys at boarding-schools, making the most of a deathbed in their midst, particularly if it was a child's. Nowadays, Geoffrey Gorer has remarked, we treat death and mourning with much the same prudery and embarrassment as sexual impulses were treated a century ago: and deathbeds then certainly provided a release for emotions inhibited elsewhere.

Over literature, too, many readers, neither unbalanced nor juvenile, nor even female, would weep much more readily than was customary later. Macaulay, for instance, cried as if his heart would break over Florence Dombey; Tennyson's *Guinevere* made him weep, and Edward Lear confessed to 'blubbering, bottlesful, over it'. George Eliot read her first attempt at fiction to her consort, G. H. Lewes: 'We both cried over it, and then he came up to me and kissed me, saying, "I think your pathos is better than your fun."' There were similar scenes when Tennyson read his poems to his wife, or when Dickens read his stories to his friends or, later, to audiences of several thousand. At the first of these private readings, Dickens had the great actor Macready sobbing on the sofa: and the spoken word was not essential, though it is worth remembering how much reading was then done aloud, in the family circle, so that the literary experience was infectious rather than purely personal and silent. Macready, meeting Dickens after reading the death of Paul Dombey, found his eyes filling with tears, and he could not speak for sobs. The English stage, which Macready then dominated, was grandly emotional in its plays and its histrionic conventions: and Dickens, a powerful amateur actor as well as an effective public reader, records one occasion when, as a dying hero, he reduced everyone on stage, an audience of 2,000, and even the stagehands in the wings, to tears.

Many more such anecdotes could certainly be told, about writers themselves being deeply affected by their own work and persuading an easy audience of family and friends to share their emotion. As for the recurrent occasions for such pathos, I can only offer a few samples. A favourite situation of course was the suffering or death of a child or a young woman: 'One must have a heart of stone,' said Oscar Wilde, 'to read the death of Little Nell without laughing.' I have a heart of stone, but can scarce check my risibility over the famous scene in *East Lynne*, where little William says farewell to his brother and sister:

> His hollow breath was echoing through the room. Death was certainly coming on quickly.
> 'Good-bye, Lucy,' he said, putting out his cold, damp hand.
> 'I am not going out,' replied Lucy. 'We have only just come home.'
> 'Good-bye, Lucy,' repeated he.
> She took the little hand then, leaned over, and kissed him. 'Good-bye, William: but indeed I am not going out anywhere.'
> 'I am,' said he. 'I am going to heaven. Where's Archie? Archie, good-bye; good-bye, dear. I am going to heaven: to that bright blue sky, you know. I shall see mamma there, and I'll tell her that you and Lucy are coming soon. Don't cry, papa. I am not afraid to go. Jesus is coming for me. I dare say mamma is looking out for me now. Perhaps she is standing on the banks of the river, watching the boats. Papa, I can't think how Jesus can be in all the boats! Perhaps they don't go quite at the same time?'

The later reaction against the over-use and the treatment of these pathetic situations I shall illustrate from contemporary responses to Dickens, and then I shall hazard some explanations. Looking back in 1887, Mrs Oliphant asserted that 'that gentle

public which wept over Little Nell, and found pathos in the story
of Smike, was never the public of the critic, yet was that to which
Dickens owed much of his first acceptance.' Certainly many
readers felt that his pathos was even better than his fun, and
Dickens himself said he preferred the power of making the world
cry, rather than laugh. But the critics *had* been moved. Or take
the *Westminster Review*, not the most tender-hearted or intellectually abject of journals: in 1847 it had described Little Nell as 'the
happiest and most perfect of Dickens's sketches' and her death as
a 'tragedy of the true sort, that which softens, and yet strengthens
and elevates'. It found similar merit in Paul Dombey. Seven years
later, in an otherwise cool review of *Hard Times*, the *Westminster*
praised the true pathos of Stephen and Rachel. Ten years further
on, indeed, in 1864, it vigorously attacked just this area of
Dickens's work—but here the reviewer was echoing attacks
launched in the late Fifties by various highbrow journals, most
notably the *Saturday Review*. A few years later, Dickens's death
and the publication of Forster's *Life* soon afterwards provided
further occasions for a summary assessment of his work, and
many of the more sophisticated commentators came down
heavily against his pathos. A century hence, prophesied one critic,
it would be only 'the careless glance of curiosity, or the student's
all-ranging eye' that would turn upon the Little Nells and Paul
Dombeys; he put his money instead on Dickens's humour—'It
seems impossible to imagine a day when the world will refuse to
laugh with Dickens.' But already it was becoming difficult to
imagine the days when it had so readily wept with him. Sur-
veying Dickens's critical fortunes, Professor George Ford cites
plenty more examples of learned and sophisticated readers at the
time who wept their manly tears, and he remarks: 'It would be
difficult to find in literary history a more dramatic example of
tides of taste than the story of the vogue and decline of Little Nell
and Paul Dombey.' And of Tennyson's 'The May-Queen', much
the same has been said. When did this change in sensibility occur,
and why?

My answers to these questions must be tentative. Over Dickens, whose critical reputation I know most fully, and who provokes these questions as sharply as any author, there had indeed been dissentient voices from the start (but they had been unrepresentative), nor was the later reaction against his pathos universal. I could counter those querulous and incredulous voices from the late Fifties to the Seventies with many reverential assessments in the same years. An obituary appreciation, for instance, referring to this reaction: 'That man must, indeed, have a mind either thoroughly bedimmed with conceit, or entirely degraded with more enormous vices', who rises unaffected from reading the deaths of Paul Dombey or Little Nell. In other words, the critical consensus which had, with few exceptions, applauded Dickens's pathos in the Thirties and Forties, was beginning to show cracks in the later Fifties and a substantial fissure by the Seventies; by and large, the critically unsophisticated remained (and for long after then) faithful to Little Nell and her fellows, while the intelligentsia reacted against them.

Most of the great specimens of literary pathos by respected authors that I have cited belong indeed to the early Victorian period. To those years, too, belong the analagous instances in pictorial art, such as Landseer's famous doggy-picture, 'The Old Shepherd's Chief Mourner' (Royal Academy, 1837), described with such reverence by Ruskin in *Modern Painters*. Maybe the hero of *The Woman in White* was not just making the perennial point about the inferiority of the younger generation when he confessed that 'today'—in 1861—they were 'nothing like so hearty and so impulsive' as their elders: 'Has the great advance in education taken rather too long a stride; and are we, in these modern days, just the least trifle in the world too well brought up?' Education certainly provides an analogy to the shift in sensibility, and probably part of the explanation. David Newsome has remarked how, in the second half of the century, the earlier public school ideas of 'godliness and good learning' are modified and abandoned: 'What is particularly striking is a change of spirit: moral earnestness becomes "theumos"—the hearty enjoyment of physical pursuits, the belief that manliness and high spirits are more becoming qualities in a boy than piety and spiritual zeal. Games-playing, on an organised basis, became an important part of the school curriculum; excessive displays of emotion came in time to be regarded as bad form; patriotism and doing one's duty to country and Empire became the main sentiments which the new system sought to inculcate.' The spirit of imperialism, more un-restrained in the later decades of the century, is indeed a manifes-tation of this toughening of emotional fibre.

Another social-political context was invoked by Walter Bagehot in 1858, to explain Dickens's pathos, which he deplored: 'The unfeeling obtuseness of the early part of this century was to be corrected by an extreme, perhaps an excessive, sensibility to human suffering in the years which have followed.' By now, Bagehot thought, there was no need for the sledgehammer blow; reform had gone as far as was necessary or desirable: and other critics accounted for the rise and fall of Dickens's reputation for pathos in similar social terms. Of course, not all of Dickens's child-deaths, nor the other great occasions for early-Victorian pathos, were directly matters of social protest (the May-Queen is not dying because of the insanitary condition of rural housing), but it is certainly right to see this literary pathos in relation to reformism and benevolence, as it is to see the preoccupation with deathbeds in relation both to the rise and decline of Evangeli-calism, and to the philanthropic and parliamentary concern with infant mortality.

One other suggestion: the full-blooded, or full-teared, pathos clearly sorts with other grand emotional gestures. I referred to the theatre, and Dr Kitson Clark has compared its conventions with pulpit, platform, and literary styles; think also of the confident affirming and commanding tones of the early-Victorian sages (particularly Carlyle) and creative writers (Dickens and Tennyson may stand as examples). That there is often bluster, confusion, shouting to keep one's spirits up, under this affirmation is evident enough, but, to cite just one familiar example, what later major author could make an admired character say, as Tennyson's Sir Galahad does:

My strength is as the strength of ten,
Because my heart is pure?

Every student new to the period remarks how strange in this
climate was Clough's poetic note in his poems written around
1850:

I do not like being moved: for the will is excited, and action
Is a most dangerous thing; I tremble for something factitious,
Some malpractice of heart and illegitimate process;
We are so prone to these things with our terrible notions of
duty.

Henry Sidgwick commented on Clough, in 1869—and the rele-
vance to my discussion is obvious—'His point of view and habit
of mind are less singular in England in the year 1869 than they
were in 1859, and much less than they were in 1849. We are
growing year by year more introspective and self-conscious: the
current philosophy leads us to a close, patient, and impartial
observation and analysis of our mental processes: we more and
more say and write what we actually do think and feel, and not
what we intend to think or should desire to feel. We are growing
also more sceptical in the proper sense of the word.' The middle-
brows and the old fogies continued to provide the old emotionalism, but the critics now damned them. As Hall Caine com-
plained in 1890: 'For many years past the cynicism that has been
only too vocal in English criticism has been telling us that it is a
poor thing to give way to strong feeling, that strong feeling is the
mark of an untaught nature, and that education should help us to
control our emotions and conceal them.'

Certainly something was lost: there was point in A. C. Ben-
son's defence, in 1910 of 'The May Queen', that no *précieux*
writer, with a care for his reputation, could have dared to write
it—'and after all the deepest of all vulgarities is the studied
avoidance of what may be thought to be vulgar'. Certainly
mid-19th-century literature was not *précieux*, it took risks,
including the risk of being (in this sense) vulgar.

This suggests one final reflection, and again I can use Dickens as the representative figure. His work is often commended to us nowadays because 'he and his period were, after all, modern; the pressures and perplexities of mid-Victorian England are indeed our own'. One sees the force of such suggestions: but I find a salutary corrective in historians of literature and society who are at least as aware of the differences between Dickens's time and concerns) and ours. W. L. Burn, for instance, stressing the essential simplicity of the mid-Victorian mind: 'To itself it appeared highly complex and so in a sense it was; but rather through its fecundity and diversity than through anything particularly complicated or subtle in its thinking.'

The critics who claim Dickens as an honorary member of the 20th century are not, I notice, apt to discuss Little Nell with much animation. The current reinterpretation of Victorian literature has done little to accommodate the pathos; whether because the writing really is bad, or because we are inhibited bad readers, it remains alien and virtually ignored. To quote once again from W. L. Burn: 'Over and over again, in examining mid-Victorian England, one comes across modes of thought and action so bizarre, so little credible, that the men and women who practised them appear as the inhabitants, not just of another century but of another world.'

Nicholas Tucker

NURSERY RHYMES

Nicholas Tucker was an English teacher, and is now an educational psychologist. He has written a book called *Understanding the Mass Media*, and is working on another about children's favourite reading and the clash with adults this has frequently led to.

NURSERY RHYMES TODAY crop up almost everywhere in a child's life: they are sung in school, played on the BBC, and very often appear in the first books he is ever given. In an age when many parents worry about the effects of certain television programmes or comics upon the very young, nursery rhymes at least are felt to be safe as well as entertaining for every age, and anyone who tried challenging this today could be fairly sure of an outraged response. Yet how many people realise that, not so long ago, it was the nursery rhymes themselves that got the outraged response, being described as 'drivellings' or as 'full of something like lies, and those very shocking to the mind'. And this sort of protest did not really disappear until quite late this century.

To be fair, the first critics of nursery rhymes often had something of a point. After all, the oldest nursery rhymes were not written for children at all. Most of them, as Mr and Mrs Opie point out in one of their invaluable nursery rhyme anthologies, 'tended to come from unrelated snatches of worldly songs, adult jests, lampoons, proverbial maxims, charms and country ballads.' Some of these were often quite cheerfully vulgar, and a few rather more unpleasantly obscene. They would usually reach the ears of

middle-class children through their nursemaids, and, as the
17th-century commentator George Wither pointed out, 'Nurses
usually sing their children to sleep, and through want of pertinent
matter oft make use of unprofitable, if not worse, songs'.

On the whole, most 17th- and 18th-century parents did not
really mind this, since they were used to their children seeing adult
life in the raw, but things were certainly different in the 19th
century. Here, parents and educators came to see children as
essentially vulnerable to all sorts of evils—real and imagined. They
must therefore be protected from evil passions both from outside
and from within themselves, and watchful parents certainly would
not approve of rhymes that were too free with their vocabulary,
such as the following:

> The sow came in with a saddle,
> The little pig rocked the cradle;
> The dish jumped a'top the table,
> To see the pot wash the ladle.
> The spit that stood behind the door
> Called the dish-clout a dirty whore.

This, though, is a comparatively mild example. Some other
rhymes then in circulation would still be difficult to quote over
the BBC today. A few nursery rhyme characters, too, had a quite
different meaning at the time: for example, Elsie Marley and
Little Jumping Joan both originally referred to prostitutes. In the
same way, 'Rub-a-Dub-Dub, three men in a tub' was originally
about three *maids* in a tub being ogled, by the butcher, the baker
and the candle-stick maker, presumably at some low country fair.
Today, I suppose, they would be forming queues outside strip-
tease clubs.

One man who did a lot to make nursery rhymes respectable to
their critics was James Halliwell, later to be a brilliant Shakespearian scholar. In 1842, when he was still a very young man,
Halliwell produced the first fairly comprehensive nursery rhyme
anthology in this country. His selection was pleasantly boisterous,

but on the whole he took good care not to shock his readers. For example, rather than print anything really vulgar, Halliwell merely refers to other versions, one of which he describes tantalisingly as 'Very curious, but unfortunately too indelicate to print'. In the case of another nursery rhyme character, Nancy Dawson, who undoubtedly belongs to the same profession as Elsie Marley, Halliwell tells his readers: 'Out of the many songs relating to the heroine of the following stanza, only one has been deemed eligible for insertion in this volume.' And the one he refers to is certainly blameless enough.

The anthology was a huge success, and was quickly reprinted the following year. But even within this short time Halliwell seems to have felt he had still gone too far. In his next edition, we find the following slightly ominous note written into the preface: 'In the expectation of rendering our collection an unexceptionable contribution to a juvenile library, every allusion that could possibly offend the most fastidious reader has been carefully excluded.' And in this new edition, although it is a greatly expanded and still splendidly spirited collection, we do also find that some of the original selection has been quietly dropped.

Some of these losses are very welcome; gone now, for example, are some rather puerile verses of the 'Said Moses to Aaron' variety. Halliwell also cuts out many of the rhymes founded on portions of the Scriptures, as he finds, in his own words, 'that these facetious compositions frequently degenerate into mere vulgarities'. But there were also some rather good rhymes that were dropped, probably only because they did not seem genteel enough at the time, such as this one:

> Bryan O'Lin had no breeches to wear,
> So he bought him a sheepskin to make him a pair.
> With the skinny side out and the woolly side in,
> 'Oh, how nice and warm,' cried Bryan O'Lin.

Halliwell also leaves out the rhyme about Lucy Locket and Kitty Fisher, since as he explained in his first edition, these were two celebrated courtesans in the times of Charles II. But in this case he could have spared himself the trouble; *The Oxford Dictionary of Nursery Rhymes* now says that there is no definite proof against the virtue of these two ladies. Gone, too, are the following rousing verses, which one imagines would not have amused many Victorian parents, whatever the occasional truth behind them:

> O bonny Hobby Elliott, O canny Hobby still.
> O bonny Hobby Elliott, who lives at Harlow Hill!
> Had Hobby acted right, as he has seldom done,
> He would have kissed his wife, and let the maid alone.

In another instance, Halliwell keeps the rhyme but changes one word only. Here is the original:

> O rare Harry Parry!
> When will you marry?
> When apples and pears are ripe.
> I'll come to your wedding
> Without any bidding,
> And lie with your bride all night.

In his second edition, Halliwell now tactfully substitutes: 'And dance with your bride all night.' But in later years, even this change would not do and the line finally emerges as 'And dance and sing all the night', thus reasserting prudence at the expense of the natural rhythm of the verse.

Indeed, as time passed and the puritan grip tightened, all nursery rhyme anthologies became increasingly respectable. In his second edition, for example, Halliwell could still print this swinging little rhyme:

> Sing Jigmijole
> The pudding bowl
> The table and the frame
> My master he did cudgel me
> For kissing of my dame.

But when the last anthology directly supervised by Halliwell came out nearly 50 years later in 1890, we find that even a kiss is too much, and that the final lines have been changed to:

> My master he did cudgel me
> For speaking to my dame.

Also, in this last edition, a number of the more outspoken and energetic rhymes Halliwell managed to keep in his early editions have now disappeared or been altered. Sometimes they are replaced by rhymes like these two:

> When little Fred went to bed,
> He always said his prayers.
> He kissed his Mamma and then his Papa,
> And straightway went upstairs.

> Come when you're called,
> Do what you're bid.
> Shut the door after you,
> Never be chid.

For me, these rhymes seem far more objectionable than most of those that Halliwell omits or chops about. Of course, in general Halliwell did an enormous amount for children both now and then by helping to make so many nursery rhymes known and acceptable to parents. But there were a few losses on the way, and as Halliwell's anthologies became almost a touchstone for all future collections, we still tend to feel some of these losses today. Consider this charming original; you will probably know most of it except for the very last line:

> There was a little man,
> And he wooed a little maid,
> And he said, little maid, will you wed, wed, wed,?
> I have little more to say,
> Than will you, yea or nay?
> For the least said is soonest mended, ded, ded.

Then this little maid she said,
Little sir, you've little said,
To induce a little maid for to wed, wed, wed.
You must say a little more,
And produce a little ore,
E'er I make a little print in your bed, bed, bed.

Nowadays, of course, we have learned to substitute for the last line:

E'er I to the church will be led, led, led.

But I much prefer the original. For one thing, it is far less clumsy to read. More importantly, though, it has the great genius of so many nursery rhymes in that they introduce children to various adult concepts, in this case marriage and sexuality, in a manner that is both charming and reassuring. The same thing is celebrated, very much in the way that young children play 'Mothers and Fathers' as an unconscious type of preparation for adult life, in these verses from 'Lavender's blue':

Lavender's blue, diddle diddle,
Lavender's green;
When I am King, diddle, diddle,
You shall be Queen.
Call up your men, diddle diddle,
Set them to work,
Some to the plough, diddle, diddle,
Some to the fork,
Some to make hay, diddle, diddle,
Some to reap corn,
While you and I, diddle, diddle,
Keep the bed warm.

Actually this lovely little rhyme is itself a reformed version of a rather coarse 17th-century ballad. Yet the mention of 'bed', however charming and appropriate, proved too much for most later 19th-century editors, and even today it is rare to find this very pleasant little version in print.

Although in time most puritans gradually stopped objecting to nursery rhymes, this still left other critics. Most of these were followers of Rousseau, who had given new life to the idea, going back as far as Plato and even further, that 'Men may be taught fables, but children require naked truth'. Such critics worried lest nursery rhymes were educationally useless or even worse, confusing to the young child. One of them, a Mrs Sarah Trimmer, established a journal in 1802 whose sole purpose, in her own words, was to protect 'The Young and Innocent from the Dangers which threaten them in the form of Infantine and Juvenile literature'. Here she was free to brand nursery rhymes as only 'calculated to entertain the imagination, rather than improve the heart or cultivate the understanding'. A later American critic, R. W. Hume, repeated these objections but then went on with some ingenious suggestions for cashing in on 'these imaginative mostrosities which fill our nursery books'. 'How much better would it be to supplant them with statements proper to be acquired, which would be both consistent and real. Instead of the Cow jumped over the moon, let the child jump over the multiplication table, so that it may earlier get acquainted with the mysteries of Arithmetic. How easy also would it be to provide practical substitution for the nonsense at present obtaining—to replace the absurd and unintelligible

> Froggy would a-wooing go
> Whether his mother would let him or no.
> Heigh! Ho! Gammon!

with a sober truth like the following, which, if necessary, might also be made to jingle:

> A dollar loaned at 6 per cent
> Will yield six cents to pay the rent,
> Per annum.

Or for a baby, with a mathematical turn of mind, this might be used:

Every triangle you view
Has in it right angles two
Quod erat demonstrandum.

The latter line does not rhyme, but it might lead to useful inquiries, and on that account is added.'

Despite such ingenious advice, the campaign against nursery rhymes on this score, too, gradually faded away, especially when various distinguished people began admitting that they had once enjoyed these 'imaginative monstrosities', without any apparent bad effect. In his last anthology, Halliwell guyed some of the more solemn critics of nursery rhymes by including this so-called Quaker version of 'Hey, diddle diddle, the cat and the fiddle', which is, however, almost certainly bogus:

Hey, diddle diddle, the cat and the fiddle,
(Yes, thee may say that, for that is nonsense)
The cow jumped over the moon.
(Oh no, Mary, thee mustn't say that, for that is a falsehood; thee knows a cow could never jump over the moon; but a cow may jump under it, so thee ought to say: The cow jumped *under* the moon)
The little dog laughed . . .
(Oh Mary, stop! How can a little dog laugh? Thee knows a little dog can't laugh. Thee ought to say: The little dog *barked.*)
And the dish ran after the spoon.
(Stop Mary, stop! A dish could never run after a spoon. Thee had better say: And the *cat* ran after the spoon.)

Although there were a number of beautifully illustrated nursery rhyme books available by the end of the 19th century, there was still some intermittent resistance to come. Post-revolutionary Russia announced that in all its children's books: 'Every fantastic and religious element is carefully excluded and replaced by a healthy, bold realism calculated to stimulate children to action and the study of realities.'

The struggle was also maintained in odd pockets of America,

and in a sense by the great Italian teacher Maria Montessori. She, whilst allowing fantasy for older children, still felt that serious or even permanent damage could be done by confusing the very young over the difference between fact and fiction. As an example of this, she quotes the case of a little girl who fell out of a window trying to fly like Peter Pan, very much as parents today blame Batman for exactly the same thing. Is all this fantasy, which for most children begins with nursery rhymes, really such a bad thing at some ages? Does 'Hey, diddle, diddle, the cat and the fiddle' really confuse a child about the laws of gravity, and are we doing him a grave wrong by telling him that the distance to Babylon is three score miles and ten? In fact, it is now generally felt that if anyone tries to take all fantasy out of a small child's life, he will only substitute his own, possibly more exaggerated fictions instead. The whole point of any fantasy, whether taken from a book or from the child's own daydreaming, is that it does not have to obey all the natural rules, which in itself can lead to trouble for the odd child on the odd occasion. For example, 'Ding Dong Bell' has been accused of encouraging cruelty to cats, but whether they know the rhyme or not, I should guess that there has always been a certain amount of this amongst some children, possibly driven on by curiosity as much as anything else.

In fact, this very point—that rhymes like 'Ding Dong Bell' could lead children into trouble—was raised in the last and possibly the final campaign against nursery rhymes, which began in this country soon after the last war. This campaign was largely the creation of one man, Mr Geoffrey Hall. For nearly seven years, between 1948 and 1955, he put most of his considerable energies into what he called the 'True Aim Movement for Nursery Rhyme Reform', which eventually was to take him all over Europe and America and earn him frequent mention in the world's press. But long before this, Geoffrey Hall, who was a Manchester textile manufacturer, had been active in other humanitarian crusades. One of these, in pre-war Europe when tension was particularly high, involved a scheme whereby Hall planned to supply all the children of Europe with frocks, rompers, aprons, handkerchiefs and so on, all illustrated with pictures from *The Story of Babar,* then an international children's best-seller. By this, Hall hoped to provide a common bond and understanding between all children at the earliest age. Unfortunately, the order was under-cut by cheap foreign competition, and, even worse, a chance acquaintance pointed out to Hall that Babar's mother dies on page three of the story. For Hall, quoted in one of the many newspaper interviews he was to give, 'this destroyed the whole of the message and the guidance. What a glaring example of how blind a man can be!'

In 1948, Hall fixed upon nursery rhymes for his new campaign. He claimed that when analysed at least half of our traditional favourites, in his own words, 'harbour unsavoury elements'. These range, according to researches done by Geoffrey Handley-Taylor, then working for the True Aim movement, from 14 cases of stealing and general dishonesty right down to one case each of devouring human flesh, desiring to have a limb severed, scorning the blind, and death by shrivelling, squeezing, starvation, or cutting a human being in half.

The answer for Hall was clear. He was convinced that over 50 per cent of people can trace their childhood fears to nursery rhymes, and that because of this it was his duty to produce some reformed rhymes that would, in his own words, give all children a lasting dream of happiness. As no publisher would back him, Hall eventually published these himself under the title *New Nursery Rhymes for Old.*

You can judge for yourself whether this anthology succeeds or not. Here is Hall's version of 'Three Blind Mice'.

> Three kind mice, three kind mice,
> See how they run, see how they run;
> They all ran after the farmer's wife,
> She cut them some cheese with a carving knife;
> Did you ever see such a thing in your life
> As three kind mice?

Like the farmer's wife, the old women who lived in a shoe is also now a quite reformed character:

> There was an old women who lived in a shoe,
> She had so many children, and loved all of them too;
> She gave them good broth and pieces of bread,
> Then kissed them all soundly and put them to bed.

In 'Humpty Dumpty', originally a riddle about the impossibility of mending a broken egg, the point is rather lost in Hall's version:

> Humpty Dumpty sat on a wall,
> Humpty Dumpty had a great fall.
> All the king's horses and all the king's men
> Soon picked up Humpty Dumpty again.

Elsewhere we hear how in 'Sing a song of sixpence' the blackbirds were not really baked in the pie, but just happened to be around to sing when it was opened; that little boys are made of strength and line and all that's fine; and that Jack did not break his crown but merely 'fell down in his suit of brown'. Perhaps the greatest change though, is reserved for 'Who killed Cock Robin', which now goes:

> Who'll wed Cock Robin?
> I said the sparrow
> In a wheelbarrow
> I'll wed Cock Robin.

In the following verses, each animal is given a special duty for the wedding, and the whole thing ends with this triumphant chorus:

> All the birds in the air
> Fell a-singing and a-throbbing,
> When they heard of the love
> Of dear Cock Robin.

But Hall experienced what he called 'unexpected opposition' over this last verse, when he received a letter, which he did not seem to recognise as a leg-pull, from the Anthropology Department at Cambridge University. In this, he was assured that over the question of this last chorus: 'Competent authorities have been consulted who believe that it is sexy, and liable to arouse unworthy emotions in young people.'

In fact most of the reactions to Hall's very well-publicised campaign tended towards either ridicule or fury. Despite the publication of around half a million copies of *New Nursery Rhymes for Old*, many distributed free of charge, the campaign gradually faded away. In 1955, with typical energy, Hall announced a new campaign to reform fairy stories, beginning with *Cinderella*, who would be given a loving step-mother and two sweet step-sisters. But this never even got started, and in time the whole movement was forgotten in the next flurry of public opinion over the more urgent topic of American horror-comics, later to be banned by Act of Parliament.

In practical terms, Hall's lengthy and expensive campaign achieved very little, beyond tiny, isolated successes such as the decision of Warrington Council of Social Services to give free copies of *New Nursery Rhymes for Old* to expectant mothers attending its ante-natal clinics. Nevertheless, Hall did succeed in making people think about nursery rhymes, and some of the results of this were very interesting. For example, many critics attacked Hall for daring to reform traditional nursery rhymes without apparently realising that many of their favourite rhymes were themselves reformed versions, often dating from the 19th century. In fact, Hall would have raised far more of a public outcry if, instead of reforming nursery rhymes, he had dared print some of them in their original versions, which would then almost certainly have been seized by the police as an offence against public morals. One of the glories of older nursery rhymes is that there are no standard texts. In many cases, they tend to change over the years or from region to region, according to the tastes and tongues of those who use them and then pass them on. Hall had every right to publish his reformed versions; nursery rhymes are not in copyright, and many other people have issued reformed versions in the past which have caught on most successfully. In this, though, Hall almost certainly failed; as you have heard, his own versions were far too clumsy and generally tepid to appeal to children either then or at any time since.

Even so, it seems to me that once or twice Hall did put forward a good case for reform of a particular rhyme. For example, in the rhyme 'Old Mother Goose and the Golden Egg', one traditional verse goes like this:

> Jack sold his gold egg
> To a rogue of a Jew
> Who cheated him out of
> The half of his due.

This particular verse still crops up today for example, in Walter de la Mare's otherwise delightful collection, *Nursery Rhymes for Certain Times*. In fact, most modern anthologists now get round this verse by referring to 'a merchant untrue', but Hall's alternative phrase, 'a neighbour called Hugh', seems to me quite as acceptable and indeed necessary. Of course no national group can afford to be too over-sensitive, and the same rhyme also contains, for example, an unpleasant picture of the English country squire. But with such a tragic and long-lasting history of anti-semitism in Europe, there seems to me very little case for keeping the original stark phrase 'a rogue of a Jew' in circulation these days. It is one thing to respect the past, but quite another to hand on all its traditional attitudes, even the most disgraceful ones.

Take another example, not mentioned by Hall. The *Dictionary of Nursery Rhymes* describes it as the most popular counting-out rhyme both in England and in America:

> Eeena, meena, mina, mo,
> Catch a nigger by his toe,
> If he hollers, let him go,
> Eeena, meena, mina, mo.

Now, the first line of this rhyme, 'Eeena, meena, mina, mo,' is
of quite enormous antiquity, and in fact is thought to be the
remnants of an old Celtic numeral system. It would clearly be a
tragedy if this fascinating link with the past were to drop out of
anthologies in the future. But the fact remains that the word
'nigger' is now held, quite understandably, to be utterly offensive.
So it could be that unless a reformed version for the other part of
the verse can be found, parents and teachers in the future may well
avoid this charming but now potentially dangerous little rhyme.
As it is, many modern anthologies are already excluding it.
Actually, it would not be difficult to change this little rhyme, at
least on paper, since the original phrase in use in this country seems
to have been 'Catch a chicken by his toe'. At the moment, though,
with colour prejudice as one of the world's chief problems, I can
see little reason why we continue to tolerate the original of this
rhyme in some modern children's books which, among other
things, should surely try to help young readers to adapt themselves to present-day realities. Of course, it is never pleasant to
censor anything, but there is no reason why the 'nigger' version
could not be revived in happier times if that is what people still
wanted.

Should we, in fact, discourage all rhymes that deride national
groups? The rhyme 'Taffy was a Welshman', for example, was
often used in the past as a form of Welsh-baiting to be chanted
loudly on St David's Day, sometimes on the Welsh border itself.
One way the Welsh retaliated was to put about their own version,
which you will see goes rather differently:

Taffy is a Welshman, Taffy's not a thief,
Taffy's mutton's very good, but not so good his beef;
I went to Taffy's house, and everything I saw,
Was cleanliness and Godliness and obedience to the law.

Yet organised Welsh-baiting is now such a thing of the past
that I don't think too many bitter memories would be stirred up
today by the original rollicking story of Taffy. As one would

expect, though, Geoffrey Hall made an effort to reform it, beginning rather flatteringly:

> Taffy was a Welshman, Taffy was a chief.

But significantly it did not catch on, even in Wales, probably
because no one really minds about it any more.

Of course, there are a very few old rhymes that are so inherently
unpleasant that there seems little point in trying to keep them
alive, even by reforming them. Take this one, that actually
appeared in *Mother Goose's Nursery Rhymes*, published in 1924
and reprinted as late as 1962:

> A penn'orth of bread to feed the Pope
> A penn'orth of cheese to choke him;
> A pint of beer to wash it down,
> And a good old faggot to burn him.

Perhaps the best thing to do with this sort of rhyme is simply to
let it drop out of print altogether. An American Roman Catholic,
Frank Scully, has done his best to counter this and other possibly
heretical rhymes by producing his own reformed anthology
called *Blessed Mother Goose*, but I rather wonder if his efforts will
catch on any better than Geoffrey Hall's ever did.

Now we are back with Geoffrey Hall again, was he right about
anything else? Is there anything in his idea that some nursery
rhymes habitually terrify very little children? Again, despite all
the exaggerations Hall seemed to go in for, there does remain the
point that just a few nursery rhymes can be very frightening, and
indeed are intended to be. Listen to this quite haunting and
venerable nursery rhyme, which has been recorded, appropriately
enough, by Boris Karloff, at his most sepulchral:

> There was a man of double deed
> Sowed his garden full of seed.
> When the seed began to grow,
> 'Twas like a garden full of snow;

When the snow began to melt,
'Twas like a ship without a belt;
When the ship began to sail,
'Twas like a bird without a tail;
When the bird began to fly,
'Twas like an eagle in the sky;
When the sky began to roar,
'Twas like a lion before the door;
When the door began to crack,
'Twas like a stick across my back;
When my back began to smart,
'Twas like a penknife in my heart;
When my heart began to bleed
'Twas death and death and death indeed.

Now this sort of thing is fine for older children who want to test themselves out against something frightening but ultimately within their control. I think a younger child, though, could be quite upset by this rhyme, or by a few others, like the horrifying rhyme set in a graveyard that begins 'There was a lady all skin and bone' and traditionally ends with a piercing scream. No parent should think that the very phrase 'nursery rhyme' means that everything that follows is automatically suitable for all children at every age.

At the same time, with the exception of a few frightening verses, I think Hall was wrong about everything else he condemned as violent and cruel in nursery rhymes. At a time in a child's life when he is beginning to come to terms with his own violent fantasies, it is surely a very good thing to be able to find these in some senses reflected in nursery rhymes. It will help a child to realise that he is not the only one with such feelings, and that they can, to a certain extent, be indulged through this early literature. Very often nursery rhymes will bring into the open various quite specific infantile fantasies, for example about destruction, death or mutilation, so that they are both recognisable to the child and also within his control, since any child can control a nursery rhyme merely by learning it and then repeating it over and over again. In fact, whatever Geoffrey Hall may have said in the past, we may well be faced soon with the opposite threat: that nursery rhyme anthologies may become far too nice and respectable. This could be happening because some parents and educators, recognising the essential violence in some nursery rhymes, have become too concerned to protect their children from this side of life, rather than help them come to terms with it from an early age. Already many modern anthologies seem fearfully tame when compared with some of the older collections, which always had a good score of fairly violent rhymes, however hard they tried to avoid the more obviously erotic ones. The BBC programme *Listen with Mother*, with its enormous influence, has also adopted a clear policy of avoiding any rhyme that could conceivably upset a child, once again, with other factors, leading to a total effect that seems fatally over-sweetened and unreal for many of today's children. It would be tragic if all nursery rhyme assortments in the future lost that essential balance between depicting all the human emotions, good and bad, which they have always managed to do in the past, despite the most strenuous opposition.